The
Organization
Makers

ADMINISTRATION SERIES

Eugene E. Jennings, *Editor*

Basic Computer Programming
Decima M. Anderson

Cases in Personnel Management and Supervision
Richard P. Calhoon

Personnel Management and Supervision
Richard P. Calhoon

The Organization Makers
Orvis Collins, David G. Moore

Readings in Business Policy
Edmund R. Gray

Executive Success
Eugene E. Jennings

Organization Renewal
Gordon L. Lippitt

Readings in Management Control
Robert J. Mockler

Management in International Perspective
S. Benjamin Prasad

Research and Development Management
Daniel D. Roman

Measuring Executive Effectiveness
Frederic R. Wickert, Dalton E. McFarland

Business Policies and Decision Making
Raymond J. Ziegler

THE
ORGANIZATION
MAKERS

A BEHAVIORAL STUDY OF INDEPENDENT ENTREPRENEURS

by

ORVIS COLLINS
New York State University College at Buffalo

and

DAVID G. MOORE
New York State School of Industrial and Labor Relations
Cornell University

APPLETON-CENTURY-CROFTS

Educational Division

MEREDITH CORPORATION

New York

This book is based on *The Enterprising Man,* copyrighted
in 1964 by the Board of Trustees of Michigan State University. We wish to thank the Board and the Bureau of
Business and Economic Research of that institution for
permission to use materials from *The Enterprising Man* in
The Organization Makers.

In preparing *The Organization Makers,* we have freely
added new and dropped old textual and case materials,
and have shifted the structure of the book to change emphasis from that of a research report to a portrayal of an
important occupational group. This process of revision
has left some portions of *The Enterprising Man* practically
intact in *The Organization Makers,* while other portions of
this book are new. A listing of all the additions, deletions,
and revisions would be a major undertaking in itself.

To our wives:

June McCormick Collins
Margaret Rider Moore

Contents

Preface ix

Introduction: Organization Making and Economic
Development 1

PART ONE
THE SCHOOL FOR ENTREPRENEURS

1. The Man and the Firm 13

2. The Entrepreneur as a Child 15

3. A Psychologist Looks at the Entrepreneur 39

4. Formal Education: Dropouts and Graduates 49

5. The School of Experience 63

6. The School for Entrepreneurs: An Appraisal 85

PART TWO
PROJECTORS AND PROJECTIONS

7. The Projectors: Men in a Quandary 95

8. The Projection 115

PART THREE
CREATORS AND THE ENTERPRISE

9. Creators and the Enterprise 137

viii   CONTENTS

10. Setting Up the Firm: The Strategic Act   141

11. Through the Knothole   159

12. On Their Way at Last   179

PART FOUR

INDEPENDENT AND ADMINISTRATIVE ENTREPRENEURS: A COMPARISON

13. Business Hierarchs: Men Who Rise in
       Established Businesses   201

14. Two Pathways   215

15. The Independent Entrepreneur and the
       Large Corporation   223

Bibliography   233

Index   235

Preface

The Organization Makers is a revision of *The Enterprising Man,* a book originally published by the Bureau of Business and Economic Research, Graduate School of Business Administration, Michigan State University. Both books are based on a study conducted at Michigan State University and supported by a grant from the Small Business Administration, Washington, D.C.

Our reasons for undertaking this revision are twofold. First, we are interested in presenting the results of our research to a broader audience. Although *The Enterprising Man* was written primarily for an academic audience, many men in large and small businesses who did see the book wrote the authors. We wish to reach more of these men by issuing a revised edition. A second reason for our revision is the opportunity it presents for a second look at the data and for the incorporation of additional materials not previously used.

There is precious little known about business leaders in our society. The amount of conjecture and speculation, however, more than makes up for the lack of concrete information. Books appear with cosmic regularity in which business leaders are perceived either in terms of the projected needs of the authors or in terms of the perceived needs of the potential audience. Sometimes they are glorified and sometimes they are denigrated. They are seldom viewed as for the most part conventional, occasionally unusual people caught up in a system of social action requiring special adjustments and adaptations. If this book is unique, it is unique in that it starts with live data taken from 150 depth interviews. More than this, it focuses on a special group of business leaders in our society, organization makers who have started businesses.

The research was a team effort throughout. David Moore conceived the study and wrote up the original design. Professor Darab B.

ix

Unwalla of the College of Business, Michigan State University, was in charge of the field research, set up the sample design, directed the work of the interviewers and office staff, and gathered some of the data used in the study. Roger Coup of Social Research, Inc., Chicago, analyzed the psychological materials. Orvis Collins took the lead in the analysis of the interviews. Orvis Collins and David Moore prepared the final manuscript. And, in our current revision, we were assisted throughout by Professor June Collins.

Our deepest gratitude must go to the organization builders in our sample, who must remain anonymous, but who gave so much of their time and ideas to this study. We have come to admire and respect them as significant leaders in our business society. Throughout this book we have quoted liberally from their interviews. All quotations, however, have been thoroughly disguised. Some of the patterns of entrepreneurial behavior are sufficiently similar from one individual to the next that the reader may on occasion think he recognizes a person of his acquaintance. He can be assured ahead of time that this recognition is in error.

This book is based on research into the origins, motivations, and patterns of behavior of men who tried to create new business organizations and succeeded. How the research was designed and executed is fully described in *The Enterprising Man*. Here we wish only to say that our research approach was to go out and talk at length with 150 men in 100 business enterprises in light manufacturing founded between 1945 and 1958. We asked these men to tell us in great detail about themselves and about the events which led to their creating a business organization. Out of the thousands of pages of interview material gathered in this fashion we have drawn together the cases presented in this book. For a technical description of the research, the reader is referred to *The Enterprising Man*.

D.G.M.

The
Organization
Makers

Organization Making and
Economic Development

This book is about men who create new business enterprises, but our interest is not primarily in these men. Our interest is, rather, in the process by which new organizations come into being. We are interested in this process as a total action system, not as a narrow technical activity.

Anyone who spends an hour or two browsing through the Chicago or Manhattan Yellow Pages will be amazed by the proliferation of organizational instruments created within the last fifty years—since, say, the years of World War I. This proliferation of limited purpose organizations is one of the several fundamental transformations that has occurred in our times. It has changed our lives more fundamentally than has air travel, telephone communication, electrical and nuclear energy, space exploration, or computer technology.

Nuclear energy, we all agree, was a product of the Manhattan Project. Space exploration is a product of NASA. The Mark III is a product of the Ford Motor Company. We agree that these are products of organizations, but our preoccupation with hardware technology inhibits our asking the next two questions: Who "produced" the Manhattan Project, NASA, and the Ford Motor Company? And what was the production process?

Today men design and develop organizations by thousands. In every community, in every industry, and in every government the creation of organizations is a sustained undertaking carried out by an emergent occupational force of specialists in that field. These men create the instruments which make possible other developments in the economy and in the hardware technology.

Our world today is one in which organizations are deliberately designed and created for one limited purpose. All the significant tasks, even those of the hardware sciences, are increasingly carried forth within the vehicle of such organizations. Today organizations are made to be used as tools and weapons both in procuring economic wealth and in the struggle for social, political, and economic power. When an AID mission goes to Africa the manner in which that mission is organized is more fundamental to its success than the bulldozers and well drillers it takes along. The executive who sets up a department for research and development is making a tool for R&D. The established corporation is nothing other than a social apparatus for the production of goods and services. The union leader who combines locals into a national or international system is creating a weapon which will be used to insure corporation employees a fair share of the income from corporation products.

It is vital that, if the free world is to stay free, we have systematic knowledge of the process of organization making in those societies in which the making of organizations is not centrally controlled and administered by a party superorganization. The freedom to make, use, and discard organizations has been integral to the growth of political, religious, economic, and scientific freedom as we know it in the West. If men are to continue to make limited-purpose organization and if they are to learn how to make more effective and efficient organizations, it is crucial that we increase our knowledge and enhance our understanding of such organizations as natural phenomena. As such organizational systems become more complex, we can seek to understand them, or we can take the stance that such complex matters can only be coordinated by a central mechanism—a state apparatus operating on the basis of a master plan.

This book represents a tentative and exploratory attempt to investigate the process of organization making as carried out by one kind of maker: the independent entrepreneur who creates from nothing a new business firm. As far back as Elizabethan times, this kind of organization maker has been of peculiar importance in pioneering and innovating organizational forms in the Western World.

THE PROCESS OF ORGANIZATION MAKING

Organizations are created in two basically different ways. They are created as extensions of existing structures, such as the setting up of a new functional department or product division within an established business, a new government agency, or a new college within a university. These organizations by extension are brought about by the overhauling, or the "reorganization," of existing structures. It is the work of administrators to enact the process of organization creation by extension. When administrators in established systems engage in this activity we shall, in this book, call them "administrative entrepreneurs."

Organizations are also created as independent entities with no "formal" ties with existing structures. Business enterprise comes first to mind, but such organization making is not confined to the economic sphere. The growth of denominationalism in religion was made possible by the freedom of dissident leaders to leave established churches and create vehicles within which to practice their own theological doctrines. Political freedom is closely tied to the notion that a leader may at any time organize a party in opposition to the existing political parties. Men in the Western World create associations for purposes ranging from the study of butterflies to communication with loved ones who have "passed over" into the spiritual world. When a man engages in the creation of an organization from scratch, we shall, in this book, classify him as an "independent" entrepreneur; but for convenience in speaking of our research population we will often call him simply an "entrepreneur."

Men in Western democracies create organizations in both ways. Every day, many organizations that are extensions of existing organizations are brought into being. And yet there is the freedom to develop *de novo* organizations in competition with existing structures. One can, if one wishes, try to create a new business. One can set up a third political party. One can strive to win adherents and create a new religious organization. This does not mean that the undertaking is always an easy one. Any new organization must compete with existing establishments. Its creators must fight for its existence. We shall see in this book how intense this struggle can become, and how important the human spirit is in achieving success.

Throughout this book we shall attempt to present the process of organization making as a natural phenomenon. There are really two major problems to be dealt with in understanding this phenomenon. First, we must seek to know the social and cultural forces which give rise to the independent entrepreneur as an occupational type. Where does he come from? How is he different from other men? What are the special pathways which lead a man to try to set up an independent organization? All these questions are concerned with the events that take place before a man creates an organization. Finding the answers to these questions is crucial to understanding the process of organization making.

The second problem is that of the organization process itself. In this book we will think of an organization as a system of sustained interaction of people, and we will think of that interaction system as both created and guided by the entrepreneur. In other words, we shall think of an organization both as a "thing" and as a process. We shall think of this process as going through phases, with each phase shaped by the phases which have preceded it.

THE MAIN PHASES OF ORGANIZATION MAKING

For purposes of delineation, we shall divide organization making into three major phases.

1. The School for Independent Entrepreneurs. If we wish to understand independent organization making as a natural process, we must begin by looking not at organizations but at the men who create them. We must begin by examining the events through which men are brought to the point of striking out on their own and creating new and independent organizations. Part One, "The School for Entrepreneurs," will look at the shaping and training of independent entrepreneurs.

2. Projecting the Enterprise. Initiation of an independent organization occurs at that moment in time when one man, or a small group of men, first envisages the need for and the possibility of bringing men, machines, and materials together to undertake an activity. We shall call this the moment of "projection." A projection takes place when a man has an "idea," and when he has imaginative insight into how to implement this idea.

Projection is usually accompanied by bringing together a small group of men who may, or may not, form the nucleus of the new organization.

In the case of organization by extension, this group typically consists of men who hold office in already existing organizations such as a government agency, a foundation, or a corporation. These men form a committee, or another special-purpose device, the members of which represent the interests in the projected activity of one or more existing organizations. Plans which represent these interests and which lay out an approach to securing resources necessary to the extension are formulated. Men who project in this manner use positions within existing structures to make extensions and recombinations of existing structures.

The independent entrepreneur projecting an organization from scratch follows much the same procedure. Typically, upon making his projection he brings together a small group of men who examine resource availability and commit themselves to a "deal." An organization maker who projects an organization from scratch is not operating from an ongoing structure. He must operate outside established structures, and he is without the resources which the established organization can place at the disposal of administrative entrepreneurs.

In the case either of the administrative or of the independent entrepreneur, projecting is a phase of proposal and counter proposal, of exchange of pledges, and of entering into continuing commitments. This phase culminates in the drawing up of some kind of formal document.

Part Two of this book, "Projectors and Projections," will explore this phase.

3. Creating the Firm. The phase of projection culminates with the drawing up of a formal document such as a proposal, a legislative act, articles of incorporation, or a partnership agreement. This document, which for the independent entrepreneur states a "deal," serves to symbolize and legitimate the creation of an organization.

More realistically, the phase of creating the firm begins when men are first brought together in sustained interaction by the entrepreneur, and continues until the firm is well established.

Here, again, there is a marked difference between the creation of organizations by extension and the creation of independent organizations. Resources are usually earmarked in advance when creation by extension takes place. This means that activities can be carried forth in a rational and well-planned way. Furthermore, an organization extension which needs additional support to get itself off the ground can usually secure such support from the parent organization or organizations.

The independent entrepreneur, building his organization from scratch, must typically find support on an opportunistic and not well-planned basis. Furthermore, he cannot retrieve his errors by appeal to a sponsoring system. The new organization must stand or fall alone, and we will see that the crucial factor for the organization's survival is often the driving force of the independent entrepreneur. This phase of organization making will be treated in Part Three, "Creators and the Enterprise."

We have, strictly for purposes of delineation, divided the process of independent organization making into the three phases outlined above. These phases are examined in the first three parts of the book. Having completed this examination, we shall compare independent with administrative entrepreneurs in Part Four, "Independent and Administrative Entrepreneurs: A Comparison."

THE INDEPENDENT ENTREPRENEUR
AND THE ADMINISTRATIVE ENTREPRENEUR

Blinded by the glamor of hardware technology, we have until quite recently not seen the fundamental role of organization making in economic development. It is increasingly apparent that more is required for industrial growth than land, labor, and capital—the big three of classical economics. It is often argued that America developed industrially because of vast natural resources and scarce population. Natural resources, however, are not enough. According to David Potter, what counts is the "aptitude of a society for using" its natural resources:

> Of course, no one ought to minimize the bountiful good fortune which has befallen the American people; but is it not too simple merely to picture the American as the lucky winner of nature's lottery? In other parts of the world other peoples have eked out a meager existence amid natural resources which were technologically meaningless to them and yet were comparable to the resources of

North America. In some places there are people who still do this today. The working economic assets of a society depend not only upon the supply of natural resources but also upon the effectiveness with which resources are converted into energy or productive capacity or goods and even upon the use which is made of these goods in exchange.[1]

Professors Frederick Harbison and Charles A. Myers tested these ideas in an extensive international study of management and entrepreneurship. From their study of industrial development in eleven countries, both developed and underdeveloped, they concluded that:

. . . management is an *economic resource,* or a factor of production. In this respect, it is similar to capital, labor, or natural resources and is combined with them in varying proportions in productive processes. Managerial resources, like capital, for example, must be accumulated and effectively employed or invested in productive activity. A country's economic development may be limited by a relative shortage of this critical factor, or that development may be accelerated significantly by a high capacity to accumulate it. In many instances, moreover, management is an even more critical factor in industrialization than capital, and it is almost always more vital to development than either labor or natural resources.[2]

Harbison and Myers are institutional economists who have been somewhat critical of the sterility of impersonal economics in explaining economic change and development. They have sought to reconsider the role of the entrepreneur and to raise him from the status of an impersonal, profit-seeking computer to a flesh and blood, living human being motivated by sentiments, cultural influences, and intelligence. As such, Harbison and Myers agree with a number of modern economists who are concerned with a rejuvenation of current economic models.[3]

Although theoretical economists have made room for the entrepreneur as a decision maker and an actor in economic events, the

---

[1] David M. Potter, *People of Plenty* (Chicago: The University of Chicago Press, 1954) p. 86.
[2] Frederick Harbison and Charles A. Myers, *Management in the Industrial World* (New York: McGraw-Hill, 1959) p. 19.
[3] Our interest in the entrepreneur was stimulated by our relationship with Professor Harbison at the University of Chicago.

entrepreneur has typically been cast in the role of a rational man who makes optimal choices in an environment of very limited and highly specified dimensions.[4] As such, his function is confined to that of a kind of computational link between impersonal forces on the one hand and foregone conclusions on the other. In short, it has not been necessary to give much attention to the entrepreneur in economic analysis since any rational person seeking optimal choices within a highly specified environment would reach the same conclusion and act in the same way. Something of the same kind of disregard has occurred among economic historians who have analyzed economic events as if they were related to philosophical, cultural, and religious influences, but hardly at all to business activities and the efforts of men to build business enterprises.[5]

If we bring the entrepreneur as a person, front and center, just who is it we are talking about? Is he the man who conceives of a potential new business? Is he the man who promotes the relationships necessary for the new business to come into existence? Is he the consolidator? Is he the man who administers and operates the organization once established? Is he the man who risks his capital in new ventures? These may appear to be unimportant questions, but we are attempting to identify the catalytic agent in society which sets into motion new enterprises, new combinations of production and exchange. We are dealing with an extremely important economic function, and one which may have a great deal to do with the industrialization of underdeveloped countries and with the continued growth of our economy.

Arthur H. Cole agrees with Harbison and Myers that entrepreneurship is essentially a broad organizing and decision-making function. Cole defines entrepreneurship as "The purposeful activity (including an integrated sequence of decisions) of an individual or group of associated individuals, undertaken to initiate, maintain, or aggrandize a profit-oriented business unit for the production or distribution of economic goods and services."[6] Within certain limits, Harbison and Myers subscribe to Alfred Marshall's definition:

[4] See James C. March and Herbert A. Simon, *Organizations* (New York: Wiley, 1958) p. 137.
[5] See Thomas C. Cochran and William Miller, *The Age of Enterprise* (New York: Harper, 1961) Chapter 1.
[6] Arthur H. Cole, *Business Enterprise in its Social Setting* (Cambridge, Mass.: Harvard, 1959) p. 7.

The task of directing production so that a given effort may be most effective in supplying human wants is so difficult under the complex conditions of modern life that it has to be broken up and given into the hands of a specialized body of employers, or to use a more general term, of businessmen; who "adventure" or "undertake" its risks; who bring together the capital and labour required for the work; who arrange or "engineer" its general plan and who superintend its minor details.[7]

Both sources agree that the entrepreneurial function is generally performed by a group rather than by an individual. Cole says:

The aggregate of individuals which together and cooperatively develop the decisions might perhaps be denominated the "entrepreneurial team." It is really a team in the senses (a) that each person or office plays a particular position or represents a particular aspect of the total enterprise, and (b) that each such person or officer is in some measure a complement of the others as far as the total purposes of the unit are concerned.[8]

Harbison and Myers put it this way: "Marshall's assumption, made for purposes of abstraction, that the qualities of entrepreneurship are found in one person can apply in reality only to the very small firm. In most enterprises, a hierarchy of individuals is required to perform entrepreneurial functions."[9]

As well as Harbison and Myers, Cole makes a case for the entrepreneurial team or organization, then tends to identify one individual in the team who is superior to the others and who, in a sense, is the ultimate authority:

Perhaps it should be pointed out here that while there are a number of people involved in the development of a decision, and while the group may be looked upon as a team, there is no escaping the fact that all the members of such a team are not equals in any administrative sense. . . . There remains . . . the chief executive, president, or chairman of the board, who undoubtedly exerts more influence than any other individual in the team, and sometimes, de-

[7] Alfred Marshall quoted from Harbison and Meyers, *op. cit.,* p. 9.
[8] Cole, *loc. cit.*
[9] Harbison and Myers, *op. cit.,* p. 15.

pending on personality or force of character, may have almost the power to veto over all the rest.[10]

Harbison and Myers say:

In the hierarchy of management, the organization builder has a critical role. He may be the owner of the business, a professional manager, or a government official. In any case, he is the top manager who builds the hierarchy. He is the keystone in the arch of management; he cannot be separated from his organization but is fused with it. His function is to establish the conditions under which the other members of management can achieve their own personal goals through performing the tasks which they are assigned in the organization as it achieves its goals. This is the most difficult of all managerial functions. It requires a concept of organization building and a philosophy of management. The tone of the organization is usually sounded by its top executive, and the success of the enterprise may well depend upon whether he infuses the whole hierarchy with energy and vision or whether, through ineptness or neglect, he allows the organization to stagnate.[11]

Harbison and Myers go on to describe the organization builder who, they say, is "the catalytic agent in the process of industrialization, i.e., he acts and reacts with the economic and social environment to bring about economic change."[12] For them, the "organization builder" is the entrepreneur.

Our own view of the entrepreneur follows Harbison and Myers. Their term *organization builder* is an apt description of the entrepreneur, if by *organization* they mean an ongoing system involving productive activities as well as transaction and exchange. We are, in this book, concerned primarily with the "free enterprise" entrepreneur. Furthermore, we distinguish between organization builders who create new and independent firms and those who perform entrepreneurial functions within already established organizations. Perhaps we are, after all, thinking of the entrepreneur in the way Schumpeter viewed him: "everyone is an entrepreneur only when he actually 'carries out new combinations,' and loses that character as soon as he has built up his business."[13]

[10] Cole, *loc. cit.*
[11] Harbison and Myers, *op. cit.*, p. 15.
[12] *Ibid.*, p. 17.
[13] Joseph A. Schumpeter quoted from Harbison and Myers, *op. cit.*, p. 18.

PART ONE

THE SCHOOL
FOR
ENTREPRENEURS

CHAPTER ONE

The Man and the Firm

The creativity of the human mind and spirit takes many different forms. In Part One, we are going to study the lives of men who created business firms. Our interest in these men is not simply biographical and historical. We want to get below the surface and strive to understand the events of organization creation in terms of the drives, tensions, dreams, and actions of men who have shaped successful and ongoing business enterprises. We want to see these men as they were in the world of their childhood, as they went forth as young adults into the world of occupations, and as they were prepared for the most significant creative act of their lives: the bringing into being of a business enterprise.

From the biographical material of these men and from psychological tests taken by them, we will show variations in the "entrepreneurial mode." Our approach is not one of relating effect to cause. The reader should know at the outset that we do not, having completed this study, know "why" men become entrepreneurs.

We do know something quite different, and perhaps far more important. We know that the act of creating a new business is not an isolated and unrelated event in the lives of men. It is true that in America anyone can go into business for himself. It is even more true that only a relatively few unique men can create a business enterprise. The vast majority of us—and the statistics on business failure bear this out—would fail. Most of us would fail quickly and miserably.

For the ordinary person to attempt overnight to create a new business is tantamount to the person who cannot read music sitting down to compose a symphony. The creation of a new business, like any form of creativity, is dependent upon the mastery of fundamentals.

The creation of a business of any significant size and importance requires, however, something more than a knowledge of technique. It requires an inner force that can be translated into mastery
over the checks and setbacks, the apparently insurmountable obstacles, and the never-ending stream of difficulties with which any man
who performs a truly creative act must cope.

In the several chapters that follow we are going to abstract
those patterns of experience and of behavior that seem most relevant
to successful creation of a business enterprise. We will begin with
childhood experiences, and move on through the years of formal
education and occupational experiences that serve as preparation
for the act of creating a business. Our point of departure throughout
Part I is that the business firm established by these men is, in a
real sense, a projection of what they are. It is a creative act of the
highest order.

CHAPTER TWO

The Entrepreneur as a Child

Creating an organization from scratch requires motivation bordering on obsession, a drive that possesses a man and keeps him struggling in the face of obstacles and frustrations.

Men in government who strive to create new instruments which are extensions of already existing systems—such as NASA, TVA, or the Peace Corps—must have both persistence and patience. Men who attempt extension of an existing corporation by establishing a new product department or an overseas division must overcome the dead hand of the past, allay the suspicions of colleagues whose vested interests are threatened, and face other uncertainties contingent upon charting a new and untried course.

Such men, in positions of power and security, create new organizations by securing access to and control over resources already accumulated by existing structures. If they fail in one attempt, they have not lost everything. They still have their positions to fall back upon.

Men, on the other hand, who seek to create organizations from scratch can tap no such treasury of wealth and power. They must work with what they have, and often they have very little. The only security they can know is that security which lies within their own character.

If we are to understand the process of creating new organizations from the beginning, we must dig back into the early formative years of the men who create them. In this chapter we look at the entrepreneur as a child. We do so to find the sources of that driving force which pushed this man through the tribulations he underwent in creating his own business enterprise.

STORIES TOLD BY ENTREPRENEURS

Stories told by entrepreneurs begin, as good stories usually do, with a problem to be solved, with a danger to be faced, or with a bad guy to overcome. As in a good detective story, entrepreneurs put the body on the doorstep with a dagger through the heart in the first paragraph. Their stories cover a wide range of childhood experiences. Yet, if we seek to understand the common rather than the diverse elements in these stories, we can see the foreshadowing of behavior patterns leading to the act of creating a new business.

As they tell it, most entrepreneurs as children were caught up in dramatic, dangerous, and difficult crises. In contrast with big business and federal government executives, entrepreneurs look back on childhood as a time of storm and stress.

What makes these stories so different from those told by corporation or federal executives is not so much the objective fact reported as it is the quality of remembrance, the vividness with which these men recall childhood experiences and weave them into the fabric of their later years.

The stories are built around traditional themes in American life. The tellers talk in parables. The dramas they present convey a theme important only because it portrays the past as it bears upon the emergent present and the unfolding future.

The stories are not in an objective sense "untrue." The events imparted in them probably happened very much as set forth. Two things, however, are added: a stereotype that fits the story into accepted American values, and the presentation of the events as unique experiences of the storyteller. The storyteller is saying to his audience (and this audience includes himself), "Look, you may think this has happened many times. But pay attention, because it never happened to anyone else quite this way."

The occasion for telling the story is only overtly the interview situation. The listener feels that these tales have been told many times, sometimes with other people as the audience. Telling the story helps the teller to clarify in his own mind who he is today, and how he was magically transformed out of what he was in the beginning; and it helps him understand how he is part of his own times and his own place, how he fits into the great cultural sweep which is the history of a nation. Telling his life story also helps the entrepreneur unravel the skein of his own behavior—to answer the questions, "Why did I do it, and what did I get out of it?"

The scenes from childhood are, for most of these men, vignettes of life long ago. How long ago is seen by looking at the age distribution (Table 2-1) of entrepreneurs at the time they were interviewed.

TABLE 2-1

Age of Entrepreneurs at Time of Study

Age	Number Reporting Ages	Percentage
30–34	1	1.2
35–39	6	7.3
40–44	10	12.2
45–49	18	22.0
50–54	24	29.3
55–59	12	14.6
60–64	4	4.9
65–69	5	6.1
70+	2	2.4
Total All Ages	82	

The bulk of these men were between 45 and 60 years of age when they told us about their childhood experiences. Almost half of them were between fifty and sixty, and well over half of them were over fifty.

In telling us about their early years, most of them were reaching back mentally across a span of 40 or more eventful years. Looking back, they saw their childhood as a preparation for that moment when they would have both the skill and the character structure to create their own organizations. If we look back with them, we see through their eyes the shaping of the man who took the creative step of founding his own business.

SCENES FROM CHILDHOOD

Entrepreneurs obviously come from many different backgrounds, and these backgrounds—just as obviously—have an effect on the kinds of businesses they create. Some entrepreneurs create firms which are primarily producers of industrial products, some create professional or customer service firms, some create firms to exploit advances in engineering, some create what are primarily financial enterprises. A man's projection and creation of a firm is necessarily an extension of his early training and experience, but it is not always easy to find the connection.

Occupational Origins. Let us begin by looking (Table 2-2) at the occupations of the fathers of entrepreneurs, making some comparisons between men who created their own business organizations and men who rose to high position in established businesses.

We see that almost one fourth (24%) of the big business executives are sons of powerful and affluent major executives or owners

TABLE 2-2

Father's Principal Occupation: Entrepreneurs
Compared with Business Leaders

Father's Principal Occupation	Percentage of Entrepreneurs[a]	Percentage of Business Leaders[b]
Major executive or owners of large business	1	24
Minor executive (including foreman)	2	11
Professional man, clerk, or salesman	16	22
Farmer	19	9
Owner of small business	25	17
Laborer (skilled or unskilled)	30	15
Other	6	2

[a] Number of entrepreneurs reporting: 80.
[b] Percentages for business leaders are taken from W. Lloyd Warner and James C. Abegglen, *Occupational Mobility in American Business and Industry* (Minneapolis: University of Minnesota Press, 1955) p. 45.

of large businesses, and that an additional 11 percent are sons of minor executives with foremen included in this category. Thus, over one third (35%) of the leadership of big business is drawn from families whose heads held high or low administrative positions in the bureaucratic world.

In sharp contrast, only three percent of the fathers of independent entrepreneurs had as models for their own career aspirations men who held major or minor positions in large organizations. Entrepreneurs tend to come from the nonbureaucratic world. Nineteen percent of them are the sons of farmers, and the interview materials show that many of these were marginal farmers.

Exactly a fourth of the entrepreneurs reported that their fathers owned small businesses. These are men who in their early family experiences observed and learned about independent business as a way of life, but the interview materials show that the attitudes they learned were not always positive. Many reported that their father's business was either only marginally successful or that it had failed.

Finally, almost one third (30%) of the entrepreneurs were sons of either skilled or unskilled laborers. In some cases these sons of working men had artisan fathers who taught their sons the value of skills, but in other cases the fathers were chronically unemployed and "laborers" only by courtesy.

In general, men who enter into corporation life tend to be drawn more heavily from the world of bureaucracy than are men who create their own businesses. Men who create their own businesses are drawn largely from walks of life which are not part of the bureaucratic world of established prestige and power.

To take such bare statistics at face value would be a mistake. They tell something, but they conceal much. For example, we assessed the level of economic and financial security from the entrepreneurs' own recollections of their families of origin. Almost two-thirds of the entrepreneurs described their families as poor, twenty-nine percent said their families were affluent. The fathers of the men who described their families as poor were fairly well distributed through the occupations of farmer, owner of small business, and laborer. However, men who described their families as well off were also distributed fairly evenly through these three categories.

To put flesh and blood on these bare statistical bones, we must look at the variations in childhood experience recalled by these men.

In American thought, the figure of the independent entrepreneur is intertwined with the Horatio Alger theme. This male counterpart of Cinderella is dear to the heart of most Americans. Often stories told by entrepreneurs seem deliberately fabricated to fit this myth. However, many entrepreneurs were driven by forces and values very different from the noble virtues described in the Horatio Alger tales. Let us consider some variations in the next several paragraphs.

The Orphaned and Alone. As an example of sterling character emerging from adversity, let us take Mr. Bowman. Mr. Bowman's real name is on cherished toys found in the homes of many Americans. Unless you happen to know Mr. Bowman personally, you will not know that his interest in toys stems (in his own recollection) from his childhood. Listen to how he tells it:

> My father was from Poland. He died when I was seven years old. He was a young man—thirty-five. It was an accident, and, of course, then my mother, who was born here, had to bear the burden of raising three boys. You might say that some of my earliest influences was as a boy of ten. My mother became ill and was in the hospital; and, therefore, my brothers and I had to go away and stay with my grandfolks. You know how older people are. They just can't cope with young children, so we were put into the juvenile home for delinquent boys for six or seven months. We really weren't delinquent in any manner whatsoever, but this was the only place they had to put us. It was the delinquent home that has left an everlasting impression on me.
>
> The home was very militaristically regimented, you might say. I really learned a lot there. The boys were organized into platoons. This experience was really good for me. I had an opportunity of being put in charge of a group of boys. It wasn't given to me—you had to earn it, and I did. In fact, I was in charge of three different groups. The highest group was for boys up to sixteen years, for drilling and discipline. You can imagine me at that time, ten or eleven years old, in charge of sixteen year old boys and many of them hardened juveniles, but it gave me an opportunity to use my leadership ability. I also learned a considerable amount of diplomacy. You can imagine, a little guy like me—just a half pint—compared to some of those hard and bitter boys.

I had a little disgrace here too. There was a lead gun that one of the boys had and it looked like real. Since I was so interested in this gun, I got hold of it. One of the toughies found out that I had it and I realized that I shouldn't have had the gun, but I was so fascinated with this kind of thing that the toughy squealed on me. I was really ostracized in front of all the fellows and their kangaroo court. This left a lasting impression on me—you have to do the right thing. If you are responsible for something, you have to accept that responsibility and do what is expected of you.

As Mr. Bowman sees it, character formation is very simple and straightforward. One is put on one's own at an early age, one takes responsibility and becomes a leader; and, when one sins and falls from grace, one does not fail to learn the lesson. We shall run across Mr. Bowman many times in this book, and we shall always find him talking right out of Benjamin Franklin's *Poor Richard*. "Honesty is the best policy," he tells us again and again.

Mr. Kenney learned a quite different lesson from poverty. He was not an orphan. His father was an itinerant electrician moving from town to town, but never able to get and keep a steady job. As they went from town to town, Mr. Kenney was learning, and the lessons he learned were applied many years later to problems of considerable magnitude in finance. Here is an interviewer's summary of Mr. Kenney's first business venture:

His first big deal came at the age of eight. There were elections going on. He was delivering papers, and a candidate offered to pay him to deliver cards with the platform and a picture on them. Kenney told him, "I have a better idea. I'll slip it inside my papers and it will cost you fifty cents for all my customers. That way they'll be sure to get inside the house." The candidate was very strong for this, and Kenney subcontracted some of this kind of work to the other newsboys.

At the age of eight Mr. Kenney had already learned a basic lesson: if you have a service to sell, you can make some money. For Mr. Kenney, life has reduced itself to this fact. He soon became more sophisticated:

About this time they had a garden, and the town they lived in was beginning to boom. There was an ordnance operation nearby, and all kinds of itinerants were filling up the town to work there. They lived in tents. Kenney filled up his wagon with garden produce. The first day he went out and sold his wagonload of fruit and vegetables for a nickel apiece. The next day it went so fast, he decided to up the price to a dime. By the end of the week he was selling fruit and vegetables for a quarter apiece. He made a lot of money doing this.

He also went out and bought pigs. He contracted with people in the town for their garbage, on which he raised the pigs to market size.

By the age of ten, Mr. Kenney was making more advanced deals:

This house they had rented when they moved back was sold out from under them. They had no place to go, and there was absolutely no money in the family. He got his brothers together, including some step-brothers by this time, and made a compact with them that they would help support his proposition. He went to a real estate agent whom he finally talked into selling them a house. He bought it with the agreement that there would be no down payment. With a down payment, it would cost him $25 a month. Instead he said, "I have no down payment. I will give you $35 a month mortgage money." Finally the man met his terms, but required his father's signature. The father agreed to it.

At this tender age, Mr. Kenney had solved a family crisis by what we shall in a later chapter call the transactional mode. He kept a roof over the heads of his family by making a "deal."

Both Mr. Bowman and Mr. Kenney learned lessons from poverty. Mr. Bowman learned that honesty, hard work, and responsibility lead to fame and fortune. Mr. Kenney learned that the really smart operator can make a deal. Mr. Bowman subscribes to the virtues of sobriety and industry. Mr. Kenney subscribes to the virtues of being alert and forceful in exploiting opportunities. Mr. Bowman learned that reward comes as a natural consequence of service. And Mr. Kenney learned that profits are made by men who know how to utilize the needs and weaknesses of others.

We will meet both these men later, and will find that as adults each suffered pain and anguish applying these lessons learned in early childhood. For both men, early entrepreneurial efforts brought on insecurity and a return to poverty, but neither ever lost faith in his own version of the entrepreneurial way.

The Escape from Poverty. In mulling over their own early years, men like Bowman and Kenney seek to explain both to the interviewer and to themselves, what "caused" them to establish a business enterprise. Being human, entrepreneurs often seek an explanation within some "crisis." A remarkably large proportion of them identify this "crisis" as poverty. Stereotyped details occur throughout the stories: *The sale from under them of the house that they had rented when they moved back . . . the newspapers that were read and then used as wallpaper . . . the doubt whether there would be food on the table on any given day . . . not being able to have one's shoes resoled and having to put cardboard in them.*

When taken out of context, these details have a shopworn quality. It is only when we read them embedded in the episodes of which they are a part that we see a figure always dear to American hearts, the figure that made Dickens famous, the Oliver Twist or the David Copperfield, the hungry waif bravely facing an unfriendly and uncaring world. Again and again, these men describe how in their earliest years they were caught in the grip of poverty. Their tales of poverty usually point out morals about lessons learned. Two general stances (both rather acceptable to Americans) are taken. The first is the rags-to-riches through sterling honesty and hard work. The second is the hardboiled idea of going it alone, and reaching the top through sheer determination. These two ideas, usually couched in rigid moral precepts, generalize on what entrepreneurs themselves see as the relationship between deprivation and character development.

The theory is that the experience of poverty leads to what these men call "self-reliance" or "independence." They conceive of themselves (and this conception is more than a little grounded in reality), as men who travel fast, travel light, and travel alone. Since as children they were not dependent upon others, as men they have no need of others. Furthermore, they distrust situations in which others control their destinies.

The Escape from Insecurity. This emphasis on self-reliance does not always stem directly from poverty. It sometimes stems from the strange location of older people in the child's world, from the absence of stable and reliable adult figures. Several conditions can be delineated—most dramatic are those stories in which parental figures are removed by illness or by unexpected and violent death. The parent is also often removed from the scene in the sense that he cannot render economic support because he has to travel, or because he is emotionally withdrawn. Finally, in some cases the entrepreneur himself at a very early age removes the father and/or mother from the scene.

Death and Sudden Death. The theme of death and sudden death is often repeated: *He died when I was seven years old . . . lost his father at the age of two and his mother at the age of seven . . . Mr. Merrill's mother died when he was twelve . . . when my father died in 1929 . . . then my father, he died in 1921 or '22.* At first these appear to be mere, passing references to death, but in the entrepreneur's mind death is often associated with a sudden and dramatic turn of events for the worse.

Sometimes these death scenes are told with great vividness—as with Mr. Montague who tells us how his father gathered the ten children around his deathbed and asked them to keep together on the farm. Sometimes the story is without embellishment, stark simplicity underlying the dramatic intensity. The equation is simple: death came, the parent was gone, life became dark and hard.

The Parents Who Went Away. Similar to the parent who dies is the parent who remains alive but who physically or emotionally withdraws from the child. The impact here may be different from that arising from the death of a parent. A parent's death may leave the child with the vague feeling that the parent had rejected him, but any sense of rejection is masked by a feeling of loss and by the fact that the orphan is placed on his own. In the case of the parent removed physically, economically, or emotionally from the family, the feeling is one of pure rejection. Some entrepreneurs recall that their fathers, out of maliciousness, sloth, or incapacity, failed to provide economic support and moral leadership: *He was the laziest man I ever knew . . . in and out of business several times but never made any money at it . . . we didn't starve to death, but we were very poor.*

Such entrepreneurs speak of their fathers with frank disgust, often just before they go on to tell how they quit school at an early age to start out on their own. Often coupled with this "weak and bad" father is a long-suffering and deserving mother: *Somebody had to look after things—Dad wasn't man enough, so I took over.*

The Parents Who Were Sent Away. One curious element in

these interviews was the frequent recurrence of a half-joking or un-selfconscious inversion of the father-son role: *I deserted my father and took a job . . . as soon as I got settled, I sent for my father.*

Here the sons turn the tables on their fathers, reversing the normal relationship. This is a symbolic rejection of the father in his traditional role, but the acceptance of the father on the son's own terms. If the father falls in with this switch, there is sometimes an ensuing warmth of hothouse intensity. One entrepreneur took the interviewer into the plant and showed him the first machine that his father had ever worked on. As soon as he had established himself, the son had bought this machine; and the father, at the time of the interview, was working on it for his son.

The Poor But Honest. So far we have talked of entrepreneurs who see poverty and deprivation as the triggering experience leading to entrepreneurship. Obviously, not all entrepreneurs see things this way. Mr. Thompson, for example, lost his father when he was two, and lost his mother when he was seven. He thereafter "lived around" with relatives, and later with two older brothers. This early breaking up of his parental home seems to have left no impression whatever on Mr. Thompson. He dismisses his early childhood with a few words. When, later, the interviewer leads him back to this supposedly critical period in his life, he shrugs off the matter. Emotionally Mr. Thompson has left the home he never had. Perhaps this is because his older brothers later took special interest in him.

Other men came also from "working-class" families, but regard themselves as children of honest and reliable parents. They tell us they knew security not only from their fathers' employment, but also from a network of supportive community relations.

Such children, seldom moving from town to town, never felt alien and outcast in the communities where they grew up:

> We lived more or less in a subdivision—well, you know, in the kind of area that was going to be absorbed into the city. Our home was in a pear orchard, as a matter of fact. Our father was a machinist. He worked mostly at a manufacturing company that made bookbinding machinery. He also worked for a long time with a surface-grinding company. He retired just a few years ago.
>
> I think I got my mechanical skills from my father. I found at an early age that I like mechanical things. My cousins and others in

my family have all been in this kind of work. I have an uncle who is chief inspector in a Detroit automotive firm and who was superintendent of inspection over five plants there. He is getting ready for retirement now, so he has dropped some of the plants, but he has been in this general line all his life.

We have here the genesis of that kind of entrepreneur who is basically an artisan. Warmth toward an artisan father is here coupled with admiration for an uncle successful in the world of large corporations. This man traces his interest in "mechanical things" both to his father and to his more extended family of orientation.

Mr. Fellows also comes from one of these tight-knit artisan families, but attributes his "drive" to his mother's father:

> Mr. Fellows is the oldest of five children. One of his younger brothers graduated from college and the other brother took two years of college but quit to work with him. Mr. Fellows' father is a tool and die maker and has worked with a manufacturing company for a number of years. He is of Scandinavian descent and was a farmer in the old country. The grandfather on the father's side was also a farmer. Mr. Fellows' mother also came from Scandinavia. Her father was a farmer who also worked in the coal mines. Mr. Fellows claims that he got his drive from his mother's father, who was one of the richer men and a power in the community. He worked twelve hours in the mine and also ran the farm.

In these stable, close-knit, skilled worker families the world view of the artisan entrepreneur is shaped. Early grounding in the skilled trades is crucial technical training, but this technical training is often seen in retrospect as part of a well integrated life style:

> Mr. Yoseloff said that at noon he would walk down with his father's lunch, and then in the evening he would clean up his father's work bench and set it up for the next morning. About the same time, his brother was operating a patternmaking shop in the back yard. He worked along with him. In addition, he had his own little shop in a corner of the yard. He would bring home wood from the plant, make wagons, and sell them to the other kids.

In this account, Mr. Yoseloff is already translating his artisan skill into business enterprise by selling a product to "the other kids."

Mr. Yoseloff's early training in artisan enterprise has paid off. He created and today is president of a foundry.

These children received solid training in the skilled trades. As adults, they made good use of this training, but technical training must be viewed as only one aspect of a more general developmental process. Not least important in this process is the perception of adults as competent and hard working.

By way of contrast to these urban blue-collar children, let us now look at that nineteen percent of our sample who came off the farm.

Off the Farm. For sons of artisans the road to entrepreneurship entails following skills and attitudes learned early in life. For men, however, who were born on the farm there has to be a break with farm life. Why did these boys leave the farm and go to the city?

For some of these men there is no "reason," and they wound up in the city only because of circumstances which they now recall as diffuse and random. These men sometimes say simply that they found farm life uncongenial. Mr. Essex puts it succinctly, "I did not like feeding pigs."

For others, the reason was more compelling. They left to escape poverty and near-starvation:

> Mr. Martin was born near Montgomery, Alabama. He tells us that his mother was second or third generation Scotch-Irish and had very ardent religious convictions. She was an adherent, it is apparent from the interview, to various forms of evangelism. There were four children in his family. They lived in a tarpaper shack. The newspapers were read and then used as wallpaper in the house. There was often a doubt whether there would be food on the table on any given day.
>
> Mr. Martin says he determined early in his life that he would get away from home and earn at least a million dollars to compensate for the poverty he knew as a child.

Mr. Martin has made his million, and several more. Elsewhere in his interview he comments, "It's actually the first *two* million that are the hardest." We really cannot account for why Mr. Martin, rather than some other child born to sharecroppers, made this giant step into the world of large enterprise; but it is intriguing that Martin's older sister was also a business creator. She left home first, and started a florist shop which she expanded into a chain. She married well; her husband was also a small proprietor. Did the sister first dream the entrepreneurial dream and then inculcate her younger brother with it? Did they both read a rags-to-riches story in some now forgotten dime novel?

Other boys, as we might expect, did not choose to leave the farm, but were carried along by fathers who moved from farm to city. Sometimes the transition was gradual. For example, Mr. Brown's father left his own farm to become a supervisor at an electrical plant. However, he never completely gave up farming, but developed in his spare time a truck garden near the plant. During his boyhood, Brown and his brothers did most of the work on this farm.

The transition from the world of farming to the world of business is not always so great as we sometimes imagine, and indeed may not be as great as the transition from the unskilled worker to the business enterpriser. The farmer produces a cash crop which he must then sell. A subsistence farmer, or one who raises a single crop such as wheat, may have only occasional contact with markets. But a man such as Mr. Brown's father, who truck gardens, has problems very similar to those of a light manufacturer who produces and sells many items.

Leaving the farm need not result from a deep need to escape nor from migration of the family. Some men simply drift away because jobs are available elsewhere. As one man put it, "When I was about sixteen I left my father stranded and moved to Detroit."

Most, but not all, of the men from farms recall farm life as a life of hard work and little reward. Mr. Martin describes his father as "the laziest man I ever knew" and looks back on farm life as "hell." Mr. Hart, however, looks back upon his years on the farm as years of security and affluence. He became a blacksmith at an early age, and in his late teens he already had a shop of his own, doing work for neighboring farmers. For Mr. Hart, the transition from farmer's son to artisan entrepreneur was simple, natural, and rewarding.

In Their Father's Footsteps. About a fourth of our sample (Table 2-2) is made up of men whose fathers, as small business men, had made at least one step toward entrepreneurship. One might think that sons of such men would have an advantage in outlook and training over sons of unskilled workers, skilled workers, or farmers. Close reading of the interviews, however, shows that this is not always so. In some cases, in fact, the fathers' failures left the sons fearful and distrustful. For men who grew up while their fathers were striving for a toehold in business, life could be precarious. Mr. Fine, president of Eagle Metals, recalls his father's struggles:

> Until 1936, he was in the metals business similar to this. He was doing fine until the crash of 1929. Things were rough until 1936, when he gave up and went to work for a company that was in a similar business. This didn't work out, so he went into brokerage, selling scrap metal, and so on.
>
> He came here from England in 1908. We had an uncle who lived near Jackson, and he was in the scrap metal business. He sent my father the money for the ticket. After leaving Jackson, my father worked in Chicago for two years, then he got into the scrap business. This was all before World War I.
>
> By 1936, my father was completely broke. He did very well until about 1929, and then, as you know, the crash came along and really messed things up.

Mr. Fine's father committed himself, and was wiped out. After graduating from college, Mr. Fine tried several careers before—as he sees it, somewhat by accident—he went into manufacturing.

Mr. O'Brien's father was born into an affluent family, but in a legal fight over the grandfather's property, the father lost out. O'Brien's father subsequently made only half-hearted efforts to recoup his fortunes. He went into the oil business, and "moved around a great deal." He lived several places in the South and Panama, but "whatever he accumulated, he lost in the 1929 depression. He finally gave up trying to make his living in the oil industry and came to Michigan, where he cultivated a small farm outside Bay City." Here is a somewhat futile man whose life ended with a whimper rather than a bang.

Mr. Montague, delineating in detail his own childhood, tells a tale more in the tradition of stereotyped tragedy:

> Dad was a farmer and a contractor. In 1910, he moved to Chicago to make more money, but in 1916 he was almost broke so he moved to Alma, Michigan. Dad traded the house in Chicago on a farm there. At this time, there were ten children in the family when

mother died in 1918. Then dad was killed in a car accident in 1920. He gathered his children around the deathbed and asked that we keep together on the farm. There were five girls and five boys. A year after dad's death, my oldest brother married a widow with five children. This really made things rough. In three months we lost the farm. Joe, Sally, Ed, and I wound up in the TB sanitarium as state aid cases, and we were kept there for eight months. Then we went to Chicago, where my brother got a job. He couldn't make a go of it there, so he went to Wisconsin.

Here a small businessman lost his business and his life, and from these two events ensued the difficult circumstances under which Mr. Montague began his own career.

Montague's story is in the classic rags-to-riches theme, but in Mr. Cunningham's case the father's failures in business were coupled with a bitter estrangement:

> As far as my family life is concerned, actually, my father worked at a job until he went into the shingle business. My mother was against it terrifically. She fought him. She didn't want him to give up the security of a steady job and go into business. As a matter of fact, they fought for ten or twenty or thirty years afterwards. So my father sort of retreated from us. He would even be gone for two or three months at a time. We were a very poor family. We didn't starve to death, but we were poor.

In each unsuccessful, small-business family, the learning of technical skills may take place in a milieu of physical deprivation and psychic insecurity, but to leave matters thus is to ignore those families in which the father both taught his children the techniques of entrepreneurship and was a satisfactory career model. Mr. Snow, president of Eden Corporation, tells us how his father provided a solid platform on which Snow built his own career:

> When my father died in 1929, my two brothers and I took over my father's moving and storage business, which my father started with a horse and wagon. This was not a very big business, so we added a furniture business. Two years later, we added to this a retail coal business. Then, in 1936, I bought my father-in-law's general insurance business. Two years later, we dropped the coal business and one of my brothers went to work for Sears Roebuck. My other

brother has the furniture and moving business, and I have the insurance business.

Here is a web of organizing activities spun from the father's initial effort. With experience gained from this little group of firms, Snow went on to create a manufacturing enterprise. In such instances, a father may produce as offspring a whole generation of entrepreneurs. Mr. Marsh describes the interlocking of two generations:

My dad was a Great Lakes sailor. One of the trades that he picked up was welding. He used to do a lot of marine boiler repair work. In 1924, dad left the Lakes, and started a welding and repair business with a single portable welder.

My brother Frank—he was the oldest and I am the youngest of the family—worked with my dad and learned the welding business. Soon after we moved to Bay City, Frank married a local farm girl and went to work at a plant as a welder. He worked there for a while. In 1930, Frank and Dad went into the steel fabrication business as partners. In 1939, Frank and two men from Detroit conceived the idea for a domestic product, and Frank started to work on the idea. Two years later, he bought the two men out, and in 1952 he incorporated a separate business.

The brother, Frank, initially went into partnership with his father, and after receiving his basic training struck out on his own. Marsh, elsewhere in the interview, describes how Frank served as a sponsor for him.

The lure of entrepreneurship when learned early may be too strong for a man to follow other pursuits. Mr. Evart's father put him through law school, but Evart seized the first opportunity that came along to go into light manufacturing. He tells us:

My father worked for Ford initially, and then, in 1920, he and his partner went into business producing rubber stripping made of aluminum. He started in the basement of our home, and, as a matter of fact, as a boy I used to work on this stuff on a piece basis. I'd get so much for each piece I turned out. I can remember a friend of mine coming over and wanting to go to a show, and I said, "OK, wait a minute. I have to go downstairs and earn some money first." I would run downstairs and turn out enough pieces and get money to go to a show. In 1922, my father bought out his partner.

Such men, in becoming organization creators, are fundamentally building on a model they find appealing:

> To give you an example, I would drive the truck to pick up the workers, take them to work, pick them up the next morning. I worked with my father, and I must say I learned a lot from my father. In those days fathers were different, and the type of training and discipline we had were also different.

From the Old Families. Few entrepreneurs recall their families as ones in which affluence goes back beyond the father's generation. To round out the scenes from childhood, however, let us look at three of these.

Mr. Dixon is both old family and new American. His father, graduate of the University of London, came to this country to join the faculty of a prestigious university. He combined university research with product development, and formed a corporation to produce these products. He is now listed as a director of a bank and a director of a large corporation, in addition to being the president of the corporation he founded.

Any son, it seems, would respect and imitate so outstanding a father. Mr. Dixon, to the contrary, sees his father as a hostile, grasping, and difficult man. He tells us that, when he was projecting his own first enterprise, he applied to his father's bank for a loan. He says the father had the loan refused, but offered to buy personally enough stock to control the new enterprise. Dixon says, "He never wants to let go—he can't."

Mr. Salisbury is one of several entrepreneurs whose fathers were professional men. Such families may develop a tradition of strong commitment to a calling, but at Mr. Salisbury's generation neither he nor his four brothers entered the ministry. Mr. Salisbury indicates he has a sense of having betrayed the family tradition when he says, "My father told me that I would have made a fifth generation of ministers in our family, except that I fell down and did not do it."

Mr. Abrams also has a strong sense of family. He comes from a highly respected Jewish family, which has long been established in this country. He was born in New Orleans and is the only member of his family in five generations to leave the family town. His father was an artist, architect, and industrial engineer. In his own conversation, Mr. Abrams often refers to his family, indicating at every turn that his own behavior is shaped by what he feels is a mantle of responsibility and leadership bequeathed him by his distinguished ancestors. He sees his father as a man who meticulously adheres to the gentlemanly tradition.

SCENES FROM CHILDHOOD: AN APPRAISAL

We could seek to categorize in greater detail how the social origins of these men foreshadowed varying modes of entrepreneurship. Such pigeonholing, however, if carried very far, is a serious mistake. The thing to keep in mind is that in childhood different routes to entrepreneurship were beginning to emerge. These beginnings were nothing more than points of departure, and cannot be construed as causes leading to effects. We have seen that entrepreneurs come from the less powerful and affluent occupational categories, but that simply placing these men in these categories may mask more than it reveals.

A remarkably large proportion of entrepreneurs see their movement toward the moment when they created their own organizations as essentially a flight—an escape. The strategy is escape, and the tactic withdrawal; but the line of march is recalled as putting extreme demands on the child's reservoir of courage before, as a man, he begins to create his own organization. These men look back across the years to a child who had to leave a life that could no longer succor and protect him, and they see their careers as an escape from that life.

But, more concretely, escape from what? Many of these men, in looking back through the years, vividly relive the times when they went hungry and were cold in their houses, and when their clothes were not warm against the weather. They do not, however, think of physical hardship in and of itself. There is also fear—fear of hunger and of exposure to the cold. They learned this fear, but they also learned shame. Reaching back across the years, they recall the shame felt by the young and by the poor, and the shame felt most keenly by those who were both.

Poverty is most often, but not always, coupled in the minds of these men with emotional or economic insecurity. Aside from poverty itself, they talk of death. Sometimes as they talk, we sense that they are fondling remembrance of the death of a parent. In these stories, however, death is significant not only in that it brings in its wave destitution. Two further motifs frequently crop up.

One such motif is a kind of half-submerged guilt. Often, stories which come through to us in a hackneyed way almost become caricatures serving, we suspect, to conceal a deeper reality. Which of us, suddenly faced with the loss of a protective and loving figure, escapes unburdened by self-blame? Which of us ever puts completely to sleep that voice deep inside that insistently tells us that guilt, at least in part, lies at our door? Which of us can ever deny to ourselves that, at the very least, we could have done more to prevent the tragedy?

We can turn the psychological coin over and look at the other side. Which of these men has ever truly absolved his dead parent for going and for leaving him in a cold and alien world? The guilt is there, but there is also the sense of having been betrayed.

No matter which side of the coin we look at, death for these men figures as a reference point for the beginning of their first bout with insecurity. These stories are told to point the moral that out of tragedy a new man emerges, and that the kernel of this man is bravery. The child must leave because there is no longer nurture and protection. This, however, is the first of many leavings. The child has learned a "leaving pattern."

Closely allied with the theme of death are the stories in which the father appears so weak and incompetent that, to use the words of one man, he "might as well have been dead." Sometimes these men recall their fathers as once able and energetic men who, in the face of crisis, failed and suffered an emotional death. Sometimes they see their fathers as inherently lazy and inefficient, as models of ineffectiveness which they must avoid. Sometimes they are confused by the fact that the father turned completely inward on himself, away from his son and other members of the family, often without hope and not even looking for work. Here the father is recalled as a weak, unknowable, and strange figure who cannot be comprehended. Here, again, the burden is placed upon the son who must find the means of escape.

Sometimes we glimpse a father who was present and able to

provide for his son, but who was emotionally withdrawn from him. Still again, there is the sometimes partially hidden but always festering sore infected by conflict between father and mother. Typically, these sons recall that they tended to take the mother's side. Finally, in some interviews, there is talk of the sheer amount of time that the father was away from home. He may have been a salesman or he may have been looking for work. To these young boys, however, it amounted to the same thing: the father was not there.

In all these stories of escape from insecurity, the quality of remembrance is the same. Here is a mirror of reality, but the mirror distorts and we get a caricature. The child is left alone and unprotected by the sudden, and (for the child) undeserved, removal of the parent. The lonely child, with his grubby fists in tear-filled eyes, accepts the loss and faces up to the dangerous future. Slowly, his determination wells up and the child (a man now) takes his first steps down the lonesome road.

Running alongside, often interwoven with, the theme of the improvident father is the theme of the dominant and the untrustworthy adult. Throughout life, as we shall see, the entrepreneur meets this person. He appears as father, as schoolteacher, as boss, as sponsor, as senior partner, as purchasing agent, as banker. No matter the guise, he always demands too much and gives too little. The entrepreneur always feels that this figure is dangerous and, in a diffuse way, disgusting. At any point the figure may betray him, sometimes by deliberate design, and equally often by careless desertion. We shall see how the entrepreneur frequently defends his own behavior by reconciling it with that of such figures.

Here we are close to one theme in the character development of one kind of entrepreneur. The theme lies in the entrepreneur's relation with this figure which assumes the right to direct and to guide, and, further, the right to discipline the entrepreneur and to correct in him those weaknesses which it cannot overcome in itself. The organization maker sees this figure as one which begins by promising and intending to give all, but which, after demanding love and work, leaves the entrepreneur alone and unprotected. This is sometimes a powerful and persistent figure, but one that cannot be trusted. To recognize this figure is something many entrepreneurs learn early in life and never forget.

The manner in which he learns to cope with this figure is the very style of entrepreneurship. The entrepreneur runs if he can. Otherwise, he irrevocably severs the relationship. Often, however, he can neither cut nor run. He then suffers the presence of the figure and works manfully in spite of it.

Reaching back mentally through the years, these men often recall being trapped by the presence of another figure. This other figure is the mother, deserving and wronged, who needs love and protection. In such cases, the little boy does the only thing he can. Manfully, he steps in and does what was left undone by the delinquent father. He takes over as the man of the house, protecting mother and siblings, simply because the "real" man in the family has proven himself inadequate.

Being the man in the family, however, implies usurping the role of the father. This generates fear, which, in turn, must be escaped. The father may find him in what is rightfully the father's place. This is not to be taken in the strictly Freudian sense of sexual guilt, although in the interview material there is ample evidence to suggest that some men had this guilt feeling. It is, rather, to be taken as meaning that these men have usurped the rightful economic and familial roles belonging not only to fathers but to all male adults. The entrepreneur is, in his remembrance, still the little boy who did what he had to do, but who knows that sooner or later (and for doing what he had to do), he is going to have to face the music.

He is, consequently, always alert and poised in the face of this danger. It is energizing toward the ever present threat that accounts for much of his magnificent behavior in moments of crisis. When the old danger threatens again, he acts with great decision and courage. He must act because not to act is to slip back into an insecure and impoverished world pervaded by the brooding figures of adults who demand but cannot give.

In the chapters that follow, these adult figures reappear many times. We shall see the older man who first sponsors the entrepreneur, and then, having exacted work from him, either turns his back on him or otherwise fails him. We will see the boss who must be rejected because he is a drunkard or a fool. We will see the business partner whose place in the business must be usurped because the partner is disloyal and incompetent. We shall see backers who must be fended off because, having made only a small contribution, they seek to take all. We shall see domineering purchasing agents who attempt to intrude themselves and to "run" the company. The cast of characters changes, but the essential outlines of the drama remain the same.

THE ENTREPRENEURIAL WAY

It is the entrepreneur's relationship to these situations and figures that, in large measure, sets him off from men who, spending their lives in large organizations, uncritically accept the mandates and directives handed down to them. The independent entrepreneur, typically, cannot accept without reservation authority imposed on him either by other people or by the impersonal organization in and of itself. He cannot live within a framework of occupational activity set by others, and he cannot accept in an uncritical manner the rational and legal rules imposed by bureaucracy. He must, in the end, seek another way. It is this seeking of another way that, in the most fundamental sense, makes an independent entrepreneur of him.

In the years of childhood, this relationship with authority and with authority figures is, necessarily, focused around the figure of the father; but it is often generalized to include all adults in a cold and alien world. From their earliest years, entrepreneurs—and this could be substantiated through many lengthy interview excerpts—see these figures as demanding obedience and conformance without offering in return the physical necessities and psychological protection which is due those who conform and obey.

A central and important figure, we shall also see, is the figure who needs to be protected and nourished. This figure is an important one in the dynamics of the plot. We shall see that the entrepreneur almost always does what he does to look out for this figure, whatever its many forms and guises. Sometimes this figure is the entrepreneur's own family of procreation, sometimes it is his own morality, sometimes it is an idea, sometimes it is a defenseless colleague. In the end, it is the business which the entrepreneur has created which must be protected at all costs. Always, in his recollection, the entrepreneur has acted bravely and wisely to protect this figure.

The very act of entrepreneurship is, we shall argue, an act

patterned by modes which these men learn in early childhood. Many times we will find these men caught in situations of insecurity symbolically similar to those they knew in childhood. In such situations, the entrepreneur does not look for solutions within the existing framework of organizational controls. He goes, rather, outside the framework. We shall find that his mode of coping with insecurity and danger is never to return—in more than a tentative way—to organizational security, but to go deeper into dangerous territory. Eventually, in his seeking for a world which he can control and which is secure, he begins a new enterprise. Here he can use his own energies to create a world more tolerable to himself, a new business. This new organization is his world, and from it he hopes to exclude all those figures which have failed or betrayed, and injured him in the past. He can, however, never exclude them from that remembrance of the past that is so crucial a part of his own self. This being the case, he cannot ever, as we shall see, keep them completely out of his new business.

Although this is the way most entrepreneurs must follow, it is not—obviously—the way of all entrepreneurs. We have seen in this chapter that some entrepreneurs—although these are a relatively small group—come from families in which adults were responsible, energetic, and not overly domineering. As we go along, we shall present these cases—but as variations of what is the more characteristic entrepreneurial way.

CHAPTER THREE

A Psychologist Looks
at the Entrepreneur

In the pages above we have brought out themes in the childhood of entrepreneurs. Since the construction of such a schematic intrepretation is always open to the danger that the analyst will "read in" far more than actually is present in such protocols, we secured the aid of a psychologist, Roger Coup, of Social Research, Inc., Chicago, who approached the same problem through analysis of the Thematic Apperception Test protocols.[1] In the following pages, we shall present a cold, bald assessment of the entrepreneur as viewed by the clinical psychologist. Readers unschooled in the jargon of personality psychology may derive from it the notion that entrepreneurs are neurotic men, obsessed by guilt, and confused in their relations with their parents. The reader, however, is asked to keep in mind as he reads the report that it is not the business of a clinical psychologist to say nice things about people. It is, rather, his business to get as close as possible to the wellsprings of human behavior. Underlying patterns of behavior are inevitably the result of adjustments made early in life and often concern the fears and anxieties, as well as the pleasures, derived from the early years. Deep within each of us is a baby or an inexperienced child striving to relate himself effectively to a complex world and building his pattern of adjustment and motivation on premises laid down long before he felt adult emotions and the maturity of adult judgment.

[1] For those concerned with technicalities, the numbers of the cards used in the TAT analysis were 1, 2, 4, 6BM, 7BM, 17BM, and 19 from the "official" collection published by Harvard University Press, plus two special cards used by Social Research, Inc., Chicago, Illinois.

What follows is a summary reporting the main pattern of the personality structure of the entrepreneurs. It does not go into the many variations and direct reversals of the principal configurations. Accordingly, it is neither a report of any one entrepreneur, nor, for that matter, a summary of all of them; it is, rather, a statement only of the dominant themes running through the typical entrepreneur's personality. It is important to keep in mind that this analysis was made "blind," and without reference to the interview data. The following is an excerpt of Roger Coup's findings.

SOCIAL CHARACTER AND VALUES OF THE ENTREPRENEUR

The attitudinal and emotional set of a man is shaped by the unique experiences he has had as an individual and by the broadly shared experiences he has had as a member of a given group, social class, society, and culture. It is to the early shared social experiences that we address ourselves first in appraising the attitudinal and emotional values of the entrepreneur. These are the values which he may mildly accept, fervently believe, deny, or skillfully utilize, but which he must somehow recognize and come to grips with if he is to function as a member of society.

The social value system characteristic of the entrepreneur is steeped in middle-class mores, the "American Way," the Protestant Ethic. This is the value system to which he overtly, frequently, and consistently gives voice in his stories to the TAT cards. In reality, of course, the entrepreneur may not always live up to these values, but for most men in this sample it would appear that failure to do so would lead to feelings of guilt and perhaps to a defensive denial of that failure. One of the most striking features of the TAT stories told by the men in this sample is the infrequency with which "wrong-doing" is an element of the themes. When it does appear in the themes, it is usually but vaguely stated ("He's done something wrong"), and is invariably condemned.

There are six cardinal social values, consistent with American middle-class values, which are often evidenced and underscored in the entrepreneurial TAT stories. These are:

1. The values and experiences of childhood are basically inferior to those of adulthood.

2. Children should honor their fathers and mothers—especially the latter.

3. The mind is inherently superior to the body.

4. Conspicuous display of abilities for the purpose of self-aggrandizement is wrong.

5. Infidelity is wrong.

6. Sloth is evil.

It is apparent that values of the kind outlined above would in practice serve to maximize self-control, external compliance to authority, and industriousness—all in keeping with the values and particular needs of the middle class and of a culture embracing the Protestant Ethic. Moreover, as we shall see, these values play a significant part in the psychodynamics of the entrepreneur.

However, the social values cited above do not in themselves tell us much about the social mobility aspirations of the entrepreneur. The values are middle class, but they would conceivably do as well for the bureaucrat perpetually ensconced in a large corporation as they would for the enterprising, ambitious man who ventures forth to establish his own business.

Lack of Social Mobility Drives. What is lacking here among these entrepreneurs seems to be the value of "getting ahead," rising in a social hierarchy, and achieving positions of authority and rewards associated with power and status. Such evidence of strong mobility aspirations and values is, in fact, singularly lacking in the TAT stories told by the men in this sample. TAT stimuli which normally lead to fantasies about mobility often do not in this sample. Moreover, the instances of mobility aspirations that do occur tend to be negative rather than positive—i.e., the hero is mobile because he is attracted to some richer and more satisfying way of life. Characteristically, the entrepreneur in this sample is not *socially* upward mobile or is so only with some misgivings about the family he has left behind him.

Punishing Pursuit of Tasks and Chronic Fatigue. The entrepreneur regards himself as a very hard-working man. Nevertheless, he often feels a need to drive himself even harder. Failure to live up to this relentless standard gives rise to uneasiness or a sense of guilt. This dedicated, and often punishing, pursuit of demanding tasks serves the entrepreneur as a primary control mechanism, helping him to keep in check internal forces which he is prone to fear and cannot integrate acceptably into an overall, balanced personality structure.

Although the entreprenuer may, in fact, be a hard worker, the important point here is that his work *seems* especially hard to him because of his tendency to overexpend himself in his activities, to invest more energy than his actual objectives might warrant. To his associates he may appear as a man with "plenty of spare energy to burn," but he himself is more apt to experience a feeling of chronic fatigue or that life is unduly hectic. In some cases, this punishingly strenuous activity may be of a sporadic nature, a flurry of "make-work" activity following a period of guilt inducing "rest." The ensuing state of exhaustion is symbolically important to the entrepreneur, even though it may suggest to an objective observer that the overall output is disproportionately low, relative to the energy put into the task.

The entrepreneur, with very few exceptions, evinces no "love" for his work, devoted to it though he may be. He is not, typically, a man who knows how to enjoy his industry or the fruits of his labors. Indeed, he is sometimes suspicious of those who do enjoy their work, as though this were somehow impossible or an indication that the work must be basically unworthy or trivial. The result is that the entrepreneur is left with a feeling of never being quite able to reach any satisfactorily definable and rewarding goal. His response to this is a renewed striving for further, equally unsatisfactory goals. Hence his feeling of restlessness and need to move on to new fields. In the eyes of his associates, however, he is apt to be perceived as a man who never rests content with past successes, but who must ever strive anew for additional triumphs.

Lack of Problem Resolution. The entrepreneur does not, typically, resolve the problems he perceives in the TAT cards (half of the time he poses no outcome to his stories). At his best, he can elaborate the problems for each card *and* the kinds of solutions that would resolve these problems, but somehow he manages to avoid bringing the problems and the theoretically correct solutions together to effect a resolution. It is as though he panics at the idea of success or too much success.

As implied thus far, the ego structure of the entrepreneur tends to be weak, the super-ego dominant, and the id ever-threatening. On the one hand, the entrepreneur is keenly aware of the moral precepts (super-ego or parental-induced values), on the other hand, he is consciously or subconsciously aware of impulse needs (id or bodily induced values). But he demonstrates little in the way of a strong ego that can reconcile and integrate these forces. Consequently, the entrepreneur tends to perceive the world in rather simple terms of irreconcilable dichotomies—black *or* white, good *or* evil, mind *or* body, dominant *or* submissive, work *or* enjoyment, total abstinence *or* total abandon. A golden mean between these posited extremes is not commonly known to the entrepreneur.

The intensity, simplicity, and narrow scope of the drives of the entrepreneur may, of course, be a positive asset in the realization of his successful career pattern. His energy may be partially wasted, but what is not wasted is channeled into narrow grooves and may well be all the more effective for that. The entrepreneur is not the kind of man who tolerates extraneous issues—and he tends to include all but the most essential activities and considerations in such a category.

The Relations of the Entrepreneurs with Subordinates. The entrepreneur's relations with subordinate figures are satisfactory when on a patriarchal or patronly basis. In such instances, the relationship may be a very warm one (often with narcissistic overtones), with the entrepreneur admiring the eagerness, industriousness, and compliance of the subordinate. Often, however, it is "bad me" rather than "good me" that the entrepreneur projects onto subordinate figures—it is the latter who are condemned for entertaining the sloth, lechery, rebelliousness, and similar "vices" that the entrepreneur resists within himself. This suggests that the labor relations prevailing in the entrepreneur's plant might tend to be extremely good or bad (and/or mercurial), depending on whether employees are perceived as the embodiment of "good" or "bad" aspects of the entrepreneurial self.

Peer Relations and Partners. Relations with male peer figures tend to be the least strained of the entrepreneurial relationships.

These peer relations are most successful when they involve parallel social pursuits outside of a business organizational framework. When more serious pursuits are involved, the entrepreneur becomes apprehensive lest the peer ties be weakened or broken. Moreover, almost any peer relationship becomes a source of anxiety whenever the question of hegemony arises within the group. A peer relationship, in other words, may be seen as a relationship which is on the verge of resolving into a superordinate-subordinate relationship. This suggests that the entrepreneur is not only a man who needs to break away from a larger organization in order to establish an independent business, but also a man who would have difficulty entering into a successful partnership in that business. A need to dominate or a fear of domination would tend to make the "partnership" an unstable one.

Relations to Authority. Superordinate relations are the least effective and affective of all entrepreneurial interpersonal relationships. *Parental* authority figures are perceived as powerful and persistent beings who are usually able to secure external compliance with their wishes. In the face of this authority, the child is neither able to internalize nor able to rebel against the parental norms. There are seldom heroes or idols among the adults in the child's world, and the child does not, as a rule, independently pursue adult-approved goals. On the other hand, the child seldom *actively* resists these goals. Instead, he complies with these goals without ever making up his mind as to whether or not they are what he wants. In a sense, it is a case of having a cause without a rebel. The child's complying without conviction to the parental press is analogous to the man's driving himself without a sense of enjoyment in what he is doing or in the goals he is pursuing (as we have described the entrepreneur at the beginning of this section). The inability to resolve successfully in childhood the question of whether to internalize or reject the parental norm continues to plague the entrepreneur in adulthood.

This is not to suggest that in actual life the typical entrepreneur as a child was not actively rebellious or that as an adult he does not express overt resistance to authority figures. The need for autonomy on the part of these men is great and would at times naturally manifest itself. What the TAT data do suggest is that the area of autonomy is *still* a sensitive one to these men who have achieved *occupa-*

tional autonomy by establishing their own, independent businesses. Their sensitivity in this area is evidenced by their inability, even now, to fantasy about it with ease, either by acknowledging overt resistance to authority or by demonstrating a more mature acceptance and internalization of the value system of authority. By establishing his own business, it would appear that the entrepreneur is expressing his need to act out these unresolved childhood problems in the area of autonomy. It should be noted that in doing so he is actually bypassing the heart of his problem, for he is achieving his autonomy *outside* of the "alien" business organization—a symbolic family. He has not yet learned how to function successfully within an organization of which he is not the dominant authority, just as he could not function successfully as a child within the family dominated by the parents.

The entrepreneurial personality, in short, is characterized by an unwillingness to "submit" to authority, an inability to work with it, and a consequent need to escape from it. Even though the entrepreneur is "his own boss" in his own establishment and devoted to his business, he does not obtain a lasting sense of satisfaction and fulfillment. This suggests that the explanation in the opening sentence of this paragraph does not go far enough in accounting for the behavior of the entrepreneur. To supply this deficiency, we must look further at the nature of the entrepreneur's problems with authority figures and the special meanings that a business of his own may have for him.

Remoteness of Male Authority Figures. Male authority figures are perceived by entrepreneurs as shadowy, remote beings. They are not, characteristically, sought out for help or looked up to as models to be emulated. "Father" figures are seen as being anxious about the exercise and recognition of their authority, demanding a respect which does not appear to be fully warranted by the facts and which the "son" figures are never quite able to grant. Moreover, in about a fifth of all cases, the "father" figures are perceived as encouraging their "sons" to rationalize away their mistakes or to overlook their basic principles. The overall picture of the male authority figure is one of a remote but dominating person, who is a bit of a fraud, and a rather attractive one at that. The manner in which this fantasy is handled by the entrepreneur suggests that the following interpretation would be in order: the father figure is remote in that he is affectively cold and unsupporting; but he is close in that he is powerful—sometimes frighteningly so—hence the need to relieve anxieties by perceiving him as a god with feet of clay; he is envied by the entrepreneur, but he cannot be readily emulated because the entrepreneur resents the act of emulation.

Two Views of Females. Female authority figures tend to be perceived as either motherly (good), or seductive (bad). In the role of motherly, good women, they are the repositories of the middle-class virtues of morality and industry. It is they who insist that things be done "right" and that they be done well. In the role of seductive, bad women, they are perceived as attractive, unattainable, and undermining all of the virtues of the good women. This entrepreneurial dichotomization of the female role in turn engenders anxieties as to the proper masculine role, whether to be the "good" son or the successful lover.

As implied from the preceding, unresolved childhood conflicts are basic to the psychodynamics of a major segment of entrepreneurs. Repeatedly, analysis of the TAT themes points to the following aetiology of the entrepreneur: a sense of disillusionment, of having been deceived, especially by the mother; a desire to emulate the father, to assume his role with the now bad, but intriguing mother; a fear of punishment or castration at the hands of a powerful, jealous father.

A SUMMARY OF THE ADJUSTMENT PATTERN OF THE ENTREPRENEUR

In summary, the aetiology of the entrepreneurial personality may be stated as follows:

1. Because of unresolved fears of the father, the entrepreneur is uncomfortable in a situation which requires him to serve under strong male authority figures. In such a situation, he is apt to feel that his freedom of action is unduly restricted. In some cases, anxieties may be great enough to impede maximum development of potential skills on the job and the realization of "too much" success (which would invoke the jealous wrath of the male authority figures).

2. The entreprenuer, moreover, finds it difficult to function effectively and gratifyingly within an organization (a symbolic mother

figure) which is not his own but which belongs to a male authority (symbolic father) figure. Such a situation too closely corresponds to the traumatic childhood experience in the family.

3. By establishing a business of his own, the entrepreneur is seeking a way of symbolically working through this oedipal impasse. The business is his own mistress, so to speak, and he need not be so anxious about controlling himself in order to escape the wrath of jealous male authorities. The entrepreneur can thus act out the need which is, of course, repressed so deeply from conscious thought and expression.

4. The entrepreneur's own business, then, is symbolically the "bad" mother, which the entrepreneur has at long last come to possess. Like the father figure he has symbolically replaced, the entrepreneur, too, is a jealous being who cannot rest content without exclusive possession. For this reason, a partnership is likely to be a fragile and discordant relationship. As in its primeval counterpart, the "sons" who have banded together to acquire their rights to a business, a falling out and final struggle for exclusive possession is an expected development.

5. By this establishment of the business, his exclusive possession of the "bad" mother, the entrepreneur has come into his own. Here he can demonstrate his maleness, prove his masculinity.[2]

6. Yet, although the entrepreneur's autonomy has thus been symbolically as well as literally attained through the establishment of his own business, this autonomy is a tenuous state of affairs and one which is often apt to seem dissatisfying. It is only a symbolic solution to the problem, and even in that sense it is "wrong." A man highly disturbed in this respect might experience a vague, "groundless" anxiety even—or perhaps especially—when his business and life seem to flourish with success. Such an entrepreneur experi-

---

[2] This conforms with reported interview data to the effect that trophies, guns, and "male" paraphernalia are customarily displayed on office premises rather than on or over the family residence mantel. The TAT data also suggest, as does this arrangement of furnishings, that in the entrepreneur's dichotomized world of females the wife is required to fulfill the role of the "good" mother. The entrepreneur thus has his wife and keeps his mistress. This symbolic analysis is further supported by reported interview data that the entrepreneur often prefers to conduct business meetings at his home, away from business premises— much as a respectable man will invite his friends to his home but steer them away from his mistress's apartment.

ences a subconscious need to punish himself for his "wrongdoing" by bringing about his own failure in the enterprise.

7. Once this self-punishment has been effected, however—by financial loss or bankruptcy—anxiety would be relieved and the entrepreneur again would be free to function effectively. In actual life, such a man might be perceived by his colleagues as one who "shines" at his best the very times when he is seemingly "down and out." This ability to function well in the face of adversity and to stage a successful comeback would constitute a reservoir of strength for many of these men—just as their inability to tolerate too much success would be a serious source of weakness.

8. The observable career pattern, thus, might for a number of men take on the aspect of a rather hair-raising rollercoaster ride—a succession of ups and downs, dramatic reversals of success and failure, streaks of seemingly good and bad luck.

This ends the interpretation of the TAT material.

One point of congruence between our interview material and the TAT analysis is the place of adult figures in the world of entrepreneur. It is the entrepreneur's relationship to these figures that, more than any other one factor, sets him off from the men who spend their lives in large organizations and who uncritically accept the mandates and directives handed down by "leaders." The entrepreneur, typically, cannot accept without reservation the leadership of others. He cannot live within a framework of occupational behavior set by others. He must, in the end, seek another way. It is this seeking of another way that, in the most fundamental sense, makes an independent entrepreneur of him.

CHAPTER FOUR

Formal Education:
Dropouts and Graduates

Formal education is often compared to an escalator, each grade in school being a getting-off point. Those who get off early are relegated to poorer-paying and less prestigious jobs. The longer a man stays on, the greater his chances of reaching higher occupational levels and becoming a man of prestige and power. Usually, the formal education level a man achieves tightly bounds and controls his career opportunities. Studies of big business leaders and of executives in the Federal Government have shown that these elite positions are increasingly reserved for men with higher education.

Although entrepreneurs (Table 4-1) stay longer on the escalator than does the "average" man, they get off much earlier than corporation executives. Thirty-nine percent of the entrepreneurs failed to finish high school, but only thirteen percent of the big business leaders left the escalator at this early point. At the other extreme, twenty percent of the entrepreneurs graduated from college. This compares with fifty-seven percent of the big business leaders.

Only one in five entrepreneurs, therefore, stayed on the escalator through college graduation. In a world in which success in education is seen as leading to success in occupation, these men made it—in the overwhelming majority of cases—the hard way. Why are so many entrepreneurs drawn from the pool of the relatively undereducated?

There is an obvious connection between their relatively low occupational origins, their poverty, and their poor performance in formal education. Many studies have shown high correlations between the father's occupational or social-class origins generally, and the level of the son's educational achievement. There is, however, more to the matter. These same studies have shown that when men of lower occupational origins have moved to high positions in big business and big government, they have done so by first securing higher education. Why do men with educational deficits turn to independent entrepreneurships?

TABLE 4-1

Educational Level: Entrepreneurs Compared
with Business Leaders and General Population
in Michigan

Educational Level	Percentage of Entrepreneurs[a]	Percentage of Business Leaders[b]	Percentage of General Population in Michigan 25 years old and older[c]
Less than high school	17	4	37
Some high school	19	9	22
High school graduate	25	11	26
Some college	19	19	8
College graduate	20	57	7

[a] Number of entrepreneurs reporting level of education: 84.
[b] From Table 39 in Warner and Abegglen, *Occupational Mobility in American Business and Industry* (Minneapolis: University of Minnesota Press, 1955) p. 96.
[c] Computed from data appearing in U. S. Bureau of the Census, *U. S. Census of Population: 1960*.

Blocked Mobility. An explanation often offered is what sociologists call "blocked mobility." Many of these men, the argument runs, become entrepreneurs because they cannot envisage a future in the large bureaucracies or in the professions. Such men, finding advancement blocked, elect to set out on their own and create their own businesses. As presidents of their own companies they are hardly likely to impose a rule that presidents must be college graduates.

Entrepreneurs often tell stories which support this notion. Mr. Houton says he struck out on his own because he saw "the handwriting on the wall." He tells us that he had been in charge of an engineering operation with four men under him, but that, "after the war, they started to bring in people who were better educated." To take another instance, Mr. Peet says, "the greatest motivating force for my going into business for myself was the fact that I lacked formal education." Mr. Peet had for eighteen years worked for an automobile company and at the time he left had about 150 men under him. He felt he was blocked from advancement because he did not have an engineering degree. He struck out on his own, formed a partnership to produce sporting goods, promptly had trouble with his partner, and went broke.

The blocked mobility pattern is, therefore, present. In itself, however, it tells us little. We must look at men who left the escalator at different stages, examine the circumstances in which they left, and evaluate how their leaving patterns were preparation for their becoming business creators.

Intervening Opportunities. One common American point of view is that men leave the formal education escalator at an early age because they cannot afford to stay on it. Examination of stories told by entrepreneurs forces modification of this notion. Some of these men do recall economic deprivation and lack of financial support as decisive. Some, however, say that they dropped out because they felt restless and thought that they were not "getting anywhere."

Economic forces do influence decisions to drop out, but more often than not these forces have a "pulling" rather than a "pushing" effect. We have examples of men forced out of school by hunger, poverty, and the need to support their families. Others were drawn out of school—and this was often the more immediate factor—by eagerness to get "on their own," to get away from threatening adults, and by the occurrence of an opportunity to make the break.

OFF THE ESCALATOR AT AN EARLY AGE

The reader has already met Mr. Kenney, the son of an ineffective worker who moved around from place to place unable to hold a regular job. Fred Kenney, dropping out in the fourth grade, is part of that seventeen percent of entrepreneurs (Table 4-1) who never got to high school. We could say that Kenney did not have the "opportunity" to continue in school and we would not be far off the mark. We would, however, be leaving a good deal out. While still in his pre-teens, Fred Kenney was distributing campaign literature, handling a paper route, huckstering fruit and vegetables, and setting up a deal to buy a house. He was so engaged and moved so much from town to town that he did not go beyond the fourth grade. This is not surprising. Kenney himself, however, does not recall leaving school as having to do either with these economic enterprises or with having to look out for himself. He says, rather, that he told the teacher how to run the school and that he was "kicked out." By telling the teacher off, Fred Kenney recalls that he deliberately cut himself off from formal education and was thereafter free to concentrate on his business activities.

Like Mr. Kenney, Mr. Tyron did not graduate from grade school. Tyron's father died when he was three years old. His mother "went out as a scrubwoman and also brought laundry to the house" where Tyron helped her with it. At the age of nine, Tyron was selling papers on the streets of Cincinnati. He was a late starter, not getting his first full-time job until he was sixteen. Perhaps he was needed at home to help his mother with those dirty clothes. Unlike Kenney, Tyron attributes dropping out to brutal economic necessity.

Mr. Walden is also from a poverty stricken home, but Walden recalls that:

> I went to a Catholic school, but nothing was more terrible than going to school. I had bad grades. My parents, being poor, had no ability to pay the fees. The teacher would ask the questions in class, and I could not give the answers and I was embarrassed.

Although brute poverty was there, it was shame with Walden that was crucial.

Sheer economic distress undoubtedly takes its toll, but Mr. Herzler's father was a well-established, skilled craftsman. Herzler could have gone on, at least through high school, but he was restless. He felt that life is fleeting and that time in school is time wasted. Choosing an alternate route, he took his first full-time job at fourteen. He wanted to learn die casting, but the company did not have a job open. Consequently, he was put on a machine. He stayed on his first job about a year and a half, learning "to operate every machine in the shop." Mr. Herzler regarded formal education as a poor substitute for the kind of knowledge a man really needs.

Like Herzler, Mr. Swisher left school to get ahead with the business of life. Also like Herzler, he traded book learning for education in the world of work. He says he "found no interest in school," and adds:

> I learned more things about life going to and coming from school than in the classroom itself. As soon as I left school, I decided to become self-supporting and get out of the poverty in which my family was for such a long time. With this in mind, at the age of fourteen, I took up my first job. (He worked in a series of small plants.) By working in small places like that, I knocked around and learned quite a bit.

All the men we have talked about so far were cut off from formal education. In the excerpts from their stories, however, we see them beginning another kind of education. These men are enrolling in what used to be called the "school of hard knocks."

HIGH SCHOOL: THE INTERMEDIATE RANGE

Nineteen percent (Table 4-1) of the entrepreneurs had only some high school, and twenty-five percent were high school graduates. This makes forty-four percent, or roughly a little less than half, of the entrepreneurs.

Let us look first at some high school dropouts. Most of the men in this group recall leaving high school as both a rational and voluntary act. Economic deprivation is often mentioned in passing, but most of these men recall boredom in school and excitement in the outside world.

Some were while attending high school already working full-time. Mr. Hoebel tells us that while in high school he worked for his father in the roofing and siding business. He solicited business one day, and if he was successful he would go around the next day to do the job. Since he found enough work, he never finished high school.

Mr. Hart of Hart Forgings began as a blacksmith at about fifteen; he enjoyed working with horses and repairing farm equipment for neighbors. During those years when other men were securing education in high school, Mr. Hart was getting his basic training in a blacksmith shop.

Mr. Brown also was a high school dropout. His father, a craftsman, bought a plot of land and used his children to work it. Brown says his father "made certain that I had more than enough to do at all times; improving the land, sowing, growing, and harvesting the truck-farm crop." The father in this story apparently believed education was a useless waste of children who otherwise could be gainfully employed. Mr. Brown says he was "glad" to get away from both school and his father and to strike out on his own.

These men learned to play adult occupational roles at an age when most children are looking forward to high school dances. They were fed up with the role of student; they talk about their yearnings for financial independence and freedom from parental supervision, their desire to marry young, or their need for self-expression and creativity. They were often from families which could have financed their schooling but they preferred to go to work. They did not give up learning: they simply transferred to another kind of school.

Now let us look at some of the men who graduated from high school. This is the largest group in our sample, with 25 percent—or one out of four entrepreneurs—in it. These men fall into three rather broad groups.

For some of them a high school diploma was a solid accomplishment. They either worked and went to school simultaneously or vacillated between school and work. Some of them finished high school by correspondence or by night school. Overlapping with this group are those men who came from families in which finishing high school *is* being educated, and having achieved this goal one goes to work. Finally, there are a few men who, having finished high school, wished to go on to college. For one reason or another, they did not do so. Some of these men speak wistfully of having missed out.

Mr. Carlson found completion of high school a goal in itself. His father had decided that he should become a minister, and Carlson in his early years concurred. He finished the sixth grade, and then went to a seminary preparatory school. He attended one year, and then decided he would rather stay home and earn money than go to school. He dropped out, but believed he should complete high school and did so, by going at night and taking correspondence courses. The night school habit has stayed with him and, although he has never tried college, Carlson is still taking courses.

Consider, also, the case of Scott McDonald.

> Mr. McDonald at age twenty-eight graduated from high school. He did so with an iron obstinacy. He tells us that the farm on which he was raised was "marginal land, very hilly, clay soil and rocky." He also tells us that they made "at the end of the year only enough to pay up debts." His father, while Scott was still a boy, became deaf and "put the burden of running the farm" on Scott. As a young adult, Scott decided to go back to school. He tells us this "upset" his father. For many years, McDonald both ran the farm and went to school.

Carlson and McDonald feel that high school graduation is to be achieved at all costs. Other men recall high school graduation as the natural end of their education careers. These men were expected (by themselves and others) to go through high school, even if they held outside jobs. Mr. Fish interwove his high school with his work experience:

> Well, I worked all through high school—gas stations, other spots. Incidentally, I waited on the Al Capone mob when I was in a gas station. One of them had a place nearby. They used to tip well, a quarter. After high school I went to work in a factory at 35¢ an hour.

Some men were "pulled" out of formal education by the chance of a job, but some stayed on and finished high school because they had a narrow technical interest:

> I had decided to take up a vocation and I went through printing training. While I was in school I was able to spend four hours a day in the various print shops in the area, and I learned the trade. Upon graduation from high school in 1941, I decided I wanted to go to work as a printer in some small print shop. I enjoyed this kind of work, and I found it was best suited for my talent. In school I was terrible in English. In fact, I even flunked bookkeeping. All

through high school, even to this day, I don't know how to write. I did learn how to write my name so that I could sign checks, but as of now, that is the only thing which I can write. The rest of it, whenever I have to communicate with anyone, I have to print it.

Only a handful of high school graduates express regret that they did not go on to college. Mr. Shea expressed such regret, but then tells us that he graduated from high school when only sixteen, and among the top four in his class. He wanted to go to Notre Dame University, but he says that, in this context, all through his early years he had trouble with his father. When his father decided against Notre Dame, Shea put aside the idea of college. At sixteen he left home and the father who would not allow him to go to Notre Dame.

It is not, therefore, educational attainment, or lack of it, that is important. It is also the way men define educational achievement. For some, high school graduation is enough. They are oblivious to the need for or the possibility of going on to college. They do not understand college, and they see no relevance for it to their lives. Often their educational aspirations beyond high school lie in special noncollege training. There are, however, a few men who feel that in missing college they have been deprived of social and work skills, and deprived, perhaps, of a deeper understanding of the world in which they live. One such high school graduate greeted the interviewer by saying, "You'll have to excuse my English. I am not an educated man. I can only talk shop."

Whatever interpretation these men place on education, elite positions in American society are increasingly the preserve of those who have gone to college.

COLLEGE MEN AND COLLEGE GRADUATES

Thirty-nine percent of the men in our sample attended college, but half of these (19%) left college without graduating.

Let us look first at men who started college but did not finish. We usually apply to college dropouts the stereotypes that we apply to high school dropouts. We think in terms of victims of deteriorating families, of poor students who run out of money or get married too early, of students pulled out by the draft. Any of these factors may be contributory, but entrepreneurs more usually leave because of intervening opportunities. Sometimes these men drift in and out of college, aimless until a precipitating incident such as a job opening finally pulls them out for good.

Mr. Powell financed his own way in college; his decision to leave was a conscious and rational one:

> Then I decided that I wanted to go to the university. Actually, before I could go to the university, I had to return to high school for about six months and repeat the last part to get ready for the university. While I was going to the university, I went into business with my father. Actually, I was a better carpenter than my father. He had learned carpentry late in life, so he used to do the outside of the house and I would do the inside finish work. So, I was running this business while I was going to the university.
>
> I registered in civil engineering and things were pretty rough at that time. They used to really weed them out. In my Sophomore year, I started second in my class, and then by the end of the term I was right down near the bottom. About this time, businessmen would come in and talk to the class and they would tell us, "Well, if you're lucky when you finish, you might get about $125 as an engineer, probably more like $85 or $90." Here I was already making $100 a week. Well, it seemed that I just couldn't handle this engineering and run the business, too, so I switched to liberal arts. I remember taking one term of psychology. That was in 1927, and I'm still a pretty good psychologist. So, with the pressure of these things, I had to leave school. Then I went into full-time business.

Increasingly caught between the role of businessman and student, and finding that college would not immediately increase his earning power, Powell left the university.

Unlike Powell, Mr. Snow came from a family well able financially to send him through college. In his case, however, a death pulled him back into the family business:

> My father was in the moving business, which he founded. I believe my father encouraged all of us to go into the business. I went to high school, then to junior college for two years. I quit school in 1929, when my father died. I left there to join my brothers in the moving and storage business.

Mr. Grant recalls that he left because the lure of the family business was irresistible. His father had started the business in the basement of their home, and Grant from his earliest years had an intimate knowledge of it. Although the business was doing fairly well and the father was providing a comfortable living for the family, Mr. Grant had always been required to work in the business. After graduating from high school he went to junior college for two years, and then:

> I thought I wanted to be a lawyer, so I went to law school at the university—it's a night school—and I stayed there until 1937— three years—and then I quit. The reason for this was that I was working part-time on the business, and I found that I got more interested in the business, and there was more work to be done there, so I finally quit law school. I was looking through some of my old law books, and I noticed down in the margins of some of the pages I was making diagrams of different forms of weather stripping so I must have been losing interest in the law school.

That leaving college is involuntary is an idea which must be reconsidered. In these stories we see men caught in two worlds, the world of education seen as preparatory for the occupational world, and the occupational world itself. It sometimes seems senseless to push on with formal education as a means of getting ahead if education is actually holding a man back. Increasing pressures of outside work and opening up of career lines lead to progressive disinvolvement in school and studies.

These men, looking back, usually regard leaving school as a step in the right direction. They do not recall being forced out, but recall the move as one opening up more immediately lucrative lines.

An intervening opportunity may disrupt the pursuit of higher education, but there are also men who do graduate from college because no such opportunity presents itself. These men stay in college through graduation because they have nothing better to do. Mr. Forester puts it this way:

> About the time I graduated from high school, Dad beat up on Mom again and left us for the last and final time. We were on relief and I got in the three-C's awhile, but I couldn't take the chicken and went over the hill. I rated a dishonorable discharge for that, but I talked them out of it. Then I was out of work and hanging around home eating food that ought to have gone to the little kids, and I was pretty sick of it. Then these fellows I knew in high school came

by the house. They asked what I was doing and I said I couldn't find anything to do. They said, "Why don't you come up to the university? You can always make a living in college, and it's a real soft life." Well, tuition was low, and I qualified for odd jobs through the school.

I was on NYA, and then I found out as a college student I could get a pretty good job in the summer. Well, I kind of drifted through college, and I had more money of my own to spend than I've really ever had since. The feeling of having money like that, I mean. Well, I guess I drifted through college marking time for something to come up. Nothing ever did, and I woke up one day and found out I was a college graduate. Nothing ever surprised me so much, and I figured it was time I got down to work.

These college years may have been a little more difficult than Forester's nostalgic remembrance portrays them. Later in the interview he comments:

These kids that give you this "working your way through college" routine. How hard it is. I just give them a sympathetic smile. I never let on I did it myself and it was easy. That would be taking something away. When you're real young it is hard. Everything is hard. It's only later you find out what hard really is.

In contrast to Forester, some of the men did have a strong desire to go to college. Mr. Buck, president and sole owner of a large business, is one such man. Buck's family was hard hit, with no food in the house at times, and moving from place to place in a constant search for work. Buck tells us how he dreamed of college and how, out of his early jobs and deals, he collected enough money to start. The war came along and, returning from service, he qualified for the G.I. Bill. This introduced complications into what had been a rather placid college life before the war:

In February, I came back to college. I had the G.I. Bill at that time which made it much easier for me. In addition to this, I got into the counseling service. I don't exactly recall how, but I might have suggested it. Anyway, I saw a good chance to get a job doing counseling, and they gave me a job as a counselor. This helped me a lot. They gave me a nice private room with a bath and a telephone. Also, I got my board and room. It was a nice deal. I might say that I was one of the more affluent students since I had everything paid for and my G.I. Bill was on top of that. I decided I wanted more liberal arts.

Buck goes on to tell us how opportunities intruded until finally he had to rush through the last phase of college as if the devil were on his tail:

> Towards the end of my college life, I was getting very anxious to get out. I always had a burning desire to finish college, but I was anxious as hell to get on with a career. It was a battle royal with myself whether to finish or to go to work. I ran into a fellow that had an item that I really thought would go. It looked like something had to be done on it very quickly, so I went around to all my professors and explained what the situation was. They all let me out of the final exams except one professor of philosophy. He was a visiting professor from an out-of-state university. He agreed that if I sent him some reports that he would let me off the final. Actually, I still haven't sent him those reports and I still feel guilty about it.

Buck barely made it, getting his degree before the world of work gobbled him up.

There were, of course, men in our sample who went through college supported by their families and who viewed college as an expected part of growing up. Mr. Kuhn was one such man. When he returned during vacations to his home town, he worked with his hands in his father's business but this seems to have been nothing more than a symbolic gesture.

Six or seven men went on to take advanced degrees in the professions or in the sciences. They are of special interest to us because they may foreshadow the coming onto the scene of a new kind of independent organization maker: the man who leaves a high-level professional position to strike out on his own and create an organization in an advanced technological field. Since high level of education is so integral to their organization creation, we will discuss their education when we talk about them as projectors and creators.

FORMAL EDUCATION: INVOLVEMENT AND MOTIVATION

It is clear that a man's social and occupational origins place a ceiling on his level of education. Neither Kenney nor Tyron really had any chance at college. This door slammed in their faces, they took a route through shops and city streets, learning their skills through jobs and through the setting up of deals. The education they received was not that dispensed in formal schooling. These men never finished grade school, and this in itself is perhaps a reaffirmation of the Horatio Alger theme. Other entrepreneurs did stay on the escalator, with a half dozen taking advanced degrees. These men were by no means only from affluent families.

These entrepreneurs have their own "explanations" of why at some given point they left or remained in school. These reasons are set forth in anecdotes which tend (like the scenes from childhood), to be stereotypes of education themes in American culture. A life situation is presented as a setting for a drama in which the entrepreneur is the principal actor. He then delineates the action and, at the same time, like a one-man Greek chorus, explains the motivational and situational factors that govern this action.

The life situation in itself is always mediated by the entrepreneur as role player. It is his personality, his attitudes, his values, and his goals which in his own eyes determine the level of education he achieves. The life situation is regarded as a chance happening brought about by the wheel of fate. The plot develops in the way it does because the actor is there and is playing the central role. It is his own character that shapes the action to resolution. For our immediate purposes, the resolution lies in the level of education. But, more important, the way he plays this role in the educational setting foreshadows the way he will play his roles later in life.

These men do not see themselves, during their school years, as passive recipients of destiny. On the other hand, they do not see themselves as in absolute control. Their view is pragmatic and realistic. As the life situation unfolds, it presents choices. At each point factors balance so that the correct choice is made: to remain in school or to leave. In their own eyes, these men always make choices intelligently and decisively.

The choice is always made in the face of a precipitating incident which is posed as a conflict of status or role. Most men leave the education escalator early, and this decision to do so bars them from bureaucratic positions and entry into the professions. In view of the fact that they became successful and powerful men, it would be impertinent for us to say that they erred in their decisions. Others began college but then dropped out. Here again, the choice was dictated by the desire for independence and for career achievement. One in five men in our sample did elect to finish college. Some of them did so in spite of severe handicaps. These men, however, did not, on the whole, look upon themselves as particularly unfortunate grinds. Both Mr. Forester and Mr. Buck got a considerable amount of enjoyment out of college life.

We see that it is not so much the level of education achieved as it is the attitude toward that achievement which is significant. When these men left school, it was because—as they see it—something important happened. In the face of this event, they acted. Action taken is later viewed as irrevocable, but is also viewed as taken at a fateful moment. Decisions made in the face of fate are, in a sense, out of the hands of the decider. He can only propitiate fate by magical adherence to the correct morality and the proper ritual.

Ritualistic adherence to the American system of education values underlies the decisions of entrepreneurs. Their reasons for leaving school were, on the whole, the *right* reasons. We see that for the overwhelming number of these men the right decisions in the face of a precipitating crisis is to leave school—to choose the relatively unstructured over the highly structured, to choose the uncharted occupational world of the adults, rather than remain in the structured world of formal schools. Later, in the chapter on projectors, we shall see how crucial to independent organization making is this pattern of leaving.

CHAPTER FIVE

The School of Experience

Between leaving family life and formal education and firmly establishing a business falls a time of trial and training. This is the true school for entrepreneurs. The "curriculum" is rough, and only men of unusual ruthlessness, courage, and ability graduate. "Credits" are earned by lost jobs, broken partnerships, exploited sponsors, and time in bankruptcy courts. As in most schools, students are not required to take work in all subjects. They may specialize in *drifting, protégéship* or *basic dealing.* "Coursework" may also be done in the exploitation of sponsors or partners, in learning technical skills, in insecure employment or in the setting up of deals.

Most men who are to become successful entrepreneurs first spend a long time, sometimes twenty years, in this school. This is expensive education, both for the man and for society. For the man, the price is paid in accumulated fatigue, mounting guilt, and moral conflict. For society, the price is paid in the high rate of business failures, and in the fact that many of its most productive people for long years do not perform effectively.

There is no alternative to the present system of training. Business colleges and university colleges of business do not offer the education that entrepreneurs need. Furthermore, the entire system of established business and finance is organized not to support but to punish the efforts of these men. A successful candidate in the school of entrepreneurship has, above all, learned the art of risk taking. The paraphernalia of society are organized not only to teach men not to take risks, but to identify and stigmatize those men who do. Consequently, a successful course in entrepreneurship involves a thorough grounding in finding financial support outside legitimate channels, or in convincing legitimate financial agencies that a risk is not present. Such skills are learned only in the school of experience.

In this chapter we are going to look at some of the coursework taken in this school. So large a school as that for entrepreneurs offers many subjects, and there are many ways in which they can be combined into "majors." We cannot present the entire catalogue in this chapter. We can, however, list a few courses and discuss the performance of some of the abler students.

DRIFTING

This course is taken primarily by orphans and sons of marginal or low-skilled workers. It is a continuation of the insecurity and deprivation learned during the family years. The course tends to reinforce distrust of superordinate figures and to instill the belief that working for other people is a situation of basic insecurity. The student who completes it has usually also acquired a battery of technical skills from holding a great variety of jobs. Candidates may begin as early as ten or as late as the age of fifty. Especially popular during the Depression, it has continued to have large enrollments through the relatively good times of the last three decades.

Review of coursework indicates that most "successful" performance has been achieved by men with a basic distrust of adult figures, a dislike for routine, and a low level of formal training. Completion of this course qualifies the candidate to go on to work in exploiting sponsors, getting rid of partners, and general bankruptcy. Mr. Segy, now president of a large tool manufacturing enterprise, describes his drifting experience:

> In 1925, I started working for 25¢ an hour. This company made measuring and scientific equipment, and I worked there for a few months. From there, in the same year, 1925, I moved to another company that made piston rings and valves. I worked there for some time, and then, in 1926, I got a job with Dodge. For about a year or so I worked for them. From there I moved to Regis Punch Press where I worked for several months between 1926 and 1927.
> In 1927, I started experiencing difficulties with my job and so I decided to go home and work on a farm. This time I could not get

work in Michigan. I finally found some farm work in Kansas—this was during the summer of 1927. Having five jobs in the period between 1925 and 1927, I once more went back to try to get a job at Dodge and this time I was fortunate in getting one. In 1928, I was laid off again, but within a short time I was able to get another job. I worked for about three months and I was laid off again. This was an extremely disappointing and frustrating experience in my life.

Webster turns in much the same report:

> Well, when I got out of school, there was no job. A younger friend of my dad was making a stab at getting started. He had a gas station, and I went to work for him doing odd jobs. I worked on a commission basis and for the first week I remember I made $2.50, so I kept looking. Finally I got a job as an apprentice. I worked on this job for a year. I liked it very much, but it was not what I wanted. I started looking around for a job in a machine shop. I finally found a job in a company which manufactured railroad valves—that I liked. I stayed about a year, at which time I thought I was at the end of my rope. Judging from what the older men were doing and how long it took them to get there, I felt I was at the end, so I quit without having a job. This was about 1937—I was nineteen at the time. I tried another job. I wanted at that time to get into the tool room but I couldn't. I stayed only about three weeks because the job was partially production work. I left and went home and told the folks, "I quit and I'm going to Detroit." They weren't very happy.
>
> So I went to Detroit. I got into a company where I worked for two months on surface grinding, but there was a recession about this time and there was a slump—they started laying off. Finally I was laid off. I didn't know what to do. In the meantime, I had two cousins working in Akron. I had been there and I liked the town. I decided to go there, and I got a job at Zenith. I got a job in the tool room. After a few months, the same thing happened as before. One of my cousins was laid off before I was, so we all packed up and came back home where I applied for unemployment compensation, but I never did draw any because I located another job as a stockroom helper.

Flick, who has established a very successful metal processing company, did a lot of drifting. His report reads:

I don't know, I guess I just wasn't satisfied—I kept looking for something. Well, I went to work in a stock room and I liked it a lot. I stayed about eight months, but then I wasn't so satisfied. I still had a tendency, however, toward mechanical work and I didn't like the carpentry end. I kept looking for a job in a shop. I located a small machine shop run by the owner and his son. I worked for them about six months—again it wasn't what I was after.

Then I saw an opportunity to get into the tool room at this automobile plant. I couldn't get right into the tool room—they told me I had to go through production. I took a job in production on the confidence that I would get into the tool room. I got married in 1940, while I was there. I worked there a year and a half. For some reason, I wasn't exactly satisfied. Looking back, I think it may have been pressure for more money, what with my being married and all.

We took a delayed honeymoon to the South. Well, on this trip, I stopped off at a couple of places to see what I might be able to make somewhere else. I applied at a plant in South Bend. After returning to my home town, I had a letter from them offering me a job so I went down to see them. They offered me a job in semi-production work at nights. I didn't accept, but while I was in South Bend, I tried some other companies. I got a job at the Ace Tool and Die at 30¢ more an hour than I was making. This looked good to me, so we moved there.

From these reports it is clear that the drifter is a person driven by a diffuse restlessness. For him, the grass is always greener just a little further on. He wants something, but it is not clear to him what this something is. He develops the reputation of an unsatisfactory worker. He displays strong indications that he will never be able to stick to any line of work.

PROTÉGÉSHIP 1: RIDING ROLLER COASTERS

Protégéship is often taken in place of drifting, but it is not a satisfactory substitute. Many times we find men completing protégéship and then taking a short course in drifting. Such refresher coursework often sharpens them in *basic dealing,* for which protégéship is an excellent preparation since students in protégéship both observe and aid their sponsors in consummating complicated deals. Protégéship is divided into two sections, each section designed to meet the special aptitudes and the psychological needs of differing kinds of students. Protégéship 1 (Riding Roller Coasters) is for students of unusual charm and ability who have a yearning to soar to commanding heights and who are willing to risk being subsequently hurled to the lowest depths. It is not a course for the faint hearted. Protégéship 2 (Biting the Hand That Feeds) is for students with especially strong aggressions toward older men, and a willingness to be guided by the fundamental rule: There is no place for friendship in business.

To engage in protégéship, the student must first attract a sponsor. Fred Phillips, at the age of twenty-two, might well have written the text for technique in acquiring a sponsor. Here is a résumé of the Phillips approach.

Phillips first came to the attention of the owners of the firm when one of the automobile companies did not receive delivery on an order it had placed. This company was a major customer. Seeing that the order was filled began with Phillips in the stockroom. The manager chewed Phillips out in front of the company president. Phillips, however, was a man who could take care of himself and he countered by pointing out that the material with which to fill the order had never been received inside the plant, and that, in any case, it was the manager's responsibility to see that orders got filled.

In choosing Phillips as the fall guy, the plant manager had made a bad tactical error, for Phillips had quietly been organizing facts and figures. With the manager, probably mouth agape, standing there, Phillips pulled out these figures and showed the top management of the firm that the system of operating the plant was "entirely wrong." The twenty-two year old then instructed the president and owner how the plant should be run. The president and owner agreed. "From that point on," Phillips complacently comments, "my rise in the firm was assured."

Shortly after, Phillips was offered the job of plant manager. He remarks that he was "young for the job," and he knew that he was "going to have trouble with the foremen." He accepted on condition that the plant be placed off limits to the former plant manager. In addition to running the plant, Phillips became the confidant of and right-hand man to the president. As he recollects it, at one time he had almost virtual control of the company. When the company expanded, buying another plant, he was placed in charge of both. Phillips says the president was losing interest in the business, and that he "acted more and more as the proprietor, making all the decisions." He was meticulously cultivating the role of son.

Suddenly he was out of the firm, broke, and with no prospects for the future. The president's other son, the one by biological descent, came home. He was made vice-president, and in Phillips' words, "placed over me. He knew nothing about the business. He came to work about ten and left at two or three. To make matters worse he boasted he was making three or four times what I was." Phillips found the situation intolerable, believing he was being completely subordinated to the son: "I was an errand boy." Having been once burned, however, he walked away with clear understanding of his next step. "I didn't know how, but I was going into business for myself."

Phillips, having caught the eye of a sponsor, went up and down in a hurry. His basic error was that he tried to stay in the protégé role too long and tried to exploit it too fully. Successful playing of the role of protégé involves the knack of knowing when it is time to move on.

Many students use the protégé-sponsor relationship to gain a set of skills and to establish themselves at a higher occupational level. Mr. Norton tells us that after some drifting, he found himself a job as an apprentice tool and die maker. Abruptly, he left this apprenticeship and went to another company. He was looking for something better than tool and die making. At this new firm, Norton got his break. With little or no training, he gained the status of a hydraulic engineer. The sequence of events was quite simple. He began by assisting an experimental engineer in developing "the first integrated hydraulic unit." Norton says there had been earlier attempts to solve this problem, but with no success. The new design had been placed on the market before he came to work, but Norton says "there was still a considerable number of bugs in it." The product was running into trouble with customers. He tells how he got his break:

> One day I was walking down the hall with this experimental engineer and the general manager accosted us. He said, "When are you going to get that damn thing figured out?" The experimental engineer said, "Well, gee, I don't know. If I just had some time to think. I am running around so much I have no time to settle down and think it out." The general manager made a decision on the spot and pointed to me and said, "All right, why don't you go and work it out instead?"

Mr. Norton immediately went to Cleveland and found a very simple device that solved the problem. He tells us that the device itself was nothing—it was so simple that it had been overlooked by everyone—but it worked. From that time on, he was rated as an hydraulic engineer. He could see, however, that lack of formal training in engineering meant that he would not receive a promotion into management. Once this became clear he cut loose and tried engineering sales. This did not work out, and Norton, for several years, fell into dark days. He drifted from job to job in engineering sales with the idea of setting up a business of his own slowly emerging.

Another simple pattern of protégéship is that of Mr. Harlow. In his career, Harlow had only one sponsor who took him in at an early age, who trained him in the trade and in relating himself to customers, and who then disappeared over the horizon. In brief, Harlow spent his formative years working with this man, went into the Coast Guard during the war, and returned to work at several jobs while he was establishing his own contracting business.

The careers of Phillips, Norton, and Harlow are relatively straightforward. They entered protégéship 1, learned a set of skills, and then went on to basic dealing. Now let us look at Mr. Powell, whom we have already met. If Powell took courses in all subjects, it was because he was a slow but thorough learner. After the family business—which he wrested away from his father—went under, he decided to take his sister and his mother to the World's Fair in Chicago:

> I started looking around at prefabricated housing. Within half an hour I realized they didn't know what they were doing. None of them were well built at all. They were just slapped together. But there was one. It was a frame house, but the frame was of structural steel. This intrigued me, so I asked the guy at the display about a job. He said, "Well, as a matter of fact there is a job available." So I got a job with this company. I went to work for Higgins Steel, and I ended up being an assistant to Joe Higgins. We sort of hit it off together, and I used to help him with his drinking and his chasing women. Actually, this is when I got my master's degree in marketing. It was a four year education I got—I traveled nationwide.

Meanwhile, Powell was instrumental in persuading Higgins to invest more and more heavily in prefabricated housing. Under the leadership of Higgins and his protégé, the corporation was heading for trouble. According to Powell, half a million dollars were sunk in prefabricated housing with a return of less than a hundred thousand. Powell maintains that Higgins was, at the same time, "making some other bad bets."

Reading over the interview material and Powell's dizzying account of the complicated financial mess in which Higgins' Corporation had involved itself, one cannot be at all certain that either Higgins or Powell knew what was happening. What ultimately did happen, however, was clear and decisive. Money brought in to tide the corporation over turned out to be controlling money. The new controlling interest corrected what it considered to be a crucial weakness, and: "I got fired. Actually, I was up in Washington when we got the word I was fired." Already in his forties, and with a big black X after his name, Powell tried his hand at drifting:

> At any rate, I was in the state of Washington when I got fired. I decided, "Well, the place to go is California." You know, everybody in Washington says this is the place to go—the sun shines all the time, and so on. So I went to California to get a job. I got into real estate, and I worked as a sales manager for a real estate company, and actually I was a carpenter. I got thirty-five bucks a week, and I was sales manager one day and carpenter the next. This went on for a while, and I was getting deeper in the hole. I couldn't even meet expenses. I was getting $6.00 a week car expenses and traveling a hundred miles.

With typical entrepreneurial willingness to cut immediate distress and accept the unknown dangers of the future, Powell quit cold. Perhaps lured by a remembrance of former success and good times, he headed for the Midwest. He says that he did not know why he was going, except that he was going "to make prefabricated houses." He thought that, after his debacle with Higgins, no reputable company would take him into its management. He was getting too old to play the protégé convincingly so he began basic dealing. After a couple of initial setbacks, he jelled a deal and was on his way.

Not all work in protégéship 1 ends with a downward plunge on the fast roller coaster. There is the case of Mr. Walden. Walden must be considered either different from other entrepreneurs or really not an entrepreneur at all. He had two sponsors in his life. The first relationship was disrupted by a hitch in the Navy.

Mr. Commons was the first person to discover my unusual business ability and judgment. He encouraged me to take a business course at the Y.M.C.A. and I also learned typing and bookkeeping and worked in several capacities in Mr. Commons' company. In the latter phase, I was an estimator and a state manager for the holdings of Mr. Commons. In 1942, I joined the Navy and was posted on the Seabee side.

Being forced into the service caused severance of his excellent relationship with Mr. Commons, but in the service Walden made a transition to a new sponsor. This two-step transition first involved becoming acquainted with another young man in the Seabees:

It was during my last year in the Navy that I got to know Dick. I got to know Dick, and within a short time, we got to know each other well enough to be good pals. I learned from Dick that his father had a machine shop. When we got out of the war in 1945, Dick discovered that his father wanted to get rid of the company, and Dick suggested to me that both of us should form a partnership and try our hand at running the plant.

Here Dick's father appears as the sponsor for the young team. The two men took over the company with an agreement with the father that if they lost more than $13,000, they would quit. The company had been steadily losing money in the past. During the first six months of the new stewardship it continued to lose money. After six months, however, the two young men had straightened the company out and it began to make money. It became apparent, however, that it would be an uphill struggle. They had trouble with the owner of the property, the building was old, and the machinery was dilapidated. As soon as they had squeezed a little cash out of the operation, they dissolved the company. They then established a new company. Dick became president, and his pal Walden became executive vice-president, treasurer, and general manager. Having established the new firm, the two young men split the operation and established a second new company. Because it had resources in terms of customers, capital, and experience in the older company, it was an immediate success and started off with a high volume of sales. Walden became its president.

At this stage in their careers, the two men had arrived at a point where they had parlayed their original sponsorship by Dick's father into each being president of a growing company. One might expect, in terms of the pattern of behavior shown by other entrepreneurs, that here would have been the breaking point. This was not, however, the case. The two men continue to work in a close and amiable division of labor. In both companies Walden handles administration and sales. In Walden's words: "We neither of us ever make a move without consulting the other. Even when buying equipment, of which I know little, Dick will consult me, and in this way we work together for the purchase of equipment and land for the plants." Dick and Walden are "great buddies." As Walden puts it, "We developed a silent understanding for each other." The two have remarkable similarity in their life patterns: both were born Protestants; both at the same time were converted to Catholicism; both are married; and both have five children.

Walden stands out in sharp conflict to the general pattern of entrepreneurial character and actions. He was able to tolerate joint protégéship with Dick under Dick's father's sponsorship. From the sociologist's point of view, his achievement was one of working in a three person relationship in which he had to adjust to both the demands of a peer (Dick) and a superordinate (the father). This is practically the only instance we have of an entrepreneur being able to handle so complicated an interpersonal situation.

By contrast, the case tends to emphasize the crucial element in the learning task set by the lab work in protégéship 1. Successful completion of work in this course is indicated (and there are few exceptions) by terminating the protégé-sponsor relationship. This is crucial for the future development of the entrepreneur. Men who do not, or cannot, sever these relationships may continue to advance in an organization. They may, eventually, assume the mantle of the sponsor and take over the sponsor's work, building it beyond what was accomplished during the stewardship of the sponsor. However, they will never themselves become entrepreneurs in the true sense of the word. To become an entrepreneur a man must break with his sponsor.

Up to a point, Walden did well in protégéship 1, but his development was arrested. He is like the perennial graduate student who does well in his coursework but who never takes his degrees. Other men in protégéship 1, some of whose moves we have examined, completed the course. Not all of our sample, however, are temperamentally able to do the work in protégéship 1. For them protégéship 2 is offered.

PROTÉGÉSHIP 2: BITING THE HAND THAT FEEDS

This section is for men who are extremely aggressive in dealing with superordinates, peers, or subordinates. When we match their work with their childhood histories, it is clear that these men learned both disgust and distrust at a very early age.

We begin discussion of coursework in protégéship 2 by reviewing a situation which developed during the course of the fieldwork for our study. We, as fieldworkers, first met Mr. Chalmers and Mr. Littler at a time when they were engaged in a bitter struggle for control of a firm.

Chalmers, after spending many years selling and attempting to set up a deal, had started a firm that required high-level engineering work. He brought in Mr. Whiffle, who supplied most of the money, to handle the administrative and financial side. Chalmers and Whiffle then brought in Littler, who apparently was known as a brilliant engineer but one with a poor work record. Littler was to handle plant management and engineering. Chalmers reserved for himself customer and vendor relationships, and the title of president.

Chalmers had at first felt himself very fortunate to secure Littler, who immediately plunged into a bad plant situation, straightened it out, and at the same time developed radically new processing techniques which put the firm in an excellent competitive position.

The situation, however, quickly went sour for Chalmers. As things stood at the time of the first field contacts, Chalmers was interviewed in a bar and Littler was interviewed in the plant, where he took great pride in showing the interviewer the technical improvements he had made. It developed that Littler had barred Chalmers from the processing area, keeping secret from the president changes which were taking place in the manufacturing end of the business. Chalmers was not greatly perturbed at this situation, implying that he and Whiffle would soon join forces to throw Littler out. Fate, however, had an unpleasant surprise in store for Chalmers. Whiffle and Littler joined forces and threw the president out. We learned from later interviews that Chalmers left, swearing that he would take the customers and vendors with him, and then where would Whiffle and Littler be? When last heard from, Chalmers was setting up a new corporation.

As Littler saw the situation, Chalmers was a man who should never have been allowed to achieve "so high a position." Chalmers was "irresponsible, he knew nothing about the technical side of the business, and he was a chronic alcoholic." He had to go not only because it was necessary for the business, but more importantly because it was morally wrong for him to stay. Littler is an extremely perceptive and intelligent man, and yet his strong sense of moral rightness forces a behavior pattern which he has repeated again and again throughout his career.

Littler begins with his father who was a small businessman of some success, and a politician at the local level. Littler indirectly implies that his father was able to provide a stable home and help for Littler in college. He describes how their business was close to the political headquarters, and how well-known political figures were in and out of their home. To Littler, however, his father was somewhat corrupt and "drank too much." Littler was at an early age out on his own, arranging little entrepreneurial ventures. Following graduation from college, he meandered from job to job, finding nothing of particular interest. He then went to law school, where he completed three of the four years necessary for a law degree. Because of job pressures, studying at night, and an "incessant problem of an ulcer," he was forced to drop out. At this time he appears to have received his first bid from a sponsor:

> The man who hired me realized that other firms had laboratory people around the plant to give it an air of distinction—men in white coats—and since he had no technically trained people in his organization, this gentleman realized there was a possibility of getting a technical man on the staff to dress up the plant. He installed me in a job and gave me considerable money to set up a lab—figuring that it was all a front—but I went to work developing idea after idea in which this man was not interested, and I merely shoved them into my briefcase for my own personal use later in life.

The basic dishonesty of this man was intolerable, so Littler quit. He drifted from one job to another during this first period, finally becoming a part owner of a business. This partnership was quickly dissolved when Littler discovered that his partner was drunk all the time.

Drinking was only one form of barbaric behavior on the part of these men. Littler tells us that during World War II a sponsor lost Mr. Littler's services when he "tried to put the screws to a Jewish fellow to get him drafted." He says, "This is behavior I simply cannot condone or go along with, and so I quit." This may have been the precipitating incident, but perhaps it was an incident that gave Mr. Littler an opportunity to quit rather than be fired. He tells us that he had married the private secretary of this sponsor. She had been the boss's confidante and very close personal associate, and had kept all his books and his private accounts and correspondence. Littler lets us know that this marriage gave him access to such information. An interesting relationship between these three people was created, and it would have been difficult for them to resolve their future relationship. Littler did not try.

In one sense, Littler's problems arose from the fact that he was not able to move on when his relationship with the sponsor had reached its peak and had begun to deteriorate. He seems, rather, to have tried to hold on, perhaps for an emotional reason. The pattern occurs with monotonous regularity in Littler's life.

A psychologist would point out the significance of Littler's rigid imposition of moral standards on himself and others, the voyeurism implied by the act of marrying the sponsor's secretary, and the compulsive work drive coupled with his refusal to allow Chalmers to look at the work. But it must not be overlooked that—at least, so far in his career—Littler has been able to harness his compulsions to advance himself, and, perhaps more importantly, to make solid technological contributions to the culture. Littler's pattern shows an extreme moral compulsion, but the next man we will discuss shows almost none.

Mr. Hertzler views life as a conflict with no rules and no quarter given. Starting work full-time at the age of fourteen, he worked at his first job about a year and a half. He claims that he learned to operate every machine in the shop. The first story he tells us illustrates his fundamental approach. He describes a conflict centered around a grinder. He says that this $45,000 machine was down for repairs every three or four days, so "repair people came from Toledo to repair it." The machine operator was given a vacation for two or three weeks, and in his absence Hertzler became an assistant to the repair people in tearing down and rebuilding the machine. During the process he learned how to operate it. He then took it over and worked on it until the regular operator came back. "During the time I worked on it, it was never stopped once and nothing was returned by the inspector." The morning the operator came back, he began moving Hertzler's equipment away from the machine. This led to a fight. The foreman settled it by saying that Mr. Hertzler was to take over for as long as he wanted to. "I worked on that machine until I had proved to everybody that anyone could work on that job." He then quit (score one for Hertzler).

Hertzler next got a job with the Blaze Company. The foreman, who had sponsored him in his previous job and who had taught him machine work there, had already gone to Blaze. Immediately upon reporting to work, Hertzler set about showing the management how much work could be done. For example, he showed them "how I could turn out a shaft in a minute and twenty seconds, which had taken other workers three-quarters of an hour to do." He became foreman, displacing the foreman who had taught him, and whom Hertzler had followed to the new job (score two for Hertzler).

From his eminence as foreman, Hertzler caught the eye of top management. He maintains that he took a leading role in the designing of a dam, although he was at this time only nineteen years old. He learned to read blueprints thoroughly, working late at night on them. At this point in his career, World War I came along, and Hertzler was able to take out some of his aggression on the Germans. Returning to this country, he got a job. As he puts it:

> I was working on my lathe one day, and the superintendent and the foreman were standing talking behind me. I overheard them say that they wished they had somebody who could work the grinder. I shut down my machine, turned, and said, "You're looking at him." They said, "What the hell do you mean?" I said, "Yes, I can. You show me to it and I'll do it. What do you want done?"
>
> We went over to the grinder and I said, "I will do my own set-up." The superintendent said, "Oh, no. There is a man over here who will do the setups for you." I said, "Hell, no. I'll do it myself." The superintendent said, "All right." So I did it. After I started on the machine the foreman came by and said to me, "That's a dollar

twenty machine." I just said, "The hell it is." I got it up to a dollar sixty an hour and then a dollar ninety an hour. I was making out on that machine. Of course, by then everybody thought I was a rat but I didn't care what they thought. I think this is important if a person is going to get ahead. The hell with what the other guys think.

The other workers were resentful and the foreman was, too. Consequently, they kept changing my grinding wheel, so that I had to set it up every morning. After this went on for a while, I went to the superintendent, and said, "I quit." The superintendent said, "Why?" I pointed to the foreman and said, "Oh, that goddamn hillbilly over there is trying to foul me up." The superintendent said, "Well, you stay and we'll get rid of him." I said, "No, I quit, I'm fed up."

He quit and he went to Melzer Company at 85¢ an hour (score three for Hertzler). So far he had shown them all.

Immediately he repeated his tactic. He chose an opportunity to show up the foreman. This time, however, he managed to make his point in the hearing of a vice-president. The vice-president said, "What the hell are you guys here doing? This young kid here can turn this out in less than an hour and that man over there takes a day and a half. What's going on?" Mr. Hertzler tells us that the foreman was "somewhat flabbergasted," as well he might have been. The foreman lost his job because of the incident (score four for Hertzler). Hertzler was taken under the wing of the vice-president, who put him in charge of the tool room. From catching the eye of the vice-president, it was simple to catch the eye of the president.

One day the president sent him on a spying mission to another firm. He got a job there and stayed for several weeks. At the end of the three weeks he was fired. He reported back to the president:

> "Well, I got fired." The president then said, "What do you mean you got fired? What did you think about the place? Do you think we ought to buy it?" I said, "Yah." The president said, "Do you think that if you took it over you could make a go of it?" I said, "Yah." The president said, "Okay, come with me." We got into the car, went down to the other plant, and the president said, "Now you tell me who fired you?" I pointed the superintendent out. The president went over to him and said, "We're buying this plant, and Norman here is going to take over. He doesn't need you anymore, so pick up your pay."

From here we go on to a discussion of Hertzler's various exploits with the Melzer Company. It is clear that, in his own mind, he rapidly became the indispensable man. However, friction was beginning to develop between Hertzler and the president. Hertzler tells us that he was something of an inventor. He developed six or eight different ideas, which he showed to the president of the firm. The president did not show his appreciation. Hertzler became quite disgruntled, but began to see the possibility of a new combination.

Things were also not going well between the president and vice-president. In the fight, Hertzler sided with the vice-president. Hertzler and the vice-president pulled out together, taking with them prime customers and a good deal of confidential information. They set up a partnership, with Hertzler owning nineteen percent of the stock of the new company. They quickly drove Melzer Company out of business. Hertzler claims that it was not his idea to drive the president of Melzer to the wall. This was really a project of Melzer's former vice-president. Mr. Hertzler feels that it was the inherent weakness of Melzer himself that led to both the breach in the relationship and the collapse of the company.

Hertzler and his partner did not hit it off too well in their new company. The break came when Hertzler took a two-month vacation. After he had been gone three weeks, his partner called him up and told Hertzler that it was time to get back to work. Hertzler told him:

> "The hell with you. I'm not coming back. I'm taking my vacation." My partner said, "Well, you come back or you're out." I said, "All right, I'm out." I hung up the phone.
>
> About this time, Mr. Melzer came to me pleading for me to come back to the Melzer Corporation and "put it back on its feet." Of course, I refused.

He was now out of both companies, but his remembrance is that neither company could exist without him. They both went through bankruptcy. Hertzler, in the meantime, began setting up a corporate venture of his own.

It is not entirely precise to say that Hertzler did not know how to play the role of protégé. He knew, in fact, how to play this role as he defined it extremely well. His definition, however, was one of using the association with a man above him as a stepping stone in his own career. It is a mistake, further, to think of Hertzler as disloyal, self-seeking, or untrustworthy. In this case, we have a man to whom such words do not apply. In Hertzler's conception of things, loyalty simply does not exist. He is blind to it as other people are color-blind to red and green. As he told the interviewer at least a dozen times, "It's dog eat dog."

Both Littler's and Hertzler's activities represent rather extreme forms of coursework in "Biting the Hand That Feeds." These protocols have been chosen from among many because they give us a consecutive delineation of the process, and because in them we see this mode of entrepreneurial behavior in its most dramatic form. Most entrepreneurs who take the course in protégéship show the characteristics described in detail in the discussion of Littler and Hertzler. Entrepreneurs cannot stand the continuing confinement of the protégé-sponsor relationship. Men who can stand this confinement may do very well in undisrupted protégé-sponsor relationships. This is one clear avenue for movement into the organization elites.

The great bureaucratic organizations of government and business are full of men who have followed a sponsor long and loyally, working hard for him, putting the sponsor's interest before their own. When these sponsors retire or die, the protégé may be called upon to assume the mantle, undertaking the obligations and privileges that go with leadership and control. Such men contribute and receive a great deal. They do not become independent entrepreneurs.

BASIC DEALING

The core course for entrepreneurs is *basic dealing*. It is usually taken at the end of or in conjunction with drifting or after protégéship has been completed. The course of study may last only a few days, or it may last for twenty or more years. Successful completion is indicated by "jelling" a deal. This deal may be very large or very small. It may lead to establishing a business, but equally often leads to the candidate being "dealt out" of the profits, or to an abortive organizational attempt ending in bankruptcy.

The purpose of this course is to teach the student the basic technique of entrepreneurship: the bringing together of ideas, people, and money in a profitable arrangement. The student should expect to undergo and learn from a set of rigorous experiences, which may include: 1) being looked upon by friends and relatives as a hopeless big talker who allows his wife and children to go hungry while he is out chasing rainbows; 2) being rejected by reputable sources of financing, and therefore forced to deal with shady individuals and finance houses; 3) being eliminated from a transaction if associates find this profitable and can accomplish it; 4) discovering, after having finessed a deal, that instead of coming out with a profit he may come out far in the hole and be tied for years to an unprofitable line of enterprise; 5) being adept at leaving creditors and other associates holding the bag, while the student slips out of any unprofitable line of enterprise; and 6) being accused of double-dealing by associates he has either dealt out or left holding the bag.

Basic dealing is not a course for the faint hearted, nor for the fair-weather entrepreneur. This course separates the men from the boys. There is no telling how many broken businesses and broken homes are left behind by students who enrolled in the course, but who did not have the character to complete it. This is part of the high price paid for the education of entrepreneurs.

One man who did complete the course was Fred Kenney. The reader first met Mr. Kenney when, at the age of ten, he was setting up deals to deliver campaign literature and was in a fruit and vegetable business. Kenney, in his report, indicated that peddling apples and potatoes was minor league compared with peddling oil tankers. His account is too long, and too detailed about persons in the shipping industry, to be quoted verbatim. Here is a résumé:

> On a job-hunting excursion to the East Coast, Kenney saw an oil tanker tied up and offered for sale. Penniless, and without a job, he decided that he would figure out some way to use that oil tanker. With no capital, and with no contacts, he started back to Detroit with his family to set up a deal. At this point, one of his minor problems was that the owners of the tanker wanted cash. Mr. Kenney describes his trip across country from New York to his home. They had no money, and displayed a certain modicum of resourcefulness. They would stop in the middle of the night at a gas station where the pump had a large glass container on the top, and they

would drain the gas from the pump into their car. Using gas remaining in the hoses of these pumps, they were able to get as far as Toledo. There, he went to a loan agency and talked them into loaning him enough money so that he could get something to eat for his family and get them back home.

There he got in contact with a man with money, and they began discussing a deal to establish a series of oil tank farms around the shores of the Great Lakes. It appears that, at the same time, Kenney was attempting to slip his tanker card into the deck. His associate was a man of considerable wealth, and had headquarters in a prestige hotel. Mr. Kenney did not have the carfare to get from home to the hotel, a distance of a little over ten miles. He walked back and forth to keep his engagements. Negotiations dragged out over a period of a year. The associate finally decided that, in view of the amount of money going into the tank farm, he would not be able to buy the oil tanker. He did, however, put Kenney in touch with other people, and Kenney attempted to raise $65,000 with which to purchase the tanker. While he was making progress in this direction, the ship was suddenly sold out from under him.

It was the people whom Kenney had come to regard as his backers who wrote him out of the deal and sold directly to the buyer. After a year of hard effort, Kenney says he was "welshed out of the deal entirely." He had no job and no prospects.

Again, in order to secure food for his family, he went back to his relatives in the East. He finally secured a job as a riveter in a shipyard. Fred Kenney's life for the next ten years was one of holding itinerant and temporary jobs while attempting, as he puts it, "to set up a deal." With monotonous regularity, the deals fell through. With monotonous regularity, Kenney tried again. All the time he was learning.

During these years, Fred Kenney appeared to his relatives to be shiftless and irresponsible. Furthermore, he was a slow student in basic dealing. This was because he was after honors in the course. Lesser men save up a down payment, negotiate a deal for a mortgage in which the bank is completely protected, and buy a hamburger stand. Mr. Kenney was a little more ambitious. Penniless—at that time he was on relief work and made the ten mile walk back and forth to his associate's hotel in work shoes, carrying his dress shoes and his suit coat wrapped in paper to protect them from the weather—

Kenney dealt in tank farms and ships. It took him about twelve years to pass the course, but today Kenney's enterprise is the largest of its kind in the Midwest.

Perhaps because he graduated from college in the forties, a period of relatively "easy" capital, and because he was initially a little less grandiose in his scheme than Kenney, Mr. Buck took the course in basic dealing with far fewer severe setbacks. He began practice while still in college, attempting to find a market and capital for a flyer in a ballpoint perfume dispenser. This little project petered out on him, but Buck, in retrospect, tends to think he knew it would. He was only practicing. His first serious attempt occurred about the time he graduated from college:

> I went back to Peoria. I started looking around for building ventures. This professor friend of mine, the one with whom I worked on the political deal, wanted to start a little business on his own. He had some money. I spent several months looking around. My cousin was an architect in Peoria, and I spent the time in his office looking around for different deals. Finally, we decided to build houses on a speculative basis. We had the whole deal set up. I found a man with some land; he would let us build on his land without paying him anything to start with and then after we started selling the buildings we would pay him off. He was completely protected on this, because, as you know, if we didn't pay him off, then the buildings on his land would be his. The whole deal was ready to go and it fell through. This man with the land got less and less enthused.

For Mr. Buck this was merely standard coursework. Such checks were only temporary setbacks, which he charged off to learning the fundamentals of jelling deals. He quickly learned the involved lessons, and thenceforth none of his operations fell through in quite the same simple way. They fell through in more complicated ways. Buck had learned basic dealing. He still had to do advanced work in "How to Keep Partners from Getting the Upper Hand," and "How to Keep Backers Off Your Back." With a solid course in basic dealing under his belt, however, Buck was able to move rapidly through this more advanced subject matter. He took each lesson only once. Thereafter, he knew it.

These two men (Kenney and Buck) were good students in basic

dealing because it never occurred to them to be anything but entrepreneurs. Almost from the time they learned to walk, they had apparently foreseen some such career.

Some men gave no attention to basic dealing during their initial period, although they may have thought of themselves as independent businessmen. Mr. Powell was one such person. We saw Powell in the last chapter, when he was going to college and was simultaneously engaged in contracting for house building. There is some evidence in the interview that this business was originally set up by Powell's father. If this was the case, by about 1927 Powell had succeeded in wresting the business from his father, and had reduced him to a status equivalent to that of a day laborer. Powell attributes this situation to his father's all-round lack of competence. By 1927, Powell had "built the contracting business into a fairly large operation." At this point in his career, he had gained control of a substantial enterprise without having learned anything about basic dealing. Then the bottom dropped out for Powell: "I went away on my honeymoon with lots of money and a good business going. When I came back in January, I was broke. You see, the Depression started on the West Coast a lot sooner than it did here."

Powell's father does not reappear in the interview protocol. Powell was then thirty-five. He took a job with his old boss, the person he had first worked under as a carpenter. "I got sort of disgusted with this house building thing. We built a great big, expensive house and built it exactly the way we built a cheap house. I felt that it was all wrong, that they were making no advances whatsoever." Whatever the merits of the plan, Powell's boss was not buying. Perhaps he was cognizant that the business which Powell had taken over from his father had just gone down the drain. Powell quit. "Actually, I was going to sort of save the world. I had a lot of ideas about prefabricated housing which I had got from reading magazines, and I felt that I could help to revolutionize housing."

We may say in retrospect that Powell would have done well to enroll in basic dealing at this point. He did not do so. Instead, he took part of the course in drifting, but dropped out before completing the work. He dropped out to take protégéship 1. We saw how he did in the last section. It was only after having completed an exhaustive study of this subject that he faced up to that fact that he was running out of sponsors and was going to have to take basic dealing.

If any one course can be called the core course in the School for Entrepreneurs, it is basic dealing. It develops theory and practice for one problem that all "true" entrepreneurs must face at least once in their lives. This is the problem of bringing resources together into a combination that makes possible the establishment of an ongoing enterprise.

Some entrepreneurs stay in basic dealing for as long as twenty years before mastering the fundamentals. These men are, on balance, by no means the least successful of the entrepreneurs. Entrepreneurship, like football, requires a good grasp of the fundamentals. Some entrepreneurs only take basic dealing when they are engaged in seting up the one business they are to own or control. This is a risky approach, and may lead to unnecessary giving away of advantages.

CHAPTER SIX

The School for Entrepreneurs:
An Appraisal

We often say to ourselves that anyone can go into business for himself. This is not the case. Organization making, like any art, requires long and rigorous training. It also requires something more. It requires strong drive and well reinforced attitudes. This is true for men who create organizational extensions, but especially true for men who build organizations from scratch.

We had in our sample men who had come to control businesses without this thorough groundwork in entrepreneurship. Close scrutiny of the life history of most of them indicated they were not entrepreneurs in the central sense of that word. Some were simply men who were continuing, under another name, enterprises begun by their fathers or by their fathers-in-law. Others had brought money or a special ability into an already established business, and had then through a chain of circumstances assumed leadership. This is not what we mean by the independent entrepreneur. *The independent entrepreneur is a man who has created out of nothing an ongoing enterprise.*

This is an involved and highly sophisticated operation. It cannot be pulled off without thorough training. By the time they establish a business, entrepreneurs are thoroughly educated men. They have earned that education the hard way, and the courses they have taken do not appear in the curricula of high schools, business colleges, or in the universities. They have gotten their education in a much tougher school, the school for entrepreneurs.

It is only when their experience as children and as young adults is looked at from this viewpoint that sense can be made of the apparently formless and pointless quality of these years. The authors of this book recall their dismay when they first sat down to the thousands of pages of interview material that had been accumulated. After a week or so of reading, the entrepreneurs emerged as a shiftless, irresponsible crew.

Entrepreneurs present themselves as ex-waifs, as men from broken homes, and of dishonest and incompetent parents. In their recollections are repeated references to themes of abandonment, of poverty, of shame, and of conflicts between parents. They describe in detail how domineering figures entered into their lives, forcing them to leave their homes and their formal schooling.

The statistics show that larger proportions of the entrepreneurs come from the lower occupational categories and leave school at an early age than do executives in government and business. The dynamic of entrepreneurship is revealed, however, not in these objective facts but in the way entrepreneurs harp upon these facts in seeking to account for their own behavior. The facts are seen as forcing a leaving, and it is this leaving (or escaping from by severing), which comes to be the pattern constantly returned to by these men. To solve a problem by going completely outside the framework in which it arises is not necessarily to be an entrepreneur, but it is a necessary prelude to independent organization making. Entrepreneurs must break away. In two senses they must break away. They have to break away because their fundamental character development makes permanent subordination intolerable. There is an emotional revolt that always, usually sooner rather than later, takes possession of them. They also have to break away because severing of prior relationships is an operational requirement necessary to establishing oneself as the central figure in one's own business.

In retrospect, independent entrepreneurs have many reasons for having broken relationships. The father let them down or double-crossed them. The teacher turned out to be unqualified. Promotion was blocked. The sponsor got into trouble and could not sustain the relationship. The protégé had learned all he could learn. But these reasons don't really matter. Unless he has learned to break away, the entrepreneur can never achieve that autonomy necessary to create a business that is uniquely and solely his own.

Many men dream of having a business of their own. It is only the man with the peculiar character structure of the entrepreneur who can make this dream a reality. It is precisely his fear of superordinates, his distrust of peers, and his tendency to cut intolerable situations rather than stay and solve them, which causes the entrepreneur sooner or later to dissolve constricting ties. It is also precisely these characteristics which cause him eventually to go into business for himself.

Childhood is the time when leaving patterns are learned. If a man is to go on and become an independent entrepreneur, however, patterns learned in childhood must be relearned and reinforced in young adulthood. One course in which this is done is drifting. It is here that the entrepreneurs seemed to the authors of this book to be at their worst. They always seemed to be either losing a job, or out of work, or finding a job. The jobs they had held read like a roster of all the poorer-paying jobs in the Midwest. These men were always one jump ahead of the sheriff. Sometimes they failed to keep one jump ahead. Further, their behavior seemed most erratic. They got good jobs and they quit them cold. They fought with bosses, or they decided the work was not right for them. When things were going well on a job, they suddenly quit and took extended vacations.

It was only slowly that the symbolic content of what these men were talking about began to sink in to the interview analysts. In recollecting experiences from as much as forty years earlier, they were talking about presses, drills, milling machines, boring heads, grinders, cranes, hydraulic valves, blueprints, lathes. They were telling us where they had got their education. They had acquired it everywhere and they had acquired it in bits and pieces.

This is not to say that on their fourteenth birthday these men said, "I am going to be an entrepreneur. I must, therefore, acquire as wide a range of technical experience as I can." The idea is ridiculous. It is even more ridiculous to say that in some mystical way these men were destined to become entrepreneurs. They might just as well have become chronic relief cases. They had all the earmarks of men who would never be able to hold steady jobs.

During this period, these men were driven by a diffuse restlessness, by an interest in learning all they could about the world around them, by a marked lack of a sense of responsibility toward either their families or their employers, by a chip-on-the-shoulder, to-hell-with-it attitude. Coupled with this was a remarkably strong interest in mechanical matters. They approached new jobs avidly, did well on them for a short time, and left. A typical comment is: "I'd learned all I could there."

What had they learned? First and most obviously, through the course in drifting, these men had picked up a repertoire of technical skills. Technical know-how, however, is only part of what is learned by drifting. These men were also broadening and deepening their grasp of what may be called the transactional mode of interpersonal relations. They were learning, at a deeper level than they had learned as children, that no relationship need carry with it a continuing commitment. They were learning to believe that relationships are to be entered into only as long as they are of benefit. The entrepreneur has to learn to have no qualms about breaking such relationships.

Viewed from this perspective, what is learned in drifting is highly similar to what is learned in protégéship. The method of learning is what is different. In drifting, the candidate learns by casting a dragnet. In protégéship, he concentrates on one or two situations. In these situations, he is an intense student of entrepreneurial behavior. He watches his sponsor, observing and digesting what he observes. However, he is not observing only the sponsor. He studies the sponsor in the sponsor's own network of entrepreneurial activity. The entrepreneur is thus learning the rudiments of bringing together resources, of setting up structures, and of severing restrictive and unprofitable relationships. In this sense, the sponsor serves as a teacher.

The learning method, however, is not that of the sedulous ape gaining mastery through uncritical imitation. Some men do learn by this method. Enterpreneurs do not, however, if they are truly of the independent mold. Their sponsors fill them with dismay and disgust. They describe them as men of folly and cupidity, and harp on their lack of foresight or skill. Their descriptions of behavior of sponsors range from charges of carnal depravity to the accusation that "he was losing interest in the business." They often point out with triumph how their worst fears were justified and how the sponsor "went under" as a result of his own stupidity.

These criticisms are symbolic of the entrepreneur's fear and dislike of the older and superordinate figure. Many good men can live through and by the goals and objectives set by older and superordinate figures. They know the art of completely subordinating themselves to the organization and/or to one or more men. This is not to say that these men lack willpower, or that they can never move on to positions of leadership and prestige. These are not inferior men, nor is theirs an inferior way. In a society characterized by a proliferation of large-scale organizations, the value of such men as administrative entrepreneurs can hardly be underestimated. The point is that they will never become independent entrepreneurs.

In this process, the entrepreneur learns as much from his observation of himself as from his observation of his sponsor. Typical remarks are: "I was getting more restless." "I felt blocked." "I was after something, I didn't know what." "I had to get out from under." "I came to know I could never stand the insecurity of working for other people."

These men were reaching an awareness of themselves. This awareness is often talked of by them as if it began with a knowledge of some kind of unfitness. They were sensing that they did not fit in, and that perhaps they would never fit in. Out of this fear was formulated the conception of themselves as people who must go it alone, and who must at all costs find freedom from restrictive, older, and superordinate figures. Once this formulation was achieved, school was out of the question. With abrupt decisiveness, they started out on their own. They were now ready for basic dealing, played for keeps. Drifting and protégéship are the transactional model in its defensive and protective modes. In learning these modes, the future entrepreneur learns never to get overly involved, and he learns to avoid involvements that may hamper his present action and restrict his future. He learns how, wherever possible, to sever such relationships quietly and neatly. He learns how, if this is not possible, to slash out wildly and angrily to break the restriction once and for all. All this is learning merely the negative and defensive modes of the transactional model. A person who learns only these modes will never become a full-fledged entrepreneur.

Full-fledged entrepreneurship involves mastery of the positive modes of the transactional model. In fact, the positive mode *is* entrepreneurship. The act of entrepreneurship is that of bringing ideas, skills, money, equipment, and markets together into a profitable combination. It is the bringing together of these elements which is the "deal" that entrepreneurs talk about so happily. The economist, the accountant, and the banker tend to look at these arrangements in terms of the financial and material resources involved. The entrepreneur sees all these, but he, typically, sees more deeply.

He sees, always, the bringing together of people into a new arrangement. This is because, always, he must move through people. He sees these people interrelated in terms of the transactional model. If, for one moment, he strays away from this model and gets involved emotionally, he is lost. Our interviews are full of instances in which the entrepreneur, still learning his trade, allowed himself to trust, without reservation, a partner or a financial backer. Our interviews are also full of such terms as "bastard" and "s.o.b." (and even more unprintable phrases). Such phrases sum up what such men now think of their one time "pals."

This tendency on the part of entrepreneurs to recall such emotional involvements as inherently crippling and, therefore, "wrong," led us at first to formulate this transactional model of relationships as a "rational" model for behavior. At first it appeared that the rationale for behavior was sheer profit. This is the cognitive map of the interpersonal process which entrepreneurs themselves often have.

This conception of their own behavior as rational in terms of economic advantage cannot be disregarded. The entrepreneurs themselves believe in it. It is deeply rooted in their Western European cultural heritage of values and sentiments. Because they do believe in it, the economic rationale of behavior does have a strong controlling influence on them. They believe it is morally correct for them to immediately sever a relationship which is no longer profitable to themselves, regardless of the economic consequences (debtors who are not paid, stockholders who lose investments, etc.) to the other parties to the transaction. They also believe that other men act in terms of the same rationale. The adult, mature entrepreneur is not a cry baby. He expects to be "welshed out" if it is to the advantage of the other party to do so. It is the entrepreneur's job to see that it is not to the advantage of others to deal him out, and to arrange things so that they cannot. By the same token, the mature entrepreneur learns how to prevent his colleagues from getting out, even when it may be advantageous to them. Such a rational model of behavior is highly acceptable to the entrepreneur and is, indeed, the acceptable rationale for business enterprise in the Western World.

It would be an error either to ignore or to minimize the importance of this cognitive map that is used by most entrepreneurs. Equally, it would be an error to use this map as an "explanation" of entrepreneurial behavior. Neither the TAT nor the interview protocols make much sense strictly in terms of profit and position enhancement. In the summary of the TAT report, there is the statement that, psychologically, these men are not "upwardly mobile." They do not share with the members of the great bureaucracies strong desires to improve their social positions. In the interview material, we do not find that the social pattern of these men is strongly motivated by a desire for success. Furthermore, in the TAT summary, we find that these men typically do not work with clearly envisaged goals (involving financial or prestige enhancement), but that they tend to dissipate their energy without finding clear-cut resolutions to their stories. They tend to want to get clear of the story without finding a logically neat solution in terms of triumph or gain on the part of the hero. This very much fits in with the abrupt arrivals and departures, the violent splits in relationships, and the sudden turnings away from situations of obvious immediate short- and long-range advantage.

The key here is that the transactional model not only fits the traditional cultural values of profit and position enhancement, but that it also fits very closely the entrepreneur's need for autonomy, and his confused and often guilt-ridden drive to remove all restrictive and threatening figures in his immediate situation. At one level, these figures must go because they threaten profit and position enhancement. (This mode of symbolic interpretation for the real entrepreneur, however, tends to mask a deeper motivational pattern.) At another level, these figures must also go, symbolically (in terms of physical space, it may be the entrepreneur who moves on) because they threaten his right to act with unrestricted power.

The basic dilemma in entrepreneurship is that the entrepreneur needs such associates to bring together the resources necessary to establishing a new business. On the other hand, he cannot long stand these figures in the picture. They threaten the very freedom which he is impelled to find. So long as they are in the picture, he has never fully escaped from the dominating, unreliable figures which have plagued him all his life. He has never escaped from his own peculiar kind of insecurity. It is in this sense that the transactional model of interpersonal relationships serves the entrepreneur so well. It gives him a culturally acceptable set of values to serve as a rationale for forming and terminating relationships, and, at the same time, it gives him the skills and techniques (the *modus operandi*) for rapidly forming and dissolving alliances.

PART TWO

PROJECTORS
AND
PROJECTIONS

CHAPTER SEVEN

The Projectors:
Men in a Quandary

Many years ago, Daniel Defoe was intrigued by a change he saw going on in England. He observed that men were everywhere leaving traditional walks of life and entering into ventures for profit. These services were new, or had previously been performed indifferently by such established institutions as the parish, the village, or the county and national government. Defoe wrote a little book which he called *An Essay on Projects*. In this book he correctly estimated fundamental changes in English life being brought about by a group of men whom Defoe called "projectors."

The words "project" and "projector" have become, in the sense in which Defoe used them, lost to the language. The terms are, however, the best we have found to describe the events we now wish to discuss.

The act of independent entrepreneurship—that is, of going into business for oneself—begins with the conception or the idea of going into business. We will refer to this as *projecting the business*. During this phase, the men we are talking about play the *social role of projectors*. This means that they have envisaged the possibility of a business and have developed the idea to the point where it has become an action directive. How is it that men first enter into this role? How is the role so handled that it merges into the second stage and the second role of entrepreneurship, the role of creator of a business?

When we first began the research on entrepreneurs we all speculated on what we felt was a question crucial to the study: Why do men go into business for themselves? One researcher argued that most entrepreneurs come from a family tradition of entrepreneurship. Another held out for the profit motive. Another argued for an idea such as an invention or an insight into a market situation that could be exploited. As the research data started to come in, we began to realize that all these guesses were valid for some entrepreneurs, but none of them accounted for all of the men in our sample.

ROLE DETERIORATION: THE TRIGGER

We began to reformulate our thinking, searching for commonalities in life situations immediately prior to their going into business for themselves. We began to see that almost all these men took action in the face of a situation which, for want of a better word, we call "role deterioration."

For almost all entrepreneurs, entering into the social role of projector begins with the shattering of a previous life pattern. Men usually become projectors in a moment of desperation. Entering the role of projector starts with the breaking down of earlier roles, and the decision never again to attempt them. Men come to realize that they can never measure up to the demands placed on them in other people's organizations. During their years in the school for entrepreneurs, they had come to realize they could not continue in situations in which their security was dependent upon forces outside themselves. Now, for the last time, the floor of their world has given way under them. They have had enough.

Blocked Mobility Again. Most entrepreneurs couple projection with an unfortunate situation in which they believed that they had committed themselves to an organization, had done all those things they should have done, and then suddenly found that they had no future in that organization. Their mobility was blocked for the final time.

Men in such situations can do one of several things. Many, fearful of making a change, eke out their years to retirement, becoming increasingly bitter. The stereotype is the wizened old codger, the unrestrained obstructionist. The cross he bears is the fact that he knows, and everyone else knows, that he has reached his ceiling.

Another line is to tackle the problem and to solve it within the organizational framework. In fact, in the observation of large systems, nothing is more fun to watch than an able man working his way out of a career cul-de-sac. Such men may consume years of their careers in a sophisticated move designed to get them back onto the main line. If, however, they elect to remain in and work it out, they will never become independent entrepreneurs. Typically, entrepreneurs handle such situations not by solving them but by leaving them. Let us look at some examples of blocked mobility.

Mr. Crampton was tardy in reaching the point of projection. Over a period of thirteen years he had been employed by the same firm. He leads the interviewer through a dismal work history in which he had, in the face of many obstacles, steadily advanced himself. Here is what he says happened:

> I had threatened to quit several times in order to get more money. Flood (his employer) had many times promised me a piece of the business, but this never came to fruition. In 1946, the eldest son of Flood returned from college as an engineer. He came into the firm and was ordering everybody about and telling them what they were not doing right, that he had a better way of doing it. I could not stomach this, and I decided to go into business for myself. I had been tithing for several months, and giving the church ten percent of my gross earnings gave me the spiritual support which I needed during this crucial period in my life. In November, I quit. Out of a job and with no money, I began looking around for something which I could do.

Circumstances converged to force Crampton to act. He assuaged his fear during the crisis by the propitiatory magic of tithing. In making his move, he was throwing away thirteen years.

Mr. Schull had far less to lose. Schull joined the Blue Ensign Company in 1932 at the age of twenty-two. He became a protégé of the owner-president and was almost at once made assistant chief tool designer. He was immediately given several important assignments. During the period from 1934 to 1937, he traveled over the United States and Europe. He says that he was young at that time and when he went on assignment to England, his youth caused his associate in that country to suspect sabotage. Although he was moving up rapidly, Schull was not a person to be balked. He tells of the events that led to his leaving Blue Ensign:

A promotion came up, and another man received it. I thought I should have had it and I let them know it. The president agreed with me that I should have had the job, but he said, "You are young, you can wait and you should wait." I thought this over and said to myself, "Why wait? Wait for what?"

He tells the interviewer, "It was true that I was very young, that I was ahead, and that therefore I could gamble." He left Blue Ensign and rented a grocery store for $35 a month in which he set up a tool design shop.

A man imbued with the qualities of the sweet and reasonable can wait his turn, but no man with the impatience of a Mr. Schull can climb the ladder of promotion in a bureaucracy. Mr. Fisk, a graduate engineer, saw a little more deeply, we assume, than Mr. Schull, but he arrived at the same conclusion:

While at Mandrake, I saw a lot of things that were intriguing. I began to get some ideas about high-pressure tubing. Also, when a man is working for someone else, he is very limited. He only goes so far. Ninety percent of the time it is the small men who stop him. The big guys are more generous. For example, at Shilling, the old man himself is a big man in anyone's book, but he had a lot of men who did not have the capacity. When I was at Mandrake, they were going to set up a new plant. I really felt as though I had the qualifications for the job, and I wanted to do it. But they told me I did not have enough experience, and they hired another man. He is now my sales manager. I quit.

Losing Out Again. Blocked mobility implies that a man's career route has become fouled up and that he is stalled. A rather different problem is faced by men who reach the top, and then find that they can lose it all. The typical entrepreneur does not like to fight losing battles:

Mr. McDonald left because his control of the firm was threatened by some of the men who had sponsored him. McDonald seems to have secured complete dominance over these sponsors, and was acting as proprietor although he had no investment in the firm. The owner of the firm died suddenly. One son immediately became president of the company. This upset McDonald a great deal. McDonald says, "The other son saw eye-to-eye with me." These two formed an alliance against the "antagonistic" son. McDonald says, however, that complete control of the company slipped away from him. He complains that the antagonistic son did not really know the business and interfered with McDonald's work. McDonald left the firm, "in the end being forced out by the legal situation." McDonald felt he had a moral right that transcended the rights of the sons by inheritance. Having learned that he could not exercise this right he never worked for another man again where somebody could "come in and take it all away from you."

This theme of having had the fruits of hard work stolen away is common in the interviews. Mr. Wallace also got hold of a situation in which he took over another man's business, but found he had gotten himself into a rough one.

Wallace had one business failure during his early years. He says, "Labor cost too much, and there was the eternal demands of the union." After this failure, he drifted on from one to another middle-management position, finally becoming manager of a fabricating company. As manager of a company in which the owner had "lost interest," Wallace felt that he had secured both autonomy and security. Examination of the company books, however, convinced Wallace of his error:

> It was ovious to me that the company was on its way out unless everyone took a drastic reduction in salary. I was now faced with the roughest decision of my life. Should I stay with the failing company, take a seventy percent cut in salary, and try to ride it out? Over a period of four or five months, while the company was breaking up under my feet, I wrestled with this problem. I kept asking my wife, "Should I go into business for myself, or should I stay where I will be assured of a salary?" I kept asking my wife, "What do you want?" And all she kept replying was, "All that I need is a new dining-room table." I kept telling her, "You do not need to go into business for buying a new table. You can get that when I am working at a regular job."

During the months when the situation deteriorated, the notion of holding on to the company's customers, of building good relations with the banks, and eventually of buying some of the failing company's machinery became stronger in Wallace's mind. He tells us that he began to realize that by running a nonunion shop, and by keeping wages extremely low, he might be able to make a go of it on his own. Wallace had made his projection.

So far we have talked only about men who left employment either because their advancement was blocked or because their job was breaking up beneath them. Many of these men, however, projected their present business because of personal difficulty with an earlier associate with whom they were involved.

Mr. Sullivan's period of role deterioration began with the decay of a firm created by one of his sponsors—an older man. For several years this partnership had prospered, but:

> Mr. Harper was the kind of person who would think of something and would never tell us, but he would go to a next-door bar and would sit there and talk to somebody else and then that somebody else would come and check with us and we wouldn't know how the whole thing got started. This was funny. Many times he would get sore with us and instead of telling us and talking it over, he would get touchy and write letters, and he was behaving in a very funny way. Not only that, but, due to his strong likes and dislikes, he had created quite a few enemies, and it seemed to me that he just didn't seem to pay much attention to the business. Most of the time he would talk about horse jockeys, and if ever you happened to start talking it (business), he would take time off to talk about the horse jockeys. Besides, he never concentrated on any job. How could he? He became forgetful and as a result the whole thing got fouled up.

Sullivan began to see that he would have to take action if he was to save the enterprise from the progressive "senility" of Mr. Harper. When Harper refused to sell his partnership and step down as president, Sullivan moved with the partners to set up a rival firm. Harper, Sullivan's former sponsor, was forced to liquidate to pay off the withdrawing partners. Sullivan says that during this time Harper was "down with cancer."

Mr. Stuart got himself involved in a family situation:

> My father-in-law wanted me to come in with him. The idea was that I was going to work for him and then possibly take over

the business some day. And he was a real bastard. He was really hard to work for. Some of these guys in my plant now think that I'm tough and that we have it tough here, but, boy, they should've had to work under him for a while. He had me doing everything. I did every damn thing you could think of. I started out on a bench. The last two years, I was working on the outside.

At any rate, in 1952 my father-in-law sold the business to a young fellow. I didn't expect this. As a matter of fact, he sold it without me even knowing it.

Stuart lost out. His projection, however, was shaped by losing out coupled with opportunities he had come across on "the outside."

Doubting and Disgusted Again. Overlapping both that group in which men were blocked and that group in which men lost out, and hard to place in relation to either, are those men who struck out on their own because they were simply disgusted.

Before World War II, Mr. Peters had several fliers at basic dealing, none of which had paid off. He returned from the war to find himself "on the street" and without a job. At this point, Peters says he had "firmly resolved to settle down to a regular job." While looking for work, he met a Mr. O'Toole, who was much impressed by Peters. He offered Peters a job as plant manager. Immediately, Peters found that his employer did not measure up to specifications. He hit the bottle rather hard and regularly, and he would be gone for two or three days at a time.

I realized that if this man could run a business this way and still make a go of it—and the business was doing quite well—then there was no reason why I myself could not go out on my own and do as well if not better. So I kept my job for close to a year, while laying the groundwork for going into business for myself. O'Toole and I hadn't hit it off so I worked for the day I could tell him off and walk out.

Peters is not at all specific, unless we call "hitting the bottle" specific, about just what was wrong. His projection germinated from the observation that so incompetent a person as his boss could get by.

Dr. Boehr was also disgusted with colleagues and superiors, and doubtful of their ability. This thread runs through Dr. Boehr's entire life. (He was the only entrepreneur who asked that he be paid for being interviewed, and said that if he was not paid he was necessarily being "exploited.")

Boehr received his doctorate in mathematics at a prestigious European university. He tells us that shortly after taking his degree he was running a large European plant, but was only rated as a minor executive. This was patently unfair, so when an American corporation offered to sponsor his coming to this country, Boehr jumped at the chance. He stayed with this company only two years, telling us that he had decided to "get out" as soon as his resident status was assured. "I was getting on a lot of stuffed shirts' nerves, and I quit to keep from getting fired." He answered a blind advertisement and became chief engineer of a fairly large corporation, but fought with the boss and was fired. Boehr had then been in the country for three years, and had no job and no prospects. "I'd saved a few hundred dollars," he says. "At this point, I realized it was not much fun working for other people, and I thought if I could get out and get into business on my own, I would make more money and would satisfy my desires to be independent."

From Boehr's interview it is clear that he never worked for a person whom he could regard as competent. He says of his last job, "They brought in a new manager, and this did not matter to me. I could work under any competent man. However, I discovered this man was not qualified for his job, and I informed top management of this fact. It was the least I could do as a loyal employee, but I was fired for my efforts."

Mr. Black also, in a rambling discussion which cannot be included verbatim because of length, develops the theme of "being at the mercy of those who are not to be trusted and, indeed, are not honest." At the cognitive level, what Black has to say about his relation with his last boss does not make much sense. It seems that Black was hired as a production superintendent in what he supposed was a prosperous firm. After he had been on the job awhile, he got wind of several large debts which the firm had not paid promptly. Mr. Black says, "these the owner had not told me about." It is not clear from the interview why Black thought that it was any of his business, but, finally, he "faced down" the owner and demanded an explanation. The owner informed Black that Black was a salaried employee and that, as such, he need have no interest in the firm's finances. Black could "not accept this being excluded from crooked dealing." We must not, however, assume that Black would have stayed on if he had been included in the crooked dealing.

Unlike Mr. Black, Mr. Reamers did have an understanding of why he left:

> Well, for example, at Mastoden. Well, there was a lack of co-ordination between the departments and then I didn't like the slip-shod methods they used in handling their equipment. Then, too, in leaving Mastoden, I just didn't want to play politics and you had to there. If you spent time working on your job, then you found these other guys that didn't, spent their time getting the knife in you. Politics, and that was how you moved up, and without it you didn't.

Mastoden is one of the nation's largest corporations. Another entrepreneur also left this firm, and recalls:

> We had a heat treatment, then we would send it to the welding department. Sometimes they would overheat it. For example, a man would put it in for heating and he would go to the bathroom, and he would come back a half hour later and it would have been overheated. This does not show, so it would go out and after while it would come back and there would be a complaint about it. It was too soft. Well, then, I would try to tell them that it was not done by me, it was done in the welding department. But if the guy in the welding department happened to be the fair-haired boy, well, I would get blamed for it. This would get charged to my department as a loss. This is one reason I didn't feel I wanted my future depending upon somebody else's decision.

The last two men are both alumni of Mastoden Corporation. Independently, they seem to have decided that they could beat this mammoth at its own game. As one of them said, "If they can make money the way they operate, I can do a hell of a lot better."

We now turn to a group who, as far as we know, might have fitted into an established organization if a disrupting event had not intervened.

Unemployment and Disemployment Again. World War II was a great dividing point in the careers of the men in our sample. The war pulled them out and in their Army homes they had the leisure to evaluate what they wanted to do with their lives.

Mr. Dane, a graduate engineer, was in the training program of a large corporation when he got his draft notice. He decided that the Army did not fit into his plans. He describes the intricate maneuvers by which he held the Selective Service at bay.

> The Army called me on a Monday and told me I was to be inducted. I told that guy that I was being married, and that the Army could go to hell. Within a half an hour a major was in the office. This major said to me, "All right, you report or I will have you arrested right now." Naturally, I went.

Dane was in the Army for five and a half years, and was discharged with the rank of major. While he was there he began to project his own business. He secured a billet in the ordnance department. Through this job, he made contact with many corporation executives, sedulously cultivating customers of his old firm. When the war was over, this firm offered him his old job. Dane turned it down:

> My father was madder than hell, because from my father's standpoint, this was the biggest thing in the world, to be sitting in an office for them in the management group. My father thought I was crazy the way I felt, but I knew if I did not do it then, I would never do it. I had one child at this time and I knew, with more children coming along, if I did not do it then I would never get around to doing it. I had a 1936 Chevrolet and $500, and I had four months' discharge pay coming to me. I had that much time to live on, even if we did not make a penny.

In the case of Mr. Pope the war did not so much interrupt a career as provide an energizing agent to a man who prior to the war seems to have been quite ineffective. In the years before the war, Pope had suffered a steady string of failures in small enterprise. His widow tells about her husband:

> He came back and we were poor. He had $700 leave pay. Well, that is not quite all we had. I had a little place that had been given to me by my parents. How we lived that winter, I do not know. Well, I do know. We scrounged. We borrowed. We somehow man-

aged. Of course, he looked around for something to do. He knew a lot of people in high places. Some were sons of founders of businesses—doing quite well. His friends all felt that, while they could not give him a job, he should go into his own business. He was the type of person who is going to make money as a symbol. All his friends who did not go into the service were making out very well. He wanted to make money, which he did, although he only lived seven years after this. In getting started in business, he was looking for something to make. His main object was to make money, and how he did it was not too important. He was basically looking for a product to make.

Mrs. Pope tells us that the war years gave her husband that sense of direction which he had lacked. In the seven years remaining to him he forged ahead. At the time of his death, his firm employed over 200 people. After he died of a heart attack, his widow took over.

The war seems to have simply deepened, on the other hand, the diffuse sense of restlessness and dissatisfaction which had gripped Mr. Abrams. Mr. Abrams is descendant from an old southern Jewish family. He tells us that his ancestors "served the Confederacy with distinction." Abrams' father was an architect, and Abrams himself received excellent training as a design engineer. He married a young woman who was heiress to one of the largest retail chain businesses in the United States. Abrams entered the business, and tells us that in the period just before World War II he was "extremely successful." He says that at this point in his life he was interested only in "wealth and power."

Driven by a motivation which he says he does not understand, Abrams enlisted in the Marines. He was on the beachhead at Tarawa, saw combat at Iwo Jima and Okinawa, and was wounded several times. Returning from the war, he reentered the clothing chain business owned by his wife's family. After a few years he was promoted to general manager. He now had an important job in a powerful company, with a secure present and a bright future. In his recollection, however, Abrams feels that he was a disappointed and unhappy man. He says, "Coming out of the war alive made me feel I had a duty to do something creative with my life." Abruptly, Abrams quit his job, and, as he remarked to the interviewer, joined "the ranks of the unemployed."

His, however, was unemployment in the grand manner. He had sufficient income from his investments to have no need to work for the rest of his life. He regarded himself, in a sense, as retired. He built a large home in a high-status suburb, doing the architecture himself and spending a considerable amount of time overseeing the work to insure that the house was built according to his plans. He tells us that during this period he was able to spend a great deal of time with his wife and family. He got into local politics, made a number of "strategic" investments, and during this year, actually made more money than during any other period in his life.

Abrams says that during this period "I was able to be more with my wife than I ever was before, or have been since." In spite of this positive aspect, Abrams looks back on this year as "the most bitter and frustrating time a man can ever know." Things were going extremely sour for him. He began looking around. He did not merely need a job or a business. He had an obscure but powerful desire to do something creative. He says he wanted "to make a positive contribution to the country." Driven by this inner force, Mr. Abrams began to look for something he could make.

The three foregoing examples illustrate the disrupting effects of military service on what might have been placid and straightforward careers. Another group of men, however, moved toward creating their own organizations simply because of unemployment or the threat of unemployment.

By the 1930's, Mr. Landry was completely fed up with the chronic disruption in his jobs. It is clear from his interview that Mr. Landry had had interpersonal difficulties with people on most of the jobs he had held. Once he had quit to set up a small shop, an enterprise that failed. By 1929, when he was laid off at General Motors, he had begun to believe that the chronic insecurity of working for other men was causing his difficulties. At this point, he decided:

I must get a job where I would not have this problem of being laid off. I got a job as a helper in a metal working plant. In such a small business, I thought I had a job which offered some security. I worked for this company until 1938. In 1938, Mr. Sherman decided to sell the company, and after six years of steady employment, I was again facing unemployment. The owner of the company was willing to sell the business for $2,000. I did not have $2,000, but he agreed to let me purchase the business on $200 per month installments.

Landry simply wanted secure employment. To get it, he projected a business. Landry owned this business until he had paid for it. He then sold it and used the capital to establish a venture in a more promising market area.

It took Mr. Landry many years to learn his lesson, but once was enough for Mr. Coles:

> They had these little pink slips they put in your pay envelope. I can't think of anything more degrading than that—not even to be told to your face not to come back. Well, I looked at that slip and I decided right then I'd never work again for some outfit like that that could just—so to speak—throw you away.

Mr. Johnson also fell into hard times because of moral indignation. Here is a simple and direct story. On his first job as a full-fledged engineer, his employer asked him to sign a patent agreement that all inventions he devised during his employment would automatically become the property of the employer:

> I said "no," and was consequently asked to leave the company. They had a blacklist—though nobody could prove it—because for ten years I was not allowed to get a job as an engineer without signing that oath. I could not get an engineering job for ten years, and I would accept no other. After knocking about a lot, it slowly dawned on me I would go into business for myself as the only way to keep people from stealing my ideas.

In Mr. Johnson's case, unemployment was, in a sense, voluntary and in adherence to a principle. Mr. Bell had a very good job, but lost it because of a heart attack. Before the heart attack, he had been "doing a little custom work in the basement" and working for an automobile firm. He quit his job, following medical advice to take a three-month vacation. He says, "I would not ever again attempt to go three months without working." He went to Florida, where he was thoroughly bored, but where he met a man who pointed out that Bell's training and skill were a "definite economic asset." In lieu of returning to regular employment, Bell went into custom making objects for quality homes. It was only several years later, when he was making a good income free-lancing, that it occurred to him to incorporate.

The Unappreciated. Throughout the materials already presented there runs the recurrent complaint that these men were not appreciated. In the following stories, however, the complaint becomes dominant.

It is extremely frustrating for a man to have a pet idea played down or disregarded by other people. One group of men recalls quite vividly this moment in their careers. Taken in context, it seems that the unappreciated idea may only have been symbolic of a relationship that was turning sour. In fact, some of the men who claimed that they left employment because of an idea that was not appreciated seem to have promptly forgotten the idea themselves. Some of them originally did not have any clear notion of establishing their own businesses, others did. Mr. Schaeffer describes his frustration:

> I went to Tritonex in 1944. At that time, the problem of developing a [description withheld for reasons of anonymity] was just beginning to open up, and the boss put me on that. We were investigating the possibilities of [name withheld] as this was prevalent in the industry at the time. In this investigation, I spent time in the East to find out what I could about the process. They were using [name withheld] for manufacturing that sort of thing. The center of this industry seemed to be in the Atlantic states. On one of these trips East, I happened to be sitting in a bar one evening, talking to a chance acquaintance. He suggested that I go over to the University and talk to a professor who had done some experimental work along this line. This I did the very next day. The process he was using was [name withheld]. This we had known about for a long time, but it was still something of a laboratory curiosity. The upshot of the whole thing was that I spent some time with the professor and came away with the idea, "That is for us—that is the way." I was sure of it. I just could not see any other way. It beat [name withheld] in a number of ways. When I got back to Tritonex I tried to sell the boss on this new process. He just could not see it. He did not care. The old process was all he could see. I fooled around with it some in the laboratory, but just could not seem to get anyone interested in it; so I started to fool around and develop it as a hobby at home.

Schaeffer's idea, which the boss could not see, was the basis for a business, which today has large annual sales with an exceptionally large profit yield.

We can accept Schaeffer's comments at face value. At another point in the interview, however, he gives us material with which to formulate an understanding not so much of Schaeffer and his boss, but of the total situation that Schaeffer was trying to escape. Schaeffer says of his research director:

> He had some success and you might call him outstanding in his field. This had the consequence that he tended to reject the ideas of the abler man coming along. He wasn't jealous. He was too big for that, but he had become rigid in what he thought. Then he surrounded himself with mediocrities, men of no talent or drive, who always told him what he wanted to hear. This one person, especially, wormed his way in, and he was always agreeing with the boss that too much money was being spent. Research is always a gamble and sometimes you go over your budget—way over. A really basic idea may take years to develop, and it's going to sound screwball at first. This guy had wormed his way in and after that nobody's ideas but the boss's could get a fair trial. He held the purse strings.

We can, again, if we wish, accept Schaeffer's statement at face value. Anyone who has ever been around research organizations recognizes the "mediocrity" who worms his way in and uses the purse strings to strangle the efforts of abler men. He probably cropped up in the washroom conversations at the first research organization that ever existed. He will probably also crop up in the washroom conversations at the last research organization that will ever exist.

The point here, however, is not so much whether this highly stereotyped figure in fact did nullify Schaeffer's ideas. We need here to understand the mechanism that this figure provided for Schaeffer's future development. He was blocked in a situation where he could not get acceptance of his idea. That the boss was "rigid," and the "mediocrity" self-seeking, adds moral justification to the course of action that Schaeffer was to take. We are made to see that there was nothing dishonest about his leaving the company, taking with him no more than an idea. In fact, he took with him an idea—into which the company had sunk considerable funds—which was no longer merely an idea, but a fully developed technique. And Schaeffer used this technique as capital with which to form his own corporation. When we consider the degree to which this violates the professional ethics of engineering, we see why Schaeffer so vividly recalls the rigid boss and the self-seeking mediocrity. He needs them.

Born to the Way. Out of over a hundred cases, we have in our samples no more than perhaps a bare half-dozen men who were "born" entrepreneurs. If one reads back through the life histories of these men, there seems to have been no time when they were not living and breathing business enterprise. For these men, the concept of role deterioration does not fully apply. They had already fully entered into the entrepreneurial role long before they projected their present business.

Mr. Davis was born in a log cabin in Kentucky. He came to the Big Town, saved his money, and bought an interest in a retail clothing store. He seemed, in a small way, well launched as a businessman. World War II, however, disrupted the pattern when his partner was drafted.

> He left the business in a horrible state—bills that were overdue and I didn't even know about. People would call up and say, "There's this bill, what are you going to do about it?" The first I'd heard of it. Then there were shortages. We hadn't been paying our bills, so when the supplier had to decide who was going to get merchandise, naturally we were last.

The little firm went under. Davis says, "I learned a lot there in bankruptcy court. I learned it wasn't the end of the world. And the creditors were even very understanding. I walked out of there knowing if I ever went bankrupt again it wouldn't be for peanuts."

With this course in basic dealing under his belt, Davis worked for an automobile company until 1944, saving his money and lining up resources. In 1944, he left the company and bought into an automobile dealership. It was quite successful, but Davis was aware that the operation was dependent upon too many factors outside his control. When he first went into the dealership, there was tremendous backlog of consumer demand for automobiles. Davis rode the crest, accumulating capital. In 1947, he began to see that the backlog was disappearing. He says, "I had to move fast, lining up a buyer before what was going to happen did happen." He says, "I found this sucker just in the nick of time. I unloaded on him." Davis then wryly comments, "That sucker is one of the half-dozen biggest automobile dealers in Michigan today. Sometimes I wonder who was the real sucker."

Davis was now unemployed. "For about a year," he says, "I looked the situation over for a setup that met my requirements." He wanted to get into manufacturing because "that always has the big growth potential." Also necessary for what he had in mind was that he take on no partners. He says, "I had to have an absolutely free hand for what I wanted to do." He finally found a manufacturing firm that was in trouble and he bought it. He then set up a new corporation and sold the buildings and equipment from the now defunct firm to this new enterprise. Davis has since used the corporation he set up to buy control in other enterprises.

Mr. Davis is as close to being a "pure" entrepreneur as any person we have in our sample. Although born in the backwoods in a situation of extreme squalor, it has apparently never occurred to him to be anything but an entrepreneur. Viewed from this point, his period of role deterioration began when his small retail business went into bankruptcy. Davis was, however, an extremely intelligent and far-sighted man. His experience in bankruptcy taught him that the risks were more apparent than real. He therefore got a job and saved money. His failure prepared him for what Davis thought of as his real future in life. His buying into the dealership, and even the subsequent purchase of a failing business, were only steps on the road back to entrepreneurship. He returned to entrepreneurship only when he was able to establish his own corporation, free from all encumbrances. This freedom was necessary to Davis because he had all along foreseen that he would use his corporation as a base from which to buy into, or manipulate, other firms.

ROLE DETERIORATION: A SUMMARY

The period of role deterioration is a crucial stage along the pathway to independent entrepreneurship. We have seen in this chapter that role deterioration takes many forms. No matter what form it may take for a particular individual, it can always be described as having certain discernible features. The period of role deterioration is a phase in the lives of these men when their world has become shattered. It is a time when the present is insecure, or when the future is unclear and confused, and the old lines of activity have been cut off. This is a period of self-analysis. It is also a period of examination of the environment. Out of it there are generated conceptions for new lines of action.

One must not, however, describe this period in its purely negative aspects. It is also a period of freedom, a period of relative lack of restrictive forces that compel a person to move only in one direction. This is why we have seen some of the men in our sample deliberately moving toward a condition of role deterioration as if they had anticipated and welcomed it. Some of the reasons they give for losing or leaving security have the quality of being "manufactured." Some of these men seem—with nice calculation—to have brought about a situation of jeopardy and of freedom. They seem to have felt that they needed to reach some such situation before they could bring themselves to take the plunge. Their instinctive desires seem to have forced them on. They seem to have felt that it was time to leave patterned security.

Not all men who undergo role deterioration, however, seek a solution by establishing a business. Many men lose their jobs in a period of depression, have rows with their supervisors, feel their advancement is blocked, or have their pet idea ignored. Most men do not, however, go into business for themselves. To the vast majority of them, the idea does not even occur. The man who does so is a unique individual.

He is a man who has passed through a long sequence of experience and trial. In his early childhood he learned that security is not to be found in highly structured situations under the wing and protection of older and wiser people. He learned, in fact, that such structured situations and such people are inherently dangerous and demeaning. The character formation of the true independent entrepreneur is such that in a moment of crisis he seeks to break away and escape the threatening situation. The antidote to insecurity is, in a sense, more insecurity. If a man's promotions are blocked, his ideas disregarded, or his authority challenged, he makes only a pugnacious and token attempt to resolve the issue within the structure. This sort of man always keeps his hat on the corner of his desk. If he is balked or reprimanded, he picks it up, puts it on, and goes out the door.

The period of role deterioration is not accidental in the lives of these men. It is an event which, given their character formation, is almost predestined to happen. It is not, however, sufficient that a man be chronically dissident and able to find reasons for quitting, getting fired, or otherwise getting into situations of role deterioration. Many men cannot permanently play the role of loyal subordinate and steady employee. We know that there are many routes open to such men. They can become artists, writers, or join the ranks of the unemployed. They can even go to graduate school and become members of "fee" professions.

Men who become independent entrepreneurs have undergone further special training and conditioning. Somewhere, they must be exposed both to the idea of entrepreneurship and to the skills involved in it. Those men who fear situations structured by others and the training required for them are those who, in the period of role deterioration, begin to evolve a project. The period of role deterioration may be viewed from the short-range view as a dangerous and trying situation. From the longer point of view, however, it is the moment of freedom from an essentially restrictive and threatening situation. It is a necessary stage in the career of the entrepreneur. This is the moment for trying one's wings. The truly independent entrepreneur is prepared for it. He begins to think about a project. At this stage of the game, it is this propensity to think about a project that marks him as an independent entrepreneur. Many men in moments of frustration will only play with ideas for businesses. The entrepreneur, if he is to be independent, must go beyond this.

CHAPTER EIGHT

The Projection

Men with patterns of work crumbling beneath their feet seek for new ways. Some seek desperately to find another job, some start collecting unemployment insurance, and some go back to school to secure additional training. In our sample, many men faced by earlier crisis in their lives had turned in these directions. This time it was to be different.

In the last chapter we left them in that role deterioration which gave them both motivation and freedom to act. Out of this period of role deterioration, often grim and dismal, comes the projection. At first, it may be vague and elusive with an ephemeral quality that cannot be pinned down, or, it may come into being full-blown at a moment of inspiration. For a few men, the project seems to have occurred, in all its ramifications and detail, in a sudden flash of insight. For others, the projection emerged so gradually that there appears to have been no one moment at which it was recognized as such.

In the folklore of entrepreneurship, much is made of the "idea for a new business." Most entrepreneurs themselves believe in the idea as a determining factor. Analysis of their comments allows us to arrange the variations of ideas in this way:

1. The idea of an invention

2. The idea of a product

3. The idea of exploiting resources

4. The idea of a market or an outlet

5. The idea of making money

A successful entrepreneur will almost always tell you about his idea, and it will probably fall into one or more of the above categories. Entrepreneurs like to tell—in circumstantial detail—how the idea came to them. They will tell you that they were in a plant, or in a bar, or awake in the night, or driving along between two specific points on a highway. They will tell you about the weather, about the season of the year, and what they had for lunch just before the idea came to them. For these men, the idea is recalled as a guiding beacon that led them out of the wilderness. Careful reading of the interviews, however, shows that the idea may be more important in recollection than it actually was in fact.

A sequence of events does take place, but it is often only later that the dramatic importance of the idea becomes clear. If we look at some of these sequences we see more clearly what happened. Some entrepreneurs first had the idea of an invention, then, only at a later stage, began creating an organization bringing together the resources to manufacture and to market the invention. Others first had the idea of making an organization, then went on to the problem of what to produce. Still others thought that they saw a spot in the economy where something was needed, went back to the organization creation stage, and finally arrived at a specific sort of product. Others were simply invited by someone else to enter into a partnership, or a business relationship, and subsequently took over. One or two had the beautifully direct and simple idea of earning a great deal of money. As one man said, "The idea was to make money. The product was to be money. With that idea, everything else began to take shape."

The idea, therefore, is a precipitating incident. It starts a line of thought. It is also clear, however, that the idea in itself is nothing. More important is the total configuration of thinking. Caught in a dangerous and insecure situation, these men began the activity which we call "projecting" an organization.

This activity is a highly cognitive mental process, and may be the most creative moment in the lives of these men. Projecting, as we see it, is a process of drawing lines of thought into the future. The entrepreneur sees how he can take available elements and begin a procedure through which, at some point in the future, these elements can be brought into a new configuration over which the entrepreneur exercises dominance. He sees how he can construct an organization.

This is not to say that "projecting" is the drawing up of a table of formal organization; it is, rather, that the entrepreneur begins seeing how to set in motion the events that he intends will lead to the creation of a firm. In many instances, he does not seem to be at all clear in his own mind what he wants his own personal future state of affairs to be.

If the desired goals are autonomy and dominance, the entrepreneur must be willing to sacrifice these long-range desires for more immediate objectives. The very nature of the projection may require this. The act of projecting at the cognitive level is an act of commitment at the emotional level. The projector, through the very act of projecting, begins to commit himself to a future line of action. He may have to delay for years the psychological gratifications he so desperately needs. Let us look at some interview material to give concreteness to the abstract notion of projecting.

THE IDEA OF AN INVENTION

The recollection that the entrepreneur created his business to produce or to market an invention runs like a golden thread through the stories. Many of these "inventions," however, were indeed pitiable. It often seems that the entrepreneur fabricates the idea of an invention to make his story fit the folkways of enterprise. We can only understand the invention motif if we look at it in the total context of projecting.

Mr. Bowman tells us how role deterioration and projecting were closely interwoven in his own career. As his first enterprise, he had established a school. After his initial success, he tells us:

> One thing led to another and by the late forties I could see the handwriting on the wall. The majority of the men who had been in service had utilized the G. I. Bill. I felt that the training business would no longer be as lucrative as it had been. I therefore sold my equipment and business.

Mr. Bowman was entering a period of role deterioration, and, in the interview, he ties his business uncertainty in with his personal life. He goes on to say:

It was in my business that I met my present wife. She worked for me in the office. Her brother was one of the instructors, and we started going together when the divorce from my first wife became final. It was shortly after I was divorced that I was married to my present wife. About this time, I began to think about some of the ideas I had had in the past, and about some other things. Here is one of the first things I thought about. [Here Mr. Bowman shows the interviewer a rather large and bulky folder containing sketches and patent documents.] See this drawing? This item that I had ideas on back in 1936 is the same identical one that has now been patented and developed by Aztec. But, at that time, nobody thought I had an idea. I did not have the money to exploit it. I got my first patent in 1938. Here are some others. [He shows them to the interviewer.] This is the one I developed and which became, for me, a big ticket item. The first one was handmade. I developed the tooling for about $4,000—that was all I salvaged from the school—and I decided to take this to the Metropolitan Show. My wife and I were there only a couple of days, but we took orders for over 10,000.

At earlier times in his life, Mr. Bowman had made several inventions and had developed several products. In the meantime, he had established the school. It served the dual function of training him in entrepreneurship and allowing him to accumulate a small amount of capital. Having used the school for these purposes, Bowman got rid of it. It was, however, only after he realized that his school was doomed to failure—and in the story he places this adjacent to his troubles with his first wife—that he decided to do something about exploiting his ideas.

In Bowman we have the embodiment of the folk theme of business success through invention. Bowman thinks of himself as an idea man who uses his organization as a vehicle for putting the toys he invents into production. He is now diversifying. He told us that he was developing an idea which, he believed, would "revolutionize the transportation industry."

An invention also figures in the story of Mr. Roland, who seems to have first become aware of such possibilities by investing in other people's ideas. Earlier in his career, he had been an investor in an invention which utilized the pressure of water at the water faucet to operate a refrigeration unit. (Incidentally, another man in our sample was at one point intrigued by the same idea.) Mr. Roland invested $2,000 in this idea, but the project failed "because they pushed it too hard and too fast in trying to make a go of it." While this little business was failing, Mr. Roland did some inventing on his own. He developed a machine that he felt had great potential, and he built a machine shop in his own basement, where he made a pilot model. When the company for which he worked asked him to sign a patent agreement, Mr. Roland quit and went on the road to try to sell his invention. When he could not find a buyer, he began projecting the notion of setting up a firm and manufacturing it himself.

Roland first saw his idea as only one invention, but having projected his business he found that he had hit upon a process which could be applied to many continuous manufacturing situations. There has developed from his original idea a family of devices.

Bowman and Roland are men whose claims to being inventor-entrepreneurs are genuine. Mr. Victor's claim is more tenuous, and for that very reason should be studied in detail. Victor was trained as a lawyer and, during the first part of his career, he practiced law. His law work put him into contact with people at the automobile companies, a circumstance that proved important. Law was, for Victor, "on the whole, extremely boring and frustrating." He says that he had reached a point in his career at which he "had to get out." Now we see how he moved through a series of steps in making his projection.

During the early days of the war, he tells us, there was a problem in making dies for aluminum castings—"that aluminum has a peculiar thermo-quality." An inventor came along with a different type of die. An organization was formed to market this new die, and Victor invested $4,000 of his personal money. Although originally thinking of himself only as an investor, Victor got drawn into the management of the enterprise. He says things were being mishandled, and he discovered that trying to save the little enterprise was "intriguing." During this adventure, Victor got his first exposure to basic dealing. Through a complicated set of circumstances which we need not detail here, the little organization failed. Victor handled the resulting legal snarl, and in the process came to own the equipment. This included a set of dies. He decided to liquidate at a loss by selling the tooling for scrap. He called the junk man to come in and remove the entire operation. He could see no future in it.

Now for the dramatic turn in the story. Driving down the street past an automobile factory he noticed that in front of the plant was a large model of a car encased in a plexiglass ball. As he drove on, the idea of making small-scale model automobiles as a promotional gimmick came to him.

He called the junk man and cancelled the order to have the dies removed, and he had a model—six or eight inches long—made of a car. Within several weeks, he had one completed, and "it was beautifully painted." He tells us that it was quite a striking toy. He decided to go over and see the people in the automobile company. His first impulse was to sell the idea to an automobile company and let them make the cars as a promotional item. The automobile people let Victor know that they were interested only in making "big" cars. It was only after this impasse was reached that Victor began projecting his own business.

Here we have in modern and secular form a version of Paul on the road to Damascus. Even as the vision changed Paul's life, this idea changed Victor's.

Victor's hegira from law to business is only ostensibly built around an invention. Stripping away the dramatics, we see that all that actually happened was that Victor had an idea for a toy. Nevertheless, each of the three men we have considered so far believes that he is primarily an inventor. He subscribes to that mode of entrepreneurship so dear to that part of all of us which is "Yankee." This is the classic theme of beginning an organization with an idea for a better mousetrap. The theme, deeply rooted in our folkways, occurs many times in the stories.

THE IDEA OF A PRODUCT

This notion that entrepreneurs have about primarily being inventors often arises from the fact that their projections involve adapting a product or a technical process to a market. Later it is quite easy to forget that they did not actually "invent" the product.

Mr. Schull also created an organization to produce an item, but this item was no different from a product made by the company he quit. We left Mr. Schull in the last chapter at a moment when he had, because of extreme youth, been refused a promotion. What did Schull do about it? He started the Schull Engineering Company with quarters in a grocery store, which he rented for $35 a month. Here Schull immediately went into a line of work identical with that of the company he had left. Several resources were, therefore, available to him. First, he thoroughly understood the technical side of the work. Second, he knew intimately the operations and the weaknesses of what had now become his major competitor. Third, he was able to take with him the good will of former customers whom he had personally serviced. As he puts it, "I felt I had built a good reputation at the company where I worked, but I was amazed at the amount of business that went with me to my new firm." Around these resources he made a projection of his new activity. Between this conception and its realization lay a shadow—it was to take Schull years to expel that shadow.

Mr. Abrams is an almost pure example of a man who projected a firm around the idea of a line of products. Abrams was in a similar situation as Schull after leaving his high-level job without future employment. There was, however, one important difference. Abrams, by this time in his career, had amassed considerable capital, and had many contacts in the financial world. He was looking around for something to do, when an activity came to his attention. This activity can hardly be called a business, but was rather the hobby of another man. Let us call this man Mr. Neil. For six years, in a small work area across the street from his sales office, Neil had been playing with advanced electronic regulating and measuring devices. Although he was employing men and investing capital, Neil apparently regarded development of these devices as an intriguing hobby. His little organization employed four people at this time, on a rather informal basis. Largely because he had nothing better to do with himself, Abrams got interested. Soon thereafter, he bought control. At this point, Mr. Abrams had really only bought something which, he says, he regarded as a toy. It was only gradually that he was able to project how he could make a creative contribution. He began to think about bringing talented men together to work on problems of measurement.

Mr. Nelson also developed his projection around a product, but in his case the product served as an outlet for his creative talents:

When I started this business, financial security was not a big factor. The main thing and the reason I started out was that I thought I would like this and it would also give me an opportunity to pursue my first love, which is shipbuilding. I have always felt that there are very few capable people who can design ships properly. It appears that nowadays in the shipbuilding field the builder is primarily a pawn with the government or your customers saying "do this or do that," and you build accordingly. Therefore, you have little opportunity for your own expression and ideas with respect to shipbuilding. I felt that this concern would give me a better chance for my own creative ability.

Mr. Nelson considers himself a fortunate and happy man, although today only about a quarter of his sales are in marine equipment. He projected his organization as a means of working in the field nearest his heart.

In Dr. Temple's case, it worked the other way. She started with creative production, and "backed into" founding a corporation both as a legal device and as a way of securing technical assistance.

Miss Temple holds a doctoral degree in the physical sciences. After taking her doctorate, she worked for several corporations in research and development. She never stayed with one firm very long. Caught between jobs, she did a little cogitating, "I realized that for a woman it was difficult to find a good position in a big company, and I thought I'd be better off if I went out on my own." Initially, she looked for consulting jobs and developed some free lance contacts. A businessman friend, in the town where she had settled, took her under his wing and served as both sponsor and instructor. He introduced her to potential clients and taught her how to keep records. As the idea of incorporating evolved in her mind, this friend seems to have coached her in her thinking to go beyond incorporation for tax purposes, and to think about incorporating as a first step in setting up research facilities and employing technical personnel.

Here the projection occurred gradually and was closely connected to an interpersonal relationship. The relationship that led to the original projection still acts as a guiding—although by no means dominating—force in the enterprise. Dr. Temple's efforts to market a high order of ability led her gradually, through the guidance of her sponsor, toward entrepreneurship.

The idea of a product, therefore, cannot realistically be abstracted from the situation in which it occurs. In the following account the idea of a product was interwoven with another idea:

> About this time, two other fellows and I got together and decided to go into business. These two fellows—Ed, who is now first vice-president, and another fellow—and I, thought that we would try and get into business. We weren't actually going in unprepared. Ed's father had had a plant in this area for many years, and Ed had worked for him, so he knew this end of it. And I had worked in house building, so I knew the cabinet working and how to do the interior work. Actually, the third partner had bought trailers for many years—had actually had about seven trailers in eight or nine years. We sort of figured out what was wrong with these trailers and decided that we could improve on them.

The possibility of a business partnership, coupled with certain skills and an interest in trailers, led to the idea of a business. The speaker was the actual entrepreneur among the three. He projected a business around the idea of improving trailers, but more importantly, around the training of the men as the basic resource.

THE IDEA OF EXPLOITING RESOURCES

This notion of the resource leads us to a type of entrepreneurship which begins in a diametrically different direction from that of the product idea. In this group are the men who have resources available, but who have, initially, no particular idea of what to do with them. These resources take several forms. First, men go into business because they realize that there are available machines, floor space, or simply, money. Second, personnel resources may be the precipitating factors. Men who have worked as tool and die makers, as sales representatives or as engineers, realize, in a period of role deterioration, that they can lead a more satisfactory and more remunerative life by working for themselves. On this foundation, they project a business.

One resource most tempting in the world of manufacturing is that of customers. A projection is sometimes made at that moment when the projector realizes that customers can be switched to a new firm. Mr. Salisbury tells us how he stole away one of his employer's best customers:

When I was working at this outfit, we had a customer in Indiana who used to bring us 200 to 300 units per night. He would produce them during the day, and then he would bring them into our plant for heat treating, and we would do it at night. I was night shift superintendent, and so these guys on the day shift just would not do a decent job. After a while he finally specified that I should be the only one to handle this heat treating, and he finally approached me one day about going into business for myself. Why shouldn't we set up a heat treating plant down in Indiana, where his plant was, rather than shipping his units 60 miles?

Mr. Salisbury became aware that he could steal a good piece of his employer's business. This was a simple and direct projection.

John Erickson, Ph.D., spent his earlier years climbing the academic ladder to full professor. As he says, during these years he had "piddled" with consulting work, and he had formed a strong alliance with several "top" men in a large corporation. During the War, these men ran a development project. With cessation of hostilities, the corporation decided not to push further into this field, and as Erickson puts it, "there was some question whether our work would ever come to fruition."

At this point in the interview, Erickson digresses into his own personal situation, saying that life had become too "snug," and that he was bored with the routine of academic life. Then one of the men in the large corporation approached Erickson with an idea that a company be formed to exploit the new process on which Erickson had worked as consultant. At first Erickson was reluctant, saying that it was very clear to him that he "could not continue on the tenured faculty while at the same time giving this thing the time and work it deserved."

One gets the idea that Erickson was dragged into entrepreneurship by his heels. Once in, however, Erickson showed a decided flair. A firm was formed, and it immediately bought from the corporation, "at a ridiculously low figure," the processes on which Erickson had worked. The interviewer comments, "It is not at all clear why the corporation was willing to part with these rights for so little." Are we wrong in guessing that the liaison between Erickson and the administrators had something to do with it? These executives became stockholders in the new venture. This new firm came into being not only to exploit an existing process, but to secure Erickson's talents on a permanent basis. Erickson is president, but devotes almost all his time to product development, saying, "I haven't much concern with the profit side."

Another resource is the entrepreneur himself. House and Grounds came into being as a firm through circumstances which were, in some ways, similar to those of Erickson's company. From the interview, however, we understand that this firm was created solely in order to exploit its creator.

Mr. Joseph was no Johnny-come-lately, although his early career had been marked by ups and downs. Joseph bought into an electrical-appliance retail business when still in his early twenties, but lost out by not getting supplies during the War. After the War, Joseph tried to cash in on the pent-up demand for household appliances and bought into a company. This firm had built a huge inventory of irons when its principal customer suddenly cancelled and left it, "with a warehouse full of them." They couldn't give them away. Joseph's solution was to dismantle the firm and to use its components to establish a new firm which made a more diversified line of pots and pans, as well as several small appliances. "I wasn't getting caught with my pants down again," Joseph tells us. "We went along with this for several years, but it was increasingly clear that we had hit our ceiling. We were hobbled by an obsolete plant and by high fixed costs."

Mr. Joseph was still a relatively young man, but one well skilled in the ins and outs of light manufacturing. He might have continued in marginal operations indefinitely had he not been approached by a delegation of creditors of a business which was about to go bankrupt. Initially, they offered Joseph a salary to "come in and straighten things out." Joseph's investigation showed him that matters were beyond straightening out. He recommended that a new firm be formed taking over the physical assets of the one which was going bankrupt and buying up the assets of the company which Joseph was currently operating himself. He was projecting the formation of House and Grounds.

Here the projection was made by Joseph around his own competence and the willingness of colleagues to invest in him. Joseph's early difficulties can be viewed as part of his development, but Mr. Sanborn was approached when his record consisted of a string of unbroken catastrophies. Sanborn's first venture ended in a bankruptcy court. He was forced out of his second, losing what little money he had invested. He then did some drifting, finally taking a job as sales director of a fairly big outfit. The treasurer of this firm was a man who had sponsored Sanborn in earlier years:

I got there, and here I found that this treasurer who was my hero was going to jail for embezzlement. Was this ever a shock to me! I worked there and then I quit. When I quit, the main reason was there was just too damn much traveling. I traveled all over this whole country. I had decided to quit, and was going to go into a partnership with another fellow. We were going to set up a distributorship—a supply house, actually. You see, I'd gotten to know their (his employer's, at the time) customers pretty well and I thought this could be built into something. This was going to be in Green Bay. My wife was up there looking for a house at the time. I'd actually sold my house. Hell, I'd even had a farewell party for me at the office.

On the Friday, this Tidings called me. He'd been after me, trying to talk to me for about a month. What I thought that he was after was a job, and I felt that, well, I couldn't talk to him. I'd put him off and stalled him because I was leaving, and because they would have a new sales manager, and I didn't want to hire the man and stick the new manager with it. I didn't know who the new man was, and I figured he should be the one to make the decision.

So, at any rate, one day Tidings phoned me and said, "I'm over at this restaurant, why don't you come down and have lunch with me." So, hell, you can't refuse that, so I went over, and here he wanted me to head up a company they were setting up.

Four men had agreed to set up a new firm, but none of these men wanted to take charge. They were all committed elsewhere, and seeing the operation as a way of investing funds, they agreed to go ahead only if they could get Sanborn as president. In this case, therefore, the four men as capitalists were in the strict sense the projectors. Their projection hinged around the availability of Sanborn.

Sanborn says that this was all "somewhat embarrassing since I didn't have anything to put in. The six thousand I mentioned I had I'd already put in this partnership, and I felt I didn't want to welsh out there." He stipulated that, since he had nothing to "put in," there should be an arrangement for part of his salary to be in the form of shares, with Sanborn having the right to acquire up to thirty percent of the shares through this device. The only remaining enigma in this case is what in the world these men saw in Sanborn. Perhaps they see more deeply than we do, for, in spite of his earlier failures, Sanborn has built the firm soberly and solidly.

In the last three cases, we have seen that the entrepreneur himself may be the resource around which a firm is projected. Projections also arise not around people but around equipment. Mr. Cooley and his brother were both artisans who, working for an automobile company, did "moonlighting" on the side. They had come to have a quite elaborate machine shop in their garage. Cooley says that from time to time people at the automobile company would tell them about small special jobs, and that they would take on these jobs as a sideline. One of these grossed five thousand dollars, but they found that working off handmade patterns and doing hand finishing was inadequate for such a large undertaking.

Perhaps they might merely have learned not to tackle anything so ambitious again. Two other factors, however, intervened. First, they decided that they were not being treated fairly at the automobile plant. Second, they went out to a disposal depot where the company auctioned obsolete machines. Cooley says, "They had many, many fairly good machines out there and no one bidding on them. If they didn't get a bid right away, then they sold them for scrap. With very little outlay we were able to buy a milling machine, a lathe bigger than the one we then had, and a good grinder. All in all, we bought six machines, partly because we'd decided in advance how much we could spend and found that, for that amount, we could buy six. We also picked up about two hundred dollars worth of cutting tools."

With such adequate equipment, they were able to finish their large order, and they started looking for more work. According to Mr. Cooley, they still had not thought of going into business. When they got another, larger order they decided "to go into business."

Many of these men got their start during that period when the government was dumping World War II matériel. This access to what otherwise would have been prohibitively expensive equipment had, for some firms, a decisive impact. Some men had already established their businesses and were struggling when they came upon such sources of equipment. In contrast, several men projected businesses suddenly—almost on the spur of the moment—upon hearing of this equipment. Mrs. Leeks had been telling us about the earlier failures of her husband. She goes on to the dramatic and precipitating incident:

> My husband had never worked in a plant before, so he just picked it up as he went along. There was this fellow, Loren, and he helped my husband. This fellow was joking and he said to my husband, "Why don't you buy a machine and go into business for yourself? You can make $40 an hour." Well, they all laughed, but my husband said to himself, "Well, why don't I?"

Although he had nothing to make on it, and no place to put it, Mr. Leeks went to an auction and bought the machine that most nearly fitted his pocketbook, apparently with little concern about what the machine would do. He hauled it home and put it in the basement of his rented house, although the house had no suitable wiring. He apparently had not thought of securing a work contract and the financing with which to buy materials, but he had, nevertheless, projected his business.

Mr. Beaverbird had something of the same simpleminded approach. In knocking around over several states, Beaverbird had developed skill as a tool and die maker. He happened to overhear a conversation to the effect that "some of the automobile companies would give you work and help you get financing in starting a tool and die shop." Out of a job, Beaverbird had decided that it was "about time I put my knowledge and skill to work for myself." These two ideas in conjunction led to Beaverbird's projection. The next morning, he went "bright and early" to the purchasing office of an automobile company.

Having learned what the company was interested in buying, Beaverbird made two more calls. He went to his father-in-law, who agreed to loan him five hundred dollars. Next, he went to the Chamber of Commerce to find out how to qualify for the purchase of war surplus equipment. Overnight, Beaverbird had made his projection.

In 1947, to take one more example, two gentlemen of experience and acumen noticed a large and modern plant was idle. Looking it over, they learned that it had been used for small ordnance war work.

One of them now says that "much of the machinery and assembly equipment was still in place and that, as a plant, it was largely intact. We began figuring what we could make if we could get our hands on that place." When the owners agreed "that they would lease if I was really interested," these two operators then made exploratory rounds of purchasing offices. Having learned that a market existed, they began looking around for working capital.

THE IDEA OF A MARKET OR AN OUTLET

Still another approach is the one which begins with an estimate of a market situation and works back from there to financing, and to products. Mr. Toller is a type case. Toller's training and experience had been in what he calls the "distribution end." Beginning as a retail salesman and advancing to store manager for a large chain, he had acquired intimate knowledge of what people buy and had thoroughly enjoyed close contact with customers. As store manager, however, he claims that he missed this contact and this made him "restless."

He quit a job with excellent prospects to go into a retail partnership. Now his troubles began. He found that he could not get merchandise that was "really appealing." Furthermore, he came to see that the profits were not in distribution, "as most people think." He did a little cogitating, and:

> The thing was plain—you had to go into plastics. That was the coming thing, although it was still very primitive and there was nothing but poor-quality stuff coming out. Stuff that if you put a little strain on it would tear like paper. I could see how everybody wanted good plastics, and stuff like (name withheld) was being produced by the chemical companies. I came to see if I could get supplies, and if I could find some really bright young designers, there was no end to the demand. All that was needed was attractive products.

Mr. Toller was far from having his business, but he had made his projection. Another man in the sample saw the same problem, but from the vantage point of engineering:

> It was a field that suffered from what you might call retarded development. It's one of the older industries, and—well, I guess—

there was a lot of built-in inertia. They always operated the good old way, and very much by rule of thumb. A customer ordered something, they made it by rule of thumb, and if it didn't fit the customers' needs that was too bad because that was all there was. Anyway, the customers didn't always know what they needed because they had no idea what could be done for them. Study a customer's problem and then tell him what he needs—that's the way we do it today.

Six young men sent by their large engineering firm to do a consulting job had a similar outlook. They were sent as a team to study a client's operations and to recommend changes. With offices in the client's plant and working closely with the client's personnel, over a year's time they came up with some rather radical innovations, which they convinced the client would put him ahead of his competitors. The changes they recommended would cost over a million dollars.

Now, as one of the young engineers recalls it, the consulting job hit a snag. The client corporation asked that the engineering firm supply and install the new equipment. Mr. Fischer, who was the real entrepreneur, tried to convince his superiors in the engineering firm that this would be profitable and would insure that the job was done properly. The engineering firm refused to go along. (Here the interview is vague about this reluctance to take on such lucrative work.)

Mr. Fischer, however, "very much annoyed and enraged at this," told the client company that he would undertake to make the changes. All six of the engineers quit as a group, and all six became partners in forming a firm. Their first customer was the former client of the engineering firm.

THE IDEA OF MAKING MONEY

Mr. Tyron, at one point in his interview, comments, "I've always been driven by the desire never to slip back into the poverty of my childhood. To earn enough so that I would never have to experience that again has always been my guiding light and beacon." Such themes run through stories of men who began life as poor boys. Usually it does not lead to the projection of a specific business.

Several men, however, maintain that they did project around this simple notion. Mr. Foote said, "The idea was to make money. With

that in mind, everything else fell in place." This comment makes sense
only in context. Jack Foote's father was a successful independent entrepreneur, and in Jack's remembrance always treated Jack as "worth-
less." Jack got into bad trouble as a teenager, but his "old man"
bailed him out. "He always held that against me, also, and would
keep bringing it up." Managing to get through high school and into
the state university, he flunked out in his first year. He says to the
graduate student interviewing him:

> My advisor told me I set some sort of record, all F's except one
> or two D's. After that, I was strictly not welcome at home. I
> bummed around a lot, and did quite a little day labor. I didn't hit
> the bottle, though, because I more or less felt that would be going
> too far and would be the finish of me. Actually, I got into shop
> work by accident. They hired me at this plant in California and I
> found I liked the cleanliness and orderliness—shall we say the pre-
> cision? I still get a kick out of walking through the plant and seeing
> a long chip curling out on the floor.

Foote gravitated, after six or seven years, back to his home town
and to his high school girl friend. Barbara, the daughter of a vice-
president of a major manufacturing firm, had lost her mother in her
early years and had been sent to live with an aunt and uncle. Foote
lets us know that Barbara had "also knocked around a lot, and maybe
more than I like to think about." After graduation from a "better
Eastern women's college," she had spent a couple of years in Paris.

They got married and continued to be angry at the world. The
precipitating incident was, Foote recalls, a visit to Barbara's father in
Maine. Foote tells us they were both treated "like dirt, and maybe
with some justification because I had this one old suit plus a jacket
and slacks, and maybe Barbara was drinking more than she should."

Driving back from Maine in the old Pontiac, Foote brooded.
That night, he woke his wife up and said, "Barbara, why don't we
make a pile of money and show these bastards we can do it."

That, Foote would like us to believe, is when he made his projection. As he said, fifteen years later, "The idea was to make money.
With that in mind, everything else fell into place."

Mr. Camp also recalls that he went into business because he
needed money, but he ties this need to a desire he shared with his

wife to leave their only child a special kind of legacy. Mr. Camp had begun as an automobile assembler, and had moved up into supervision. Then the Camp's only child was born:

> When Pete was born, it was that he was badly deformed. Nothing could be done and it was apparent he was going to have to go through life like that. As he got older, it turned out he had a good mind. He's bright, and you might possibly say brilliant. But no matter how bright he was, we felt he would never be able to get a regular job. We felt they just wouldn't want him around.
>
> My wife and I talked about it a lot. At first, we thought "put everything we could into buying him an annuity,"—something to have after we were gone. But you only do that if somebody's incompetent. He wasn't incompetent, only deformed. Then we came to the view that if he owned his own business, he couldn't be fired. That's when we began seriously thinking about going into business.

Mr. Camp says later in the interview, "It was only to be a small business. Something he could work at and would support him. We had no idea when we started how it would grow." It did grow, and Pete in his late teens takes keen interest in it. His father says of the employees and associates, "They don't see him as unnatural and odd. These are his own people and he's at home with them, and they respect him. They have a lot of respect for his mind and what he can do."

In this chapter we have looked at many circumstances under which projections occurred, but we have not exhausted the subject. In recalling this dramatic moment in their lives, men also came up with situations that have very little to do with inventions, products, markets, resources, or money. For example, let us review what Mr. Hillman told us.

To get a full picture, we must go back into Hillman's education and into his period of role deterioration. Mr. Hillman, a man of strong opinion, in his early years went through several business ventures in rapid succession. His basic problem seems to have been that he prematurely tried to get rid of business partners. At least, after sharing in setting up several firms, Hillman several times found himself forced out of the management. After these initial failures, he became protégé to the president of an established firm. At the time Hillman became manager, this firm was having labor trouble. In fact, Hillman tells us that he got the job partly because of his views on organized labor.

Immediately on Hillman's taking over, the firm was plunged into a series of strikes, walkouts, slowdowns, and finally a lockout. Hillman tells us that his intention was "to get rid of the unions," and throughout these troubles he stuck to his guns. He explains to the interviewer that this (breaking the union) was not only necessary for economic reasons, but because the union was morally "wrong" in that it interfered with the management's right to run the company. The company was not able to sustain the struggle. In the interest of what Hillman believed was a noble cause, it went into receivership. Hillman thinks, however, that the experience taught him a great deal. He began projecting a business that would be strictly nonunion, paying low wages to new men and offering no seniority or other concessions. He tells us that he "sold" the noble experiment on this basis and had no difficulty getting bank financing.

Many, although by no means the majority, of men who subscribe to the "business ethic" are irritated and disgusted by the demands and restrictions placed on management by organized labor. Hillman, however, went beyond mere irritation and frustration. He had the creative imagination to act. He projected a business not so much as a profit-making enterprise but as a crusade. He tells the interviewer he believes that being undersold will bring other firms "to their senses." No matter what we think of his cause, Hillman *is* a man with a cause. Although their views of what constitutes the "good society" are diametrically opposite, both Hillman and Abrams had strong ideological motivations interwoven in their projections.

In this part of the book we have explored that critical phase of organization creation which we call the "projecting phase." For purposes of delineation we have divided what is, in reality, one major phase into two subphases.

The first of these we have called the phase of role deterioration. In this phase, these men have reached a point where their old pattern of life has been disrupted. The disruption takes one of many forms, usually with more than one aspect being present for each man. There is a sudden or progressive loss of economic security. There is a loss of goals and aspirations. Participation with associates and friends has been violently upset. At this time in their lives, these men are anchorless. They no longer have anything to cling to. They become projectors.

It is not, of course, experiencing role deterioration which sets these men off as independent entrepreneurs. All of us at one time or another have disruptions in our lives. We fight with our bosses. We lose jobs. General unemployment catches up with us. Illness strikes. Family squabbles lead to divorce and to loss of status in the community. That these entrepreneurs underwent such disruptions does not set them apart from other human beings. On the contrary, it makes them very much like other human beings.

What sets them apart is that during this time of role deterioration they interwove their dilemmas into the projection of a business. In moments of crisis, they did not seek a situation of security. They went on into deeper insecurity. At the psychodynamic level, this is for some of them a further escape from the intolerable. They went on from the period of role deterioration to temporarily increase the insecurity and instability of their lives.

In this period of fear and doubt, however, these men found creativity. At a time when it became necessary for them to reorganize their lives and to reestablish their futures, they had the capacity not only to dream but to transmute their dreams into action. They created the business of which they were dreaming.

Between the idea and the act falls the shadow. This shadow lay immediately ahead. These men had now to organize the universe around them in such a way that they could progress in creating an organization. The first act in this direction was setting up the firm.

PART THREE

CREATORS
AND THE
ENTERPRISE

CHAPTER NINE

Creators and the Enterprise

The projection has been made. Out of the uncertain chaos of his situation, the independent entrepreneur has extended lines of thought into the future. He has no clear understanding of where these lines will lead—and often he hasn't, so early in the game, the foggiest notion of the sustained action required to transmute his projection into reality. At this point, the projection serves merely to alter his situation of role deterioration into one in which he has both the freedom to act and a purpose for acting.

This is the most creative moment in the career of the entrepreneur. Consider his position. He has broken completely and irrevocably with his past. He no longer carries his former responsibilities and obligations around on his back like the Old Man of the Sea. At this moment, he has not yet assumed a new set of responsibilities and obligations. For a fleeting instant in his life he has that autonomy which he always craves and which, at those moments when he achieves it, is so deeply disturbing to him.

From this point forward, he is going to sacrifice a good deal of that autonomy which at the moment of projection is so important to him. Turning his projection into reality is going to call for committing himself to a steadily narrowing area for maneuvering. He may find that securing resources involves a steady trading away of his autonomy for support. He may find that in the end he has traded sponsors for partners, and employers for customers. Above all, he is going to find that every move he makes reduces his possibilities, since the choice of one line of action necessarily eliminates the choosing of any other.

Just as the phase of adolescence is important to the growth of the mature man, the phase of projection is crucial to the development of the mature entrepreneur. Many men get stuck in drifting or basic dealing, and many get stuck in the phase of projecting. In the pages that follow, we will get some glimpses of these men who are perpetually in the phase of projecting, but who can never go further. In fact, we will see the maturing enterpreneurs feeding upon such arrested cases to further their own enterpreneurial objectives. A man in the arrested state of projection is like the novelist who talks away his story in the public house because he cannot accept the immediate sacrifice of staying home and putting it painstakingly through the typewriter.

The independent entrepreneur is set apart by the fact that he can make such sacrifices. He is able to take the longer view, and can always sacrifice his burning immediate desires for his anticipation of the day when he can more fully enjoy the fruits of his efforts. We shall see that for the entrepreneur, as for the general condition of Man, that day never comes. We shall see that the entrepreneur continually trades away his present for his anticipation of the future. In this, however, his tragedy is in no small part shared by all men.

Creation is not a short-term activity that takes place only directly after the act of projecting. It is not a simple and direct act of drawing up papers of incorporation or of partnership. It does not end with the lining up of capital, personnel, floor space, and customers. It is, rather, a usually difficult and often extended undertaking that begins with the moment of projection and goes on until the moment when the entrepreneur has secured control over an established and expanding enterprise.

The process of creation does not in reality exist in neatly separated compartments, with one phase always ending before the next begins. There is a flow of events involved. These events can be conceptually isolated, but the flow is an integral movement. For the purpose of delineation, we can think of three tasks that the entrepreneur must accomplish in creating a new enterprise.

The first task is that of gathering in and organizing resources necessary to turn the projection into a line of action. We call this "setting up the firm." In this phase the entrepreneur is finding money, men, materials, and equipment necessary for getting operations going. We shall see that during this period he necessarily sacrifices—in one form or another—the very autonomy and control that is his own long-range objective. We shall see that, in fact, at the end of this phase the entrepreneur has often temporarily sacrificed almost all control over his enterprise. In his eagerness to get things going, he may have given away almost everything he is working toward. If he has permanently given it away, he has, of course, failed. In the School for Entrepreneurs we have seen cases where this happened. When it does happen, the entrepreneur is not ready. What might have been an act of creation ends as another lesson in basic dealing.

Almost before the entrepreneur has his firm set up, the second phase begins. We call this phase "getting through the knothole." For most entrepreneurs this is a period of long hours, low monetary return, and almost unbearable uncertainty. It is in this phase that entrepreneurs, as men of action, show at their best. They are men who appear to perform with peak effectiveness in a crisis.

This is the period when the costs of compromises and sacrifices made while setting up the firm are forcefully driven home to the entrepreneur. He finds that he is undercapitalized and cannot meet the payroll to get his first order out. He finds that the partner to whom he has sold half the enterprise is lazy, dishonest, and drunken. He finds that he needs tools he does not have. He finds that the union cannot furnish him with adequate skilled labor. The loft he rents is sold out from under him. Purchasing agents cancel orders without what he regards as sufficient notice or cause. Almost any catastrophe the reader can think of can be found in the stories told of going through the knothole.

If the entrepreneur is energetic, experienced, and lucky, he comes through the knothole. His next task is to clean up a house that has gotten dangerously messy. With a backlog of orders, a little cash on hand, suitable equipment, and a firm source of materials, he has achieved a first level of stability. Unless he has the insight to understand the problems that now face him, and the courage to act decisively on them, he can never achieve full control, and the firm can never truly prosper. We have called this phase of reorganizing "getting rid of partners," not because getting rid of a partner is always involved here, but because the phrase denotes something of the ruthless and unequivocal action required of the entrepreneur at this point. The opportunity presented here is often never repeated. If the entrepreneur allows matters to drift along, the structure of the firm will jell into a configuration he can never subsequently change.

In setting up the firm and in getting through the knothole, he has many times needed financial and other support. In acquiring such support he necessarily gives up many aspects of his control over the enterprise. Each individual who has furnished support has done so at a price. He has, in one or more of several ways, established a foothold within the firm. The entrepreneur has got to have the kind of character formation that makes it imperative that he drive these intruders out.

The situation in many ways parallels the relationship with adult figures in the entrepreneur's childhood. He must either drive these figures away or leave himself. We have seen that as a child and as a young man the entrepreneur did both. Now he really does not have a choice. The domineering and unpredictable figures must give up their hold on the entrepreneur's future. We shall see that these figures do not always have to leave the firm. They may remain in the firm, and may even continue to be officers and have the legal status of partners. If they do remain, however, it must be on the entrepreneur's terms. They must be subordinate to him and work "for" rather than "with" him.

In the next three chapters, we deal with the three phases separately.

CHAPTER TEN

Setting Up the Firm: The Strategic Act

Which of us has not, while driving along a road, said, "A filling station right there would make a fortune"? Which of us has not seen a new device and said, "You know, if a guy had some capital he could market that and . . ."? Which of us has not said, "Why don't they come out with something that will . . . "? Which one of us has not said, "With my experience, I'll bet I could set up a business and . . . "? Many Americans have probably even given a little thought to what might be required before actually "doing something about it." For most people, however, the idea either dies right there or after a few initial inquiries. Most of us hurry on to work or to a P.T.A. meeting, forgetting all about it. It never becomes a projection. What sets the independent entrepreneur off from the rest of us is his capacity to take some such idea and project from it lines of action.

Projection, however, is not enough. The entrepreneur must act, and he is able to act because his projection ties an initial and precipitating idea together with a clear-cut first step. Beyond this first action, the entrepreneur may have no detailed conceptual map of what he is going to do next; but he must have a general and guiding notion about where it is all going to lead, and he must be less afraid of the unknown future than of the known present. The step beyond projecting is, then, making the initial act.

THE VARIETIES OF INITIAL ACTS

In their remembrance, most entrepreneurs think of a strategic and crucial act which they regard as a sort of magical key unlocking the door to the future. Strictly for purposes of delineation, we can group these acts:

1. Getting money

2. Securing physical assets such as tools, space, or materials

3. Enlisting special talent

4. Lining up initial customers

We will find that these groupings do not hold up in the reality we will be discussing. They merely give us a framework within which to make our presentation.

Getting Money. Money is, of course, the common denominator for expressing inputs and outputs of transactions. It is hardly possible, therefore, for entrepreneurs to talk about setting up firms without, at one or another point, referring to this medium. One large group of entrepreneurs recall the securing of money as the first in a series of steps. Others see the acquiring of other resources (such as tools, talent, or customers) as the key step, with the securing of financing following and contingent upon that key step.

Mr. Brown states, probably as well as anyone, the view that money is the one strategic element.

> I had a place to get the tooling and the customer had given me an informal understanding he would buy, but he wasn't going to get pinned down until he had a better understanding I would deliver. That was reasonable. I needed money, and I needed it right now. I got on long distance to these loan sharks, right through to the president. I wouldn't talk to anybody else. I gave him the deal right over the phone and he said, "Okay, but have you had any experience?" I said right back, "I've been through bankruptcy for over a million." We talked about how I'd paid off all but a few hundred thousand. He said, "You've got experience." They had a man out on the plane the next day. I had to pay high interest, but I had the money when I needed it. They took the risk, and they earned their interest. A bank wouldn't touch me.

Brown had lined up tooling and a customer, but he needed money to get his firm going. Consequently, he remembers securing a loan as the one strategic problem. For many, it is the one problem that cannot be licked, and many projections die because a projector cannot secure a little working capital. At this stage in the game, one peculiar difficulty of the independent entrepreneur is that he has often, while gaining experience, accumulated a record as a "poor risk." Attempting to get financing, he frequently has to go to large bureaucratic organizations staffed by men who, in their very personality structure, abhor the thought of risk. These include purchasing agents charged by their companies with supporting new enterprises as future sources of component supply, loan officers in banks, and members of groups (with state and federal support) formed to aid new businesses.

Our impression is that the chances of the risk-taking entrepreneur getting financial support from any of these sources are indeed dismal. Men in charge of these funds are not, by their very nature, risk-takers. Furthermore, as in the case of banks, government regulations greatly restrict their taking a fling in such undertakings.

We interviewed six such men to gain insight into the entrepreneur's problems here, and we will report on one. To protect his anonymity, we will not describe the kind of institution he is in.

The interviewer, after being shown into the office of Mr. X, comments, "Fresh from interviewing in the alley shops, I was much impressed by the spacious suite with its carpeted floors, and the fact that the windows were big and clean." After the research was outlined to him, Mr. X went into a long discussion of how federal laws are intended to help small business, and how these laws are put into effect through such organizations as the one Mr. X heads. In an effort to pull the conversation down out of the stratosphere of national policy and high altruism, the interviewer asked how many loans the organization had made and how many applications they had had. Mr. X said they had processed almost 200 applications, and they had made four loans. He went on to express his opinion that most people who apply for such loans are not qualified: "Most of these people do not have collateral, real or potential, which means that you have to bank on the possibility of the firm and this possibility emanates strictly from the personal abilities of the entrepreneur."

The interviewer agreed with this, and then asked how Mr. X went about determining the abilities of applicants for loans. Mr. X replied that he owed his position to the fact that he was "an expert in this." When pressed on how this evaluation was made, Mr. X said, "There is really no one way. You just have to develop a feel for the entire situation." He indicated that it was important to check on the financial history of the applicant. In the case of the four loans that had been made, all to established businesses, Mr. X indicated that he had contacted suppliers to check on their relationship, and that he also "investigated" the firm's relationship with customers. Then, since the firms could furnish collateral, he went ahead with the momentous risk.

The interviewer was intrigued to know what made this loan organization, which did not make loans, tick. Mr. X, in response to a question about how he used his own time, pointed out that the consulting side of the operation takes an inordinate amount of it. Here he shifted to a similar organization, not talking about his own. He pointed out that this other organization had evolved a process requiring an applicant to pay a consultant fee "and get sound advice on how he should handle his financial situation in the future." A consulting fee of $100 an hour is charged the applicant, "and this applies to the processing of the loan." Mr. X pointed out that this activity has become the more lucrative side of this "other business" he was talking about. This development, he thinks, has real possibilities.

Mr. X also indicated that he was pushing for an amalgamation at the state level of the sort of organization he heads. In the course of this activity, he is attempting to attract more capital into his own system. He indicated that he was much interested in getting banks to invest in his organization, since he could "tap a potential which by their banking regulation restrictions they could not touch." He felt that, both in terms of the tax picture and in terms of the investment restrictions, this should be very attractive to financial houses. "They can then extend lending facilities into an area where a serious gap now exists."

A third problem with which Mr. X was wrestling at the time of the interview also involved making his kind of investment company more attractive—not to borrowers, but to investors. This stems from a unique advantage which these organizations have. Mr. X indicated that, "in the future," his kind of organization will not be so much interested in making "straight line" loans as it will be in extending credit in the form of debentures on the borrowing companies. This involves an agreement that, at a later point, the lender can either collect his money or convert it into stock in the borrowing firm. He thought that this was very attractive to people putting money into the lending agency, and this the interviewer could understand. Mr. X also thought that this second guessing on his efforts would also be attractive to the entrepreneur, but this the interviewer could not understand.

In our cases, we have several firms that have borrowed through banks or directly from government sources. We have, to our knowledge, no firms that have taken advantage of the unique opportunities offered them by Mr. X and his altruistic undertaking. It is possible that Mr. X's high altruism makes them feel like charity cases. It is also possible that they do not like the minute scrutiny they must undergo, and that they feel some reservation about the dealing in futures represented by the stock option plan. Being the kind of men they are, most entrepreneurs feel that they want to know it when someone has them by the throat. Finally, of course, Mr. X moves in university, banking, and government circles. His is the world of established and respectable bureaucratic activity. He has, we assume from the interview, little contextual knowledge about the entrepreneur. It is also likely that the entrepreneur knows very little about him.

In lieu of money from such clean and highly moral places, the entrepreneur must grub for capital where he can find it. His personal record, his immediate desperate situation, and his business and moral outlook may close "legitimate" sources to him. To him, money, like gold, is where you find it.

Some of our men—and we will discuss one such man in the next chapter—have, at one time or another, received support from what can be called "shady" or underworld sources. They paid off these debts and were not found in ditches with bullet holes in their nostrils. Perhaps there are entrepreneurs who have suffered such ends, but they, of course, do not appear in our sample; by our system of classification, they would not qualify as "successful."

Mr. French's mode of arranging financing was typical, if indeed there is a typical mode:

> I got ten thousand from this friend, and then he invested an additional ten thousand of his own. The first ten thousand he lent me as a personal loan, and this I put in as my investment. Then I found a third person to put in some money. He put in ten thousand. I had never met this fellow before. I just went to his office and told him the deal. He wrote out his check and slid it across the desk to me. He didn't even have my hat for security. He liked the game, and the action costs.

Entrepreneurs who started by going directly to a person for capital usually had, also, to pay for the action. Such comments as, "Joe and I went into partnership with about four thousand. He put up two thousand, and I scrounged the other two somewhere," usually preface narrations of a long series of difficulties. Mr. Justice was fortunate:

> I needed a building plus about twenty-five thousand and I went to a bank. But you can do business with a bank only if you have lots of collateral and two or three solid cosigners [pause] . . . But they did give me a name. This banker told me about him. He was in Tampa, and I flew down there and I came back with the twenty-five thousand. The deal was I wasn't putting in any cash, but we were equal partners right down the middle. Then this fellow turned around and gave five percent of his to the banker. This set up a watchdog over me.

Mr. Mann was not so fortunate:

> After that, I began to see I could make out. I quit and began working on it night and day—not just nights. But leaving my job like that meant I didn't have a paycheck coming in, and it was going to be weeks before I could make a delivery. This Al, he had three thousand and I tried to talk him out of it on a loan basis—a personal loan—but he wouldn't and so I took him in as a partner. He was hard-working, but he couldn't read a blueprint; he was so dumb.

Mann goes on to tell the interviewer how Al's "foul mouth" and "sarcastic way" was to cost the little firm, which was struggling through the winter months in a garage heated "only by a coal stove," its major customer. This, however, anticipates our story.

In the cast of artisan and engineering entrepreneurs, the search for money is often crucial—not only because it is needed to buy materials and equipment, but because it forces the entrepreneur to regularize his operation. Formally entering into a partnership, or setting up a corporation, may be a more important outcome than securing money itself.

Mr. Milford shows how the search for money led him to incorporate:

> I worked like a dog. I went out and bought equipment, and I started doing it all by myself. Well, actually, there was one other

fellow working for me. I found I had to file a tax report on him—then, other things. I found I was doing an ungodly amount of work for the small return. Sitting down and figuring it out, I saw I would be better off on an hourly rate.

I could see it was I needed proper machines; since in one operation I actually hand-punched thousands of holes that could have been done on a press. But to get the machines, I needed money and so then the next thing I knew I decided to incorporate and sell shares. Actually, I got two other guys to come in with me and it was really a partnership; but we thought it was better that way—That way, if any one of us wanted to reduce his investment he could sell part of the shares to the other two. It was a closed corporation. We had an understanding we would only buy and sell to each other.

This man was in production before he went into business. The quest for money led him to regularize his activities.

Securing Physical Assets. Many men mentioned financing, but not as the crucial problem. This is the case, especially, with men who had the old-fashioned foresight to "save up" before launching a business. Such men, often waiting years for the right combination, moved to set up the firm when the "right" opportunity presented itself.

Holding Brothers is about as family owned and operated as a business can be. The business is essentially an extension of the home in which the five brothers grew up together. Ed Holding, the oldest and the president of the firm, tells us about it:

When our father died, we all agreed we would hold together and be together. We all went to work, one after another, at the same automobile company after high school. We agreed we needed to have different skills; and I went into tool and die making; and Harry went into heat treating; and Art was on the production line. We moved between jobs some, and this is only an example of how we were picking up skills.

As early as 1938, we were thinking about going into business and we even leased some floor space. But the War came along and we had to hold this in abeyance. We all saved our money, and worked to pay off the mortgages on our houses, because after the War we wanted to have our money in liquid form, and even borrow on our houses.

The Holdings were not only close-knit and far-sighted: they were patient. It was not until 1946 that they decided to make their move:

During the War they (an automobile company) had been able to replace their grinders and other machines because they were on War contract, and the government paid for this. After the War, they decided to sell their old equipment which they had been storing, and I kept a very careful eye on this. Then they'd built this plant out along Belt Road. It was an emergency measure and wasn't too profitable since it was a long way from their other operations. They decided to close this plant, and I heard about it from a friend of mine. I got my brothers together. Actually, I didn't get them together. It was at a picnic out at Black Lake. We were out there, and I said, "This is it. Now is the time if there ever was a time."

The years during which the Holdings had waited and saved now paid off. Drawing on savings and borrowing on their homes, the brothers were able to capitalize at over a hundred thousand dollars. Although they had projected going into business from childhood, they did not make their move until physical facilities could be acquired at bargain basement prices.

Mr. Brogan, in contrast to the careful Holdings, moved rapidly when he got himself an order from a typewriter company. He went to a public auction house and bought several punch presses. So far so good, but Brogan looked at his check book and found that he was running out of money. The strategic problem then became one of finding space. His solution may not have been brilliant, but it worked:

There was this vacant lot, and I rented it for two months, thirty dollars a month. I bought this big tent at surplus and had it put up. That was my plant. We had wiring run in there, and the machines. The fellows, they were wearing boots and sloshing around in the mud, but they were really turning out parts.

The president of the typewriter company got worried about this and came to see what the hell was going on. He was afraid he wouldn't get delivery on his parts. He looked it over and said to me, "If you can turn out precision work under these conditions you ought to be sitting in my chair." Later, when we were making deliveries, I went to see him in his office. When I came in, he got up and motioned I was to sit in his chair. I just said, "Sit down. I don't want your chair." I didn't. I don't want to sit in any chair but my own.

Brogan never seriously considered either borrowing money or taking in partners. He tells us that as a young man he got "stung" by a deceitful partner. Furthermore, "Why should I take somebody in who is a millstone, who eats off you because he owns part of you, and you cannot buy him off because the value of his investment has increased due to your very own efforts." Brogan is a cash-and-carry entrepreneur, paying as he goes. This may have retarded his growth, but he has also avoided much anguish. He says about banks, "Why should I go to them and be as a poor man? I'm not a poor man. I pay for what I need. If I can't pay for it, then I don't need it."

The Holdings are highly rational people. They laid plans, moved ahead cautiously, and waited for the right combination. If they paid off mortgages early in life, it was so that their homes could be used as collateral. Brogan's approach is at once more erratic and more constricted. He did not hesitate to get in over his ears, but an emotional set barred him from getting out by borrowing or by taking in a partner.

Enlisting Special Talent. Sometimes the firm can be set up only if skills of unusual order can be secured, and this may be done in several ways. A projector may simply go out and hire needed skills or talents, or a person may "deal" with another organization to "borrow" such specialized help. Finally, the entrepreneur may take in partners or shareholders who then make up an entrepreneurial team, and who also supply the financing.

In the last chapter, we left Mr. Abrams projecting an organization to make advanced measuring and regulating devices. He was a wealthy man, and he was going first class. His initial hurdle was neither securing financing nor physical assets. These were not problems. Talent was, partly because Abrams was venturing into a technical area about which he had no knowledge.

His initial act was, therefore, signing up talented and highly trained men. He spent weeks visiting laboratories and research centers at universities and corporations across the country, uncovering those men rated as the most promising by colleagues and administrators. He then offered these men high salaries and other inducements. He says that his raiding expedition yielded commitments from "top men in the field." Having solved the key problem, Abrams then bought up the activity which had attracted his attention.

Abrams did not borrow money until, with his firm established, he took on a large government contract. When he did borrow—and here again we anticipate our story—it was because, "I didn't want to be owing all that money to myself. It didn't make sense for the business I owned to be borrowing money from me. I took outside finance because I could write off the interest and it wouldn't be income to myself."

Abrams was going first class, but Mr. McDonald was not so lucky. We have seen how the impending failure of the firm that he was managing drove McDonald into projecting by cannibalizing its assets.

Equipment and customers were not, as Mr. McDonald recalls, crucial, since this was an industry employing highly skilled artisans to make production tooling:

> Before I signed the papers, there was something I had to do first. I went around to the homes of these men and talked to them. I told them what the chances were, and that we were starting out on a shoestring, and that we might not make it, that they might be out of a job in six months. All the ones I wanted—all the good ones, that is—said they'd come to work for me. With that I could go ahead.

Mr. Hanson started out with no more than an order to make specialized tooling. An artisan of many years training and sound reputation, he was approached by a large corporation as "the one man they wanted to perform this work." Hanson refused to go on their payroll, but said that he would "supply them the dies, jigs and other fixtures on a contract basis." This was converted into a purchase order.

He now had an order but no shop and no specialized help. Securing the specialized help was crucial, since "There is only a handful of (kind of artisans) in a given area."

> When it came time to write the purchase order, this guy in their purchasing department suggested they'd rather write it to a firm. He said, "Why don't you file papers. We'll help you draw them up." Actually, he did sitting right there. This seems not to be too unusual because they had the forms in their office. Actually, it was he who thought up the name. He said, "Why don't you call yourself *Hanson Tooling*?" I thought, "Why not?" There was tax advantages in this, too. He pointed this out to me.

Hanson, therefore, recalls that a purchasing agent coached him to make a projection. With his firm on paper, and his purchase order signed, Hanson then made the following proposition:

Why didn't they let me make the (name withheld) right there in their own tooling shop? They had the equipment and the men, and we could try them out right there as we made them. I pointed out they would get them faster and wouldn't be sitting doing nothing and waiting for me to deliver. Their inspectors could test them as they were finished, so there wouldn't be a delay if there was anything wrong. Actually, there was a big hidden advantage in this for me. I didn't have the money or facilities and couldn't get the help. As it turned out I didn't have to pay for the help in advance. What they did, they charged costs against the purchase order. Their charges turned out to be ridiculously low. They could almost be called token.

Here, advice in setting up the firm, and use of equipment and skilled labor, were all drawn from an initial customer.

Financing is often given as the primary reason for taking in partners or for selling shares, but often the capital needed was not so much money as ability. A man's ability can be "locked in" by making him a part owner.

We left Foote in the last chapter suggesting to his wife, Barbara, that they make "a pile of money." Since Foote was broke, we might suppose that his first step would have been to scrounge a little cash. Jack knew—and perhaps he had learned this from his entrepreneur father—that the more crucial problem was to bring together able men:

> There had to be four of us. Frst, we needed an engineer. I knew something about production, but with what I knew we would never get beyond the alley shop stage. We needed someone who could set up an operation, and I thought right away of Tom. Tom is a graduate engineer, and I started figuring how to get him. Then we needed somebody who could get out and find jobs for us. Ned was the man because he was already in selling and knew quite a few people. Then, we needed somebody who could handle the financial side—taxes and all that. Actually, we never found that person. I took that on myself by default, and actually in the process I've become a pretty good accountant.

This man began with abilities and worked back from there to financing. His firm has been successful in no small part because Foote built it around abilities rather than finances. Partnerships based on

finances are brittle and will often shatter as soon as the supporting cup
of mutual financial need is removed. In Foote's team talents are complementary, and the men have a reciprocal and continuing need for
one another.

Lining Up Initial Customers. The first step is sometimes neither
one of securing financing, nor of finding equipment, nor of enlisting
special abilities. It may rather be opening up a market. With every
other problem under control, all may hinge on this one vital factor.

Mr. Rollings, starting production in a garage, had problems neither of financing nor of plant facilities. Furthermore, his product
could be turned out by unskilled help, and working capital was not
necessary as the product could be sold from day to day. With all this
going for him, Rollings still managed to get into trouble:

> At any rate, I started working full time on it. My mother was
> working on it now, and I was working on it full time. My wife, she
> would bring out coffee and sandwiches, and then she'd stick around
> and work along through the afternoon. We were really turning out
> the stuff.
>
> How to get rid of it? That was the question. I got this brain-
> storm and I went down to an advertising agency. It doesn't make
> sense now. Why an ad agency? But they gave me advice: run blind
> ads and get salesmen. Then they designed this kit for us. It was real
> flashy, and it had our name all over it—The Rollings Corporation.
> Of course, the customer didn't know the Rollings Corporation was
> a man and two women in a garage.
>
> There was a lot of southerners from their other jobs worked
> for us—part time, and then when they got laid off, full time. They
> got sixty percent, and there was still profit for us. Then they'd go
> back South, and they'd take their kits with them, or write for one,
> and we were shipping all over the South.
>
> And the next thing we were hiring; and we had five garages—
> three next door, and another one. I kept thinking I'd forget where all
> these garages were. Then the salesmen—they'd come in with their
> orders and I'd make change right out of my pocket. My mother kept
> saying we ought to go into business in a regular way.

This man's initial problem was securing an outlet for a product
that could be manufactured at home on homemade equipment and
with a small running investment in materials. With ebullient lack of

forethought he acted on the first idea that popped into his mind, that of going to an advertising agency. This paid off handsomely, and he was on his way.

THE LINE OF STRATEGIC ACTION

The reader must, by now, be aware that our groupings of initial acts has not been very successful. Entrepreneurs themselves tend to believe that one key act—securing financing, assets, talents, markets, or customers—is the magical step which makes possible creating an organization. It is convenient to accept this belief and to examine their notions by grouping them as we have done; but we now see that such simple groupings leave out a vital element.

Although they like to pick out and dwell on one crucial problem and the action with which they solved that problem, their own stories show us that this is not at all the way it happens. Entrepreneurs abstract one factor, we suspect, in part because in a world of specialists it is fashionable to do so. The lawyer sees the setting up of the firm as a legal problem, the accountant sees it as a financial problem, and the engineer sees it as a production problem. The entrepreneur often, in subscribing to these specialized views, is not cognizant that he is also describing his own speciality: the bringing together of men, money, materials, and machines and structuring these elements into a system of ongoing action.

Looking at it from this angle, we see that what the entrepreneur recalls as the strategic first step was really nothing more than one in a series of steps composing a strategic line of action. Since Mr. Kenney thinks that he was launched by one big break, let us look more deeply at his story:

Fred Kenney, like Rollings, was looking around for an opening. Unlike Rollings, however, Kenney had been looking for years. During these years he had never held a steady job. He had always been after the gold at the end of the rainbow. One follows his progress through a steady succession of deals that fell through, sensing the futility of this stubborn and incurably romantic man. Through the years he had accumulated in his backyard all sorts of discarded marine equipment. Suddenly Kenney got his big break.

A ship had sunk in the channel of a harbor. Bids were invited for raising this obstruction and clearing the channel. The established salvage companies made a routine examination and placed routine bids. Kenney, however, made a careful investigation. As a result, he was able to make a bid which he describes as about half what the companies bid. He got the contract. Hiring a diver, he loaded his beat-up truck with equipment and drove to the scene. By use of a technical process that we cannot describe here, the two men floated the wreck in twenty-four hours. Kenney went home with thirty thousand profit in his pocket. Furthermore, he was immediately able to sell the hulk for additional profit. From this point on, Kenney believes, he had the golden touch.

Taking this account at face value, we might classify it as a case of the setting up of a firm being contingent on securing financing. It was certainly this, but we must keep in mind that Kenney had served a long and arduous apprenticeship. His long years in basic dealing had finally paid off. His intimate knowledge of peripheral enterprise in the marine area was probably excelled by no man. He had now, in addition, some capital. He was no longer the perpetual outsider wistfully watching and trying to talk himself into a deal. He had the ante to get into the game.

The thirty thousand dollars was lightning which, had it not hit Kenney at this point, would probably have hit him at another. At this stage in his career, Kenney had already set up two business firms; but neither of them had had any "real" money in them. They did not go into bankruptcy, but simply atrophied from lack of activity. With his windfall from the salvage job, Kenney tried again. He made it stick this third time, not because of the nest egg but because Kenney knew how to use that money in an ongoing sequence of acts.

Some entrepreneurs, on the other hand, both recall and can describe the setting up of the firm as a line of strategic action. Mr. Peters is one such man.

His account would warm the heart of a professor of business. He came from a family that for two generations had been engaged, in a small way, in producing an essential material. The product was of such bulk and weight that shipping was a major factor. The family business was located a long way from what Peters believed would be the growing market. He tells us that his father was "content to drift along, leaving things pretty much as they were." Peters, however, was made of more energetic stuff. Upon his father's death, Peters began making plans to liquidate the company.

In the meantime, he toured the country. He went to those regions of rapid growth, examined records on income and studied probable employment in the future. He studied the supply and the shipping set-ups. He talked with bankers to get the financing picture. After such painstaking research, he eliminated all possibilities except one small town in the Midwest, a suburb of a great city. The town had everything from an enterprise point of view, and in addition was a good place to raise children. Peters was ready to act. He liquidated the family business and put the proceeds into a new company. He then secured a bank loan and bought production space. Peters was never to experience the anguish of going through the knothole. His plans were carefully laid, and his enterprise developed almost at once into a flourishing undertaking.

Peters, then, describes creating an organization as a series of moves in a well thought-out campaign. Another man in our sample tells how he played through a set of carefully laid plans. Unlike Peters, however, this man had to lay his plans in a cloak-and-dagger atmosphere. We shall call him Mr. Able. To bring the story up to date, Able had been experiencing a peculiar kind of role deterioration. He had bought stock in a rather large firm and was employed by that firm as a customer representative. He tells us how the firm was being mismanaged and how this affected his relations with customers.

> I'd go in to see them and I'd be met by the damnedest blast you ever heard. Every time, there was something wrong. A needed delivery hadn't come through, or parts were delivered that weren't up to specs, or even sometimes they weren't even the right parts at all. I'd scurry around trying to make adjustments but it was no good. These men, they were absolutely dependent on Lacey as a source of supply, and they couldn't help feeling that because I was their personal friend I was letting them down. I couldn't help feeling it, too. These fellows, they were my friends. It was most embarrassing.

Mr. Able goes on to tell the interviewer it was increasingly clear that something had to be done:

I began feeling them out, asking them what they thought. This was tricky because these buyers, they were supposed to be maintaining good relations with Lacey. And then I was actually employed by Lacey. I was on salary there and I couldn't appear to be disloyal. It slowly became clear to me that some of them, some of the big ones, were ripe to make a switch if they could be assured of a reliable supplier.

With these customers in his pocket, Able was set to make his next move. This one was inherently more dangerous. So far he had simply exchanged sentiments with some of the more dissident customers. He now set about gathering in resources. He needed engineers, he needed production men, and he needed financing. All these resources existed in the Lacey Company. Able had, perhaps—as he wishes us to believe—not consciously or deliberately, learned through daily contact which men in the company were disgruntled with their career prospects and disenchanted with the future of the Lacey Company. These men, with the addition of a couple of outside men to contribute financing, were the men Able had to have. He fully understood the risk he was taking. Keeping his own counsel, he spent several months designing the new enterprise. He estimated the amount of capital he would need, and determined exactly where and how that capital would be forthcoming. He located a building available for leasing and quietly deposited a "hold" on it. He checked into the equipment and supply situation. Now he was ready. He says:

> This was strictly a one shot proposition. I wasn't going to have a second chance. If Lacey got wind of it, they'd move against me immediately. A few promotions and a few promises and they could queer my whole proposition. If I didn't get them [the recruits he needed] in the first fifteen minutes I was never going to get them. I knew this.

Able called a meeting in a hotel room. He told none of those invited what the meeting was to be about. We get a view of that meeting through the eyes of one of the participants, a man Able had earmarked to bring both professional talent and money into the projected firm.

> He [Able] said Bill Appleby would be there, so I thought it was probably some company matter and didn't think any more about

it . . . He had a big organization chart drawn up, and he pointed to it and said to me, "This is you. You're vice-president in charge of this department." I told him I wasn't interested in getting tied up in a business. He went on, "For you it isn't an either-or proposition. You don't have to give up your practice to be vice-president. For some of these other fellows it's different."

Late that night, when the meeting broke up, Able had his new business.

The range of initial action extends from the simple technique of borrowing money without security to Mr. Able's careful and (one can say) brilliantly conceived and executed scheme. The central problem is to develop a line of action around the original projection. Entrepreneurs tend to recall one essential barrier that has to be passed. Once this barrier is passed, they in their own minds conceive of their business as having been established. Entrepreneurs recall one key act that has to be performed, and this first step is for them a kind of "ritual magic."

This key act, however, taken out of the matrix of action, is nothing in itself; but it is important because it is a key to carrying out other acts. The crucial action is all those individual acts which result in creating the organization.

Some of these men carried out this initial action sequence wisely, with foresight of anticipated and unanticipated consequences. Others, we shall see in the next chapter, acted unwisely either because they knew no better or because under pressure to get things moving they did not think about consequences. They were, before they got things on an even keel, to pay a high price.

These men were, in general, at this point not looking beyond the initial step of setting up the firm. It is not that they lacked the imagination and experience necessary to a longer vision. If, in fact, they had lacked these qualities, their endeavor would eventually have failed. If they did not look ahead, it was for another reason. The interview dramas have here a vividly real and immediate quality about them. Recounting the experience, these men relive a moment of urgency and of thrilling risk. This was the time when the slightest hitch or the slightest holding back could permanently inhibit the entire undertaking. They had to act, they had to act fast, and they had to act fast and right.

Their whole attention seems to have been focused on the immediate situation. They had no time or no energy for the longer view, or for the eventual consequences of the immediate choices they were making. From a psychological view, this was all to the good. If these men could have seen in clear and precise detail the grief, the long hours, and the risks they were to take, many of them would have ventured no further along this particular pathway. This is not to say they would not have explored other pathways, for the true entrepreneur is compelled. Some told us, after describing early failures, "At this point I was ready to settle down to a steady job." They could not.

CHAPTER ELEVEN

Through the Knothole

There may be a moment after the firm is set up when the outlook is for serene weather, but the entrepreneur who sees only blue skies ahead may suddenly find he is clawing his tiny craft off a lee shore. Squalls may sweep in from any quarter, and sometimes from all quarters at once.

Setting up the firm has called for some intricate dealings, and the entrepreneur often finds he is in for more than he bargained. The machinery which he went into debt to buy may prove inadequate, the customer he counted on may be lost, or the item he was going to make may not be salable. He may find that the infant firm is feeding too many mouths, that he cannot wait until receipts start coming in, or that he has the wrong skills for the field he has entered. He may lose his plant space, or he may find that short-term loans will not be extended. He may find that supplies cannot be obtained, or he may get embroiled with tax or labor trouble. Finally, the long hours and anxiety may take such a toll that he cannot continue.

In working through these troubles he must enlist every aid and use every trick he knows. He may find that each expedient gets him, perhaps, out of an immediate crisis; but that he has only stalled off the moment of reckoning. During this phase of getting through the knothole his tactic is simply to try to keep going, and this may mean making deals with men who rescue at a price. Ultimately, he is going to have to square accounts with these rescuers.

Getting through the knothole varies, of course, from man to man. Some of the men we have already met never really experienced it. Peters, who made a detailed advance study and also inherited money from his father, was one such man. Financially well-off, Abrams was another. Still again, the Holding Brothers had pooled among themselves enough resources so that the beginning years, when their sales were small, caused them no great anxiety. By far the larger proportion of entrepreneurs, however, experience a squeeze for periods ranging from a few months to more than a few years.

MEETING SHORT-TERM LOANS

As an extreme example of the tribulations of a man with a note about to fall due, consider Joe Cleaveland. Joe had set up his business around one order for machine parts. In order to buy equipment and to sustain his family until he could make his first delivery, Joe had gone to a rather shady character in "another state." Joe tells us that this man made money through dog racing, through investing in gambling houses, and through other activities which were barely on the right side of the law. This man agreed to lend to Cleaveland at the hardly attractive rate of ten percent a month. Momentarily, everything looked rosy. But Joe goes on with his story:

> I was working sixteen hours a day trying to finish that damn order, and I'd fall into bed without eating or even taking my clothes off. My wife was worried sick. Then I began to see that even when they took delivery, I wasn't going to make out. I wasn't going to be able to pay even part of that loan.
> I'd fall into bed and I'd sleep about an hour and then I'd be wide-awake and laying there in the dark in a cold sweat wondering what I was going to do. You see, this guy, he had a real nasty reputation. He was supposed to be a killer. I was scared and I prayed.

Joe may have been scared, but he was also a man of courage. He went to see the "killer":

> I sat there and my hands were all clammy, and he talked baseball like we didn't have a care in the world. Finally, I couldn't take it no more and I kind of shouted out right in the middle of what he was saying, "Look, I'm not going to be able to pay off my loan." "Okay," he says, "you're not going to be able to pay off the loan," and he goes right on talking about Mickey Mantle or some damn guy. Then that really scared me. I got up enough courage and asked him, "And then what happens?" He gives me a long stare and then

leaned back in his chair and laughed. "Who's been filling you with that crap? I'm a businessman. I take a piece of your operation and it doesn't pay out. You get hurt worse than I do, and so you're supposed to wind up in the East River with concrete shoes. Son, you've got the wrong department. I'm not Edward G. Robinson. You get him, you got to go to Hollywood."

Fifteen years later, sitting in the presidential office of the flourishing business he has built, Cleaveland still gets excited as he tells this story. We wonder how much it has improved with each retelling. Cleaveland puts the cap on it:

> When I get up to leave, he follows me to the door. We shake hands, and he kind of puts his arm around my shoulder. "Son," he says, "simmer down a little. Sure, I want my money out and I won't get a dime if you funk out on me. Take your time. I'm stopping all interest as of right now. You pay me off if and whenever you get in the clear. Not a minute before."

No matter how much the story has grown through the years, we feel that Cleaveland left that office with a great sense of release. With the bogeyman laid to rest, he was able to take rational and decisive action. He went immediately to the purchasing agent from whom he had obtained the original contract and explained his difficulties. The purchasing agent agreed to take immediate delivery on the parts that Cleaveland had finished, and gave him a "bigger and better order on the spot." A lesser man, at this point, might have paid off his gambler friend and gotten out. Cleaveland was made of tougher stuff:

> I turned right around and hired another man. That way I could keep that machine going right around the clock. This guy took it from eight to eight in the day, and I took it from eight to eight at night. That way, I had the day free to line up more business. It was like having three machines—three eight-hour shifts. Hank was a real worker and he never had to be told what to do. Hell, that machine went down and I wasn't there he fixed it. One day I came home and one of the neighbor kids was screaming bloody murder. The machine went down, and Hank ripped up this kid's kiddy car and made a part. It was a neighbor kid and I had to take him right out and buy him a brand new trike. Hank had the right idea. Keep that machine humping no matter what. That was our bread and butter.

Hank is today one of Cleaveland's superintendents. But it was to be another long and dismal year before Joe Cleaveland squeezed through the knothole. We get the picture from him of what so many craftsman type entrepreneurs experience during this period: the yard of the house beaten and gouged, dusty in summer, ankle-deep in mud in bad weather; the rusty stacks of parts, finished and unfinished, around the garage that housed the all-important machine; most of all, perhaps, the lonely hours of night work. "That first year I didn't take a dime out. Every cent went right back in. The kids went to school with holes in their shoes and at the end of the year I had almost $25,000 in the bank." Looking back, Cleaveland considers the eyesore his operation created and the complaints of the neighbors about the incessant thumping of the machine. "They even had the sheriff in, and I told him that if he ever lost an election, I could use a good man. Actually, I did that town a lot of good. Because of me, they've got the toughest zoning ordinances in the state."

Joe Cleaveland finally "paid out" his underworld backer, whom he recalls as "a real gentleman." It was this incautious and perhaps unwise debt contracted early in his firm's history that caused him the greatest anguish. The next time Joe borrowed it was from a bank, and it was to build his own plant.

TAKING IN NEW BLOOD

A man newly in business, once he has an order to make something and something to make it with, can usually secure a short-term loan against prospective "accounts receivable." Banks and financial houses are prepared to enter into such arrangements where the anticipated income fully covers the loan. They usually will not—and, to be fair, cannot—touch that imaginative operator who is playing both ends against the middle. Such men sometimes "take in new money," by admitting a partner. This new partner is often a gambler, but he may get restless when he finds out how speculative the venture really is.

Desperate men, to stay alive a little longer, accept transfusions and only later discover that the blood is not of their type. Jack Reusch had to enter into such an unwise arrangement. Reusch, like Cleaveland, was an artisan-type entrepreneur starting on a shoestring. To secure enough money to go ahead, he had to take in a partner. Reusch tells us that this man was "lazy and a liar." After describing in detail his partner's personal attributes, Reusch describes the relationship to us:

> He wanted a deal that he could take his money and get out any time he wanted to. Right then I smelled a rat. That tipped me off the kind of guy he was. My lawyer friend advised me, "Don't make that kind of deal under any circumstance. It's not a real partnership." All right, but what could I do? I needed the money that week, or the whole deal fell through. I signed the partnership papers. He thought he had me over a barrel.

Reusch, a wily bird in his own right, went ahead with the business operation. He says of this stage, "He [the partner] didn't know what was going on. He didn't come around to work, so he didn't know what I was up to." Reusch was "up to" an operation that involved exploiting a loose credit situation that he had found with a supplier. This supplier, unable to move his line in a tight market situation, was in reality carrying the infant firm on an extended credit line. It was around this strategic situation that Reusch was developing his operation. He insists several times in the interview that there was no fraud involved, and that the supplier "knew exactly what I was up to."

This difficulty in finding new investors after the firm has been set up is compounded by the fact that any search for additional working capital may suggest in itself that the enterprise is failing. The entrepreneur needs, at this point, all the tricks that he has learned. Jack Foote, in his first year of operations, saw a golden opportunity. One of his customers, pleased with their work on a small order, approached Foote's firm with "a very large order." Before they could accept the order, they needed over $20,000 for tooling to buy a machine and to meet labor costs. Foote, disregarding years of bad feeling, went to see his father:

> We only talked about ten minutes. He informed me the money could not be loaned on any basis whatsoever, but that he personally would put up the money as an investment in the firm. He wanted us to recapitalize and he would take about three-fourths of the new stock. This would give us enough money so we could make it.
> That's what he was after. He wanted to reduce us all to working for him. All he wanted was to get his hooks into me again. I told

him to go to hell, and walked out of there. I've seen him one time since, and that time I had to because of a family matter.

Foote went back to the potential customer. After a very hard sell:

> He finally leaned over the table and said, yes, he would advance me ten thousand dollars. This was against delivery. "Now, damn it, go get the job done." We went ahead and it was a close fit; but once we were in production we had something to show. I went back and got some more money out of him.

At this point, Foote could see a little daylight, but his troubles were far from over. By the time he had made final delivery, he had borrowed to the extent of the proceeds. Foote says, "The whole deal was a kind of industrial sharecropping, except that they did pay for the machine."

John Quimby was not as skillful in avoiding a similar trap:

> Well, the money came in from my father-in-law. What happened was I used to go over to his place for lunch. I was living off him. Hell, my son's doing that right now. I was telling him about this and how I wanted to bid on it. He said, "That sounds good, why don't you do it?" I told him I didn't have the money for the bond, and couldn't afford to order parts. He offered to come in for halves—to buy half the company. So he put in nine thousand. I didn't even know he had that kind of money. Later, he put in more and this made some difficulty. He kept telling me how to do things.

Mr. Quimby, under pressure to get some work for his infant business, had succumbed to temptation. As it turned out, he had not quite passed the point of no return. Later, he was able to buy back his father-in-law's investment, but at over double the original amount.

Mr. Kahl had a similar experience. Slipping steadily behind, over a five-year period, he had been borrowing from an acquaintance who always seemed "to have a few thousand to lend when it was needed." He says, "Money was loaned to me on such a basis that I never realized how much I owed this man and what the terms and what the implications had been." The implications suddenly became clear: Kahl owed twenty-thousand dollars. His backer suddenly announced that "he was tired of waiting for his money." In lieu of cash, Kahl had to give up a share of his business. He says, "This defeated my purpose in starting the firm in the first place. This twenty-thousand dollars gave him forty percent of the business, and in the end I had to buy him out for almost twenty times the original amount. Namely, $400,000, which I finished doing in 1958. This caused me considerable difficulty."

New money is, therefore, often taken in as the only way to keep going. The cost may well be high, but whether or not it is prohibitive depends on how important it is that the man save his firm. Some of these men had earlier in their careers abandoned businesses when the financial burden became too heavy. This time, they stuck it out.

HOLDING OLD MONEY

The entrepreneur may find early in the game that he is the only one who sees building the business as an objective in itself. Partners may, in reality, be investors interested in a high and short-term profit. Such fair-weather partners may, for many reasons, want to get out, but these reasons cannot matter to the entrepreneur. He has to hold their money in as long as he needs it.

We saw in the last section how Reusch concealed from his partner the indebtedness that was being contracted by their firm. At a later point, Reusch used this to hold the partner in. Somehow, the partner became aware of the extent of the indebtedness. Reusch, with some relish, described the resulting scene:

> He came storming in and demanded his money. He said he'd found out I was a crook and he was getting out. I tried to calm him down, but all the time the fact he thought I was a crook kept going around in my mind. That really gave me leverage, although I didn't need that much leverage. Finally, I slammed the table and acted like I was real mad. It was all acting. "You asked for it. Now I'll tell you what I'm going to do. I'm going to pick up the phone and call and tell them [the supplier] we can't pay a dime. I'll tell them we're into them for four times our assets. I'll tell them to put us into receivership." That really shook him. He could see his paltry little two or three thousand going down the drain. I waited a minute and then broke it to him gently. "Of course," I said, "they'll want to take

action for fraud. This partnership has always lied to them about our financial situation, and they've got the letters to prove it. We'll both wind up in jail."

That really tore it. He got out of there like I was poison. In the meantime my own accounts receivable started coming in, and I was out of the woods. This guy had gone on vacation, so I called him and told him there was no way out. I told him there was just enough money to buy him out, and I'd buy. I'd gotten him into the mess and the last thing I did, I'd get him out. The damn fool, if we were going under, he couldn't get out. We couldn't take his money out with all the debts we had. That *would* have been fraud. The firm bought him out for exactly what he put in. Not a cent more. Hell, we'd been making deliveries and the checks were coming in. We were in good shape, although we didn't have much cash. He didn't stop to think or to investigate. He was a coward.

Most entrepreneurs are eager, especially during this early stage, to put the best possible face on things. Reusch, however, was able to profit by putting an exactly opposite interpretation on matters. Reusch, through his attention to detail and daily application to problems, knew what was "actually" going on. He knew the true relationship with the supplier and he knew that the firm had real assets and orders to be filled. This was knowledge that the partner did not have, although it is not clear from the interview protocol whether Reusch was concealing this knowledge or whether the partner had simply never bothered to find out.

Sometimes the threat to dissolve a partnership is nothing other than a power play. A partner may suddenly evoke a buy-sell agreement. One man took in as partner a man who already had a going business. After the first year, with prospects looking good, the partner told him that he wanted to break up:

He wanted either to buy my half or sell his half to me. He thought he had me in a bind because I had no money personally. I'd even mortgaged my house to put up my original investment. It was insulting. He was offering me just about what I'd put in in the first place. There was nothing to show for my year's work. I told him, "All right, put it in writing." That made it a firm offer which he was stuck with if I could meet it.

Then I went to this young friend of mine, he was rich—that is, his father was rich. He talked to his father, and told me, "Okay, we're in." What actually happened was this. We went to the bank and he made me a personal loan which went into my personal account. I then got a certified check and went to this guy's office. "Here's your money. I'm meeting your offer." His face fell a mile. He had no idea I had that kind of money in cash. He tried to renege and withdraw his offer, but we had anticipated that. I laid another check for five thousand on his desk and said, "This is for getting out without making trouble. Of course, I can always take this to court and cost us both plenty." He accepted.

This man by fancy footwork avoided catastrophe, but Mr. Bergstrom was caught in a trap from which he could not so easily extricate himself. He had formed a partnership with his father and with a brother. They had each put up one third, but Bergstrom was the only one to actively work at the business. For this he received what he calls a "nominal" salary. "My wife and two girls were living in an apartment. Really a tenement. We had barely enough to live on."

After several years, the business had accumulated machinery and they had begun to purchase a building. Bergstrom felt that no profits could be taken out—every cent was needed to make the firm more competitive—when the father and the brother suddenly demanded that the partnership be dissolved:

My father wanted to retire and he wanted this cash to buy a place in Texas, and my brother got the real estate bug. He wanted to go into a development in California with these guys, and he wanted his money to put in. He was going to make a killing.

After a bitter family squabble, Bergstrom convinced his two inconstant relatives, but:

They would come to the plant and look at that equipment, and they thought that was a lot. That one operation, it cost us fifty-thousand dollars to put in. Paid for out of profits, but without a buyer who could use it it was just a pile of junk. I said, "Find a buyer—somebody who'll take over for the amount we've put in. Do that, and we'll liquidate the partnership." They couldn't find one, but I could have. I knew where to look, but it was up to them—not me.

A resolution equally unsatisfactory to all parties was finally achieved. Bergstrom agreed that his father and brother were to draw salaries identical to his own, "although they did no work and were not even in the State." Bergstrom also agreed to incorporate the firm, and to declare a dividend every year. "I stalled on this (paying dividends) from year to year, and they never did anything about it."

Bergstrom has been slowly gaining control by buying shares from his father's estate. He says, "My brother has had no success since then. From time to time he needs money and I buy a few shares from him. Actually, I still have to borrow to do this. This has all greatly curtailed my ability to grow."

BREAKING THE COST BARRIER

An entrepreneur starting out is hungry. Keeping going is crucial and he is liable to take any work that comes along. His strong desire to keep busy and to make a strong showing may betray him into ignoring his own costs, or he may have no way of estimating what his costs are. Getting accurate cost estimates is not especially difficult for the one-man operation, or for the operation that produces an item for one or two customers. It is not difficult because this entrepreneur can make only one mistake. If he produces one order over cost, he is out. His problems are solved.

The entrepreneur who must compete for a large number of small jobs often finds himself initially at a disadvantage in competing with established firms. We explored this problem and found that it had several facets. One difficulty is that during this initial phase the new firm may not know what its costs are:

> At that time we were being hurt by what you might call hidden costs—although they weren't really hidden but just all sorts of small things we weren't getting into our cost picture because for us at that time they had never come up in quite that way, and we had to learn through experience what we would have to include in the future.

Here the firm is like a newly commissioned ship on its shake-down cruise. Bugs keep coming up and need to be corrected. The entrepreneur who does not learn to estimate the cost of these bugs may find that although business is booming, he is sailing right into bankruptcy. Entrepreneurs tend to feel that, at this early stage, traditional cost analysis cannot provide much help. One such man, who held an advanced degree in engineering, expressed this succinctly:

> An established firm has a rhythm and it's this steady heartbeat that makes really good, professional, cost analysis possible. A top cost analysis man can get a very good picture of where the money is going—labor, taxes, downtime, seasonal layoffs. He can see what's going to come up and he can begin setting aside money out of current jobs to take care of it. Then, he can help you build a contingency fund. In a new business, nobody knows what is going to come up. Everything is contingency, and it makes no sense to have a contingency fund. Every dime you've got is in the contingency fund.

Mr. Jones, in a big hurry, had some equipment made, produced one job on it, and lost money. In a competitive field, he could not increase his prices. He had made a blunder, and took a decisive step to remedy his error:

> Those (kinds of equipment) were very poorly made. They were very poorly designed and they weren't properly built. The thing was, I had to have something to show prospects we could deliver and to show the backers where their money was going. We really just knocked them up in a hurry, and then we found out we would never be able to make a profit on them. One morning I told the men to get busy and tear them all right out of there and we were going to start over. It was the most momentous decision of my life, but actually I had no choice because I could see it had to be done.

THE GOVERNMENT "INTERVENES"

Mr. McDonald, whom we have earlier watched salvaging parts of one firm to create another, got into trouble with the government. We have seen that McDonald put together by direct recruitment a small labor force. He tells us that he had "decided" that his shop was not to be unionized, but . . .

> . . . towards the end of the first year I was served with a summons to appear in court as a defendant in a case in which the plaintiff was NRLB. The NRLB claimed that we were not a new com-

pany but only an extension of Blue Ridge, and, therefore, we should employ union members rather than the employees we had. So we submitted material proving that we were a separate company. We explained that I'd never owned part of Blue Ridge and that I was the largest owner in our new company, and so forth. However, the court ruled against us and we were required to hire these union members, plus pay them $33,000 in back wages. Through negotiations with the union and showing them we had a loss that year, we were able to reduce this somewhat.

This sudden encounter, a heavy blow to a small firm already running in the red, left a bitter taste in McDonald's mouth:

This is another example of how a union can make or break a company. In this case, I was lucky I was able to withstand the power but I don't want you to misunderstand. I was a union man once and I was a good union man. It was just in this instance that I felt that they were—and if they had been successful they might have destroyed me as a small business man.

Old sins and old obligations can also pop up in the form of back taxes. Mr. Harvey tells us that he had set up a new company which immediately purchased the physical assets of an older one. This gentleman had apparently hoped that, because this older firm had been liquidated, its tax bill would be forgiven.

And they were adamant about this. They were going to force me to sell my holdings so they could collect the taxes. I had not told my (new) associates about this, and it was most embarrassing because at first it appeared to jeopardize our operation. But they (the tax collectors) were fair and reasonable about this. They let me make payments out of my current income and thus it did not become a concern of the (new) business.

A more unreasonable set of tax collectors might have finished this operation off in short order.

BUILDING UP CUSTOMERS

Many small businesses begin with one or two orders from one customer. When these first orders are completed, new orders must be found in a hurry. A business, once under way, is a money eater. It is committed to certain costs. Lee Jack describes how he secured new customers:

> I'd go to them [purchasing agents] and tell them, "Our bid is ridiculously low, and you know that it's ridiculously low. All I want is, I want just a small part of your business to prove something to you, and this not simply to prove to you we can give you the parts for nothing, because you and I know that's what we're doing this time— but we can't go on doing that. Not and stay in business—but what I want to do is prove to you we can give you a better job with less grief to you, and never miss delivery, and still save you money. We just want a crack at it. That's all."
>
> And I'd say, "We just ship one bad piece—one piece that isn't up to spec—and you get that shipment free. You get the entire lot and it doesn't cost you a dime." I was out to dig the ground out from under those slobs [competitors]. They were fat, and I was out to cut the ground right out from under them. And I did it, too.

Mr. Jack had to be quite convincing, but he also had a hidden capability going for him. What he was not telling his prospects was that his low bids were not as ridiculous as they looked. He and his two partners had rented an abandoned house and had set up operations in it. He had chosen his partners well, and not the least important factor was the attitude and physical capabilities of their wives. The three men and their wives were the work force:

> And these girls, they were not tramps and they'd never seen a [machine] when we started up. They all came from respectable homes and they'd been well looked after, and the difference was they had good blood, and not like these tramps out there [waving toward the plant area], so when they saw what the score was, nothing would hold them back, and they hired this baby-sitter, and they'd take the kids over to Mabel's house for the day, and one of them came in ten minutes late, I'd bawl hell out of her, "We start at seven and you want to work here you get here or you're fired." That was a big laugh because, of course, they weren't paid anything, and we were only taking eating money out. That was a big laugh, and they'd show up in jeans and in the summer in shorts, and they'd outwork any man. Hell, today none of them, if they don't want to, ever so much as puts her hands in dishwater again the rest of her life. They've got it made.

With this little menage in full swing, Jack had a certain edge over his competitors. For almost two years, he neither invested in equipment nor took more than "living money" out of the firm. He was investing in customers:

> They'd come to me and say, "Can you make this? We don't have anybody to make this." Hell, I wouldn't even take a good look at it. I wouldn't even check back with Jim [the engineer partner]. I'd say, "We can make anything. Give us a big enough order, and we can make anything."

Today Jack is president and major stockholder in a company employing several hundred. He is completely dominant over his partners (and their wives), and has now a different perspective on customers: "I'm sorting them and I'm weeding them. The small fry I throw back. We have no time for them. They only louse things up. And the slow payer—he's through. Just once, and he's through. We don't wait for our money."

ASSURING SOURCES OF SUPPLY

During this period, if a man is not in trouble at one end he may be at the other. If he has customers and can sell the stuff, he may not be able to get supplies with which to make it. In one field, basically a manufacturing field, the competition requires entering into a kind of symbiotic relationship with competitors. Tom Gilbert, a newcomer in the field, points out that a man must have "contacts" with competitors in order to get into the game:

> It's somewhat unique because this is as much a trading situation as it is production. This is because you have no set source of supply. It works this way. A man in Seattle calls you and says he needs a carload of [a reusable material]. You don't have any, but maybe you've picked up information that a man in Knoxville has a carload in Portland. The local people are putting together a carload for him there. The man in Knoxville says he has it and he quotes you a price, and then you call the man in Seattle and quote him a price. You see, this time you're acting as a kind of broker. You take a hundred or two [dollars] for this. No more. You take more and the word gets around. They freeze you out. Of course, you do most of your buying on the floor in [a commodity market], but when you're

on a spot you're absolutely dependent on these contacts. A carload in L.A. isn't going to help you a bit if you're under the gun to deliver a rush order in two weeks.

Gilbert recalls establishing contacts as the most difficult aspect of his own journey through the knothole. He describes how all his cash had been tied up in a plant. For several months things had gone well. They had gotten orders and delivered on them. Profits, however, were eaten away by unanticipated costs. Gilbert was not a novice, and he may have expected this. He did not expect, he tells us, that suddenly they could get no more business. For weeks the plant stood idle, the men were laid off and the doors closed. "This was killing us. You have no idea how expensive a down plant can be—you have no idea at all." He tells us how he made the rounds of potential customers, "hat in hand, begging—I was crying." It is very clear that the enterprise was about to fold, but then:

> About midnight the phone rang and I picked it up. I don't remember what I expected. It was this guy Swanson (a purchasing agent), I'd been around to see the week before. He said he'd just got out of a production meeting, and they'd taken a very large order with 150 day delivery. They were going to need first delivery of parts in ten days. I had no idea how I was going to do it, but I said to count on me and I would do it. Before he hung up, I asked him to get some paper to me first thing in the morning. He knew I was going to need that paper to raise some working capital.

Gilbert dressed and went down to his office. Through the small hours of the morning he placed calls around the country, everywhere getting the same reply: no material was available.

> Things were tight and they were holding either for their own use or because the market would be going up. My trouble was this was Friday night and Monday was a holiday. I couldn't wait to buy Tuesday on the market. I offered them all kinds of premiums, and they wouldn't bite. This is like a club, see. They weren't trying to gouge me. They weren't letting me in.

In desperation, he remembered a friend of his father who had been in the business years before. He called this friend. In thirty minutes the friend called back.

He had a carload for me and it was only fifty miles from me—Fifty miles from my plant, and I'd almost gone under because I couldn't find that one lousy carload. The only trouble now was this is always a cash deal. These people operate on a close margin, and they've always got to have cash. This guy wanted the money when he opened for business Tuesday. This stopped me for a minute, and then I called Swanson (the purchasing agent) back. It was about five in the morning then. I said I needed an advance check for ten thousand first thing in the morning. He said, "Okay, can do," and hung up. That did it. I was over the hump.

Although he was "over the hump," Gilbert still had a busy day ahead of him. Finding that the carload could not reach him for forty-eight hours by rail, he had to get a contractor with a trailer to haul the material. He had to arrange for Swanson's company to deliver the special tools he would need. Finally, he had to start the wheels rolling to get his work force reassembled. He went into production at four o'clock that Saturday afternoon. From this harrowing experience he learned one lesson. His lack of ready access to material had almost ruined his big opportunity. He began buying and selling "strictly to get in the club."

As a further example of what supply shortages can do to a firm, consider Blue Bird Metals. The interviewer, intrigued by the word "Metals," which seemed to be a misnomer, asked about it, and:

Well, that does often confuse people. It's very simple, really. When we started out back in '52 we were going into making (withheld). Our first big order was for making parts for Trijac which, as you know, is a big producer of arms. We would never have been able to complete that order if they hadn't been able to get the steel for us. Steel was in very short supply because of Korea.

The second year, our sales fell from eighty thousand to four thousand. We were trying to get war work so we could buy steel on priority; but no one would subcontract to us. It was most discouraging. And then we started taking on plastics work. That's how we got into plastics. At first we took a few jobs for other people, and then we found it was lucrative to design our own product.

Here a firm which was originally projected to enter light metal manufacturing switched over to a new field. The experience must have been traumatic, but the firm got into a new field at a time of rapid expansion. The entrepreneur says, "We have never regretted it." He adds, "I suppose we should change our name, but I am somewhat superstitious about this. It seems somehow unlucky. Anyway, we intend to go back into metal working."

These infant enterprises cannot afford to carry heavy supply inventories. A strike in the supplier industry, therefore, can cripple or even kill them. They are, furthermore, not really attractive to larger suppliers. If a supplier must make a choice of which delivery date to meet, or which order to take in the first place, he is naturally inclined to give preferential treatment to a larger and older firm.

RIDING HOT LINES

Mr. Verde had this harrowing experience:

> We were doing very well and I even think we were doing too well because we were losing a balanced view. We had a really hot line and the salesmen were shooting orders at us, and so I think I tended to lose track. My mind was completely oriented toward production, and at that time I was concentrating on keeping the stuff moving out of there. Looking back, I hadn't heard much from sales for several weeks. One morning I walked into the shipping area. The foreman said to me, "Who shall I ship to?" There was no one to ship to. The lines had clogged up all the way back to us.

Verde goes on to say that up until that moment he had believed that the supply of retail buyers for his item was unlimited. He left the plant, "walking around while I got used to the idea." He went into a department store where his item was displayed. "They had a dusty look and I could see that they hadn't been moving for weeks." Verde was faced with the sobering reality that in the craze market what goes up must come down.

He had been bankrupt once, and he said, "I didn't want to go through that again." Going back to the plant, he called his key personnel together. They went out to the manufacturing area as a group, and:

> I said, "There it is, boys. Look at it and tell me what we can make on that junk." Well, we all started walking around the machines and when a guy had an idea he'd call it out. Some of them

were pretty ridiculous, but I'd write it down. Then the machine operators got interested, and they shut down the machines and started joining right in, and in maybe an hour or two we had a list of more than fifty items. Those women on the presses, they thought in terms of household gadgets and some of them were right to the point. A woman, she naturally thinks about what can be used around the house.

Having secured a list of possibilities, Mr. Verde led his little entourage of key personnel back to his office. There they went back and forth over the list, culling and selecting. "Two things we had to decide on. How much would the tooling cost? Who could we sell it to?" At the end of a long day, the list had been reduced to about "a half dozen real possibilities. These I took home and mulled over that night."

Verde spent the next day calling buyers in the larger department stores around the country, outlining ideas, and asking first for orders and second for opinions. He says quite smugly, "My success with the (a hot item) had made my name almost a byword with these people." The responses of the buyers were mixed. Some liked items on his list, while others suggested modifications that in essence amounted to new ideas. Toward the end of the second day, Verde had four items which he thought were "the ones that would go." Verde got his designer to work, contacted a die-making company, then called his sales representatives in:

I showed them these rough sketches and said, "Get out and sell these like your jobs depended on it, because they do. All our jobs depend on it." I started handing these sketches out. One guy—he'd always been a poor producer—said, "But can't we have some models to show, or at least something on decent paper?" I told him on the spot he was through. Those guys had been getting fat just taking orders. Now they were going to have to work.

None of the four items really caught on, although they did bring in enough business to keep the plant operating on a limited scale. Verde, however, had learned his lesson. He would never again be caught without a diversified line.

The dangers of riding a hot item are manifest, yet few entrepreneurs in light industry can quite resist. These fast-moving lines have the quality of an Eldorado for these men. Many of them nurse in their innermost hearts a secret yearning for the big item that gets on the market first and swamps the country. To only a few does this ever happen, and then the occasion can easily prove to be more grievous than joyous. The lure, however, is always there. One entrepreneur met the interviewers at the door, and leaving the door open returned to his desk. Midway in the interview he suddenly said, "You may have wondered why I left that door open, and I can tell you it is always open. Someday somebody is going to walk through that door with an idea that will make me a million dollars." He paused, and then told this story:

> We were over on East Street then in a thirty-by-thirty work area we were subleasing from this guy. There was only the two of us and we were hardly making expenses. I was working on the grinder, and all of a sudden I looked up and here was this guy. He had this toy gun. A mock-up he had made out of wood, and it was pretty crude, but it intrigued me. This guy had the idea of making a toy gun that looked exactly like a real revolver. And he'd figured out how to make the moving parts just like a real revolver. It's commonplace now, but at that time it was a brand new idea.

The entrepreneur goes on to tell how the inventor wanted to sell the idea outright:

> I pointed out there was nothing to buy. There was nothing patentable, but I said I thought it had real possibilities. I told him I'd take it on and give him ten percent after all costs. He needed some cash but I didn't have any to give him. Finally he agreed, and went away leaving the gun with me, feeling real low. It was the only decent thing I could do. Hell, he had no protection and the most he could have expected was a few hundred bucks, but this way he wound up with a nice little fortune. He really retired on it—he didn't want to work.

He tells us that while he was talking to the inventor, "An idea had clicked in my mind. I asked myself, 'Who is the biggest name cowboy in the business?' and right away I knew." The combination of the realism of the gun with the name of the most popular cowboy clicked. The entrepreneur worked out a deal by which he produced the guns, and the cowboy's publicity firm handled the publicity. The item was an instantaneous success. "We sold millions of them. It's amazing how many of something like that can be sold once it catches on. Every kid in the country had one. That gun got us off East Street and into our own building. It also got us some decent equipment."

For entrepreneurs, this *is* the Cinderella story. As such, it is a high note with which to end this chapter. The reader must not think, however, that this is the way through the knothole for the typical entrepreneur. For him the way is grubbing for customers, fighting for materials, long hours of hard work, and sleepless nights wondering how the next obstacle can be surmounted or knocked down.

CHAPTER TWELVE

On Their Way at Last

The entrepreneur comes through the knothole. If he is resourceful, determined, and lucky, somehow he makes it. Looking back, he may recall his own behavior with a touch of awe. When an interviewer, after listening to one describe getting through the knothole by the skin of his teeth, commented, "You were lucky," the man looked out the window to think it over. "No," he said, swiveling his chair back to face the interviewer, "I wasn't lucky. I was me."

The moment comes when the entrepreneur can stop and catch his breath. Customers are lined up. Production is moving. Supplies are assured. Ninety-day notes are being met. Those respectable sources of capital which only a short time before were looking down their noses are sniffing hungrily with those same noses. The firm is fairly launched. The entrepreneur now counts the cost. In adding it all up, he may find that to solve immediate and pressing problems he has compromised his long-range desires and goals. The organization maker, having come through the knothole, turns his attention to retrieving and consolidating his organization.

Here, once more, the entrepreneur must change his ways. He may have been a recalcitrant son and a reluctant schoolboy. He may have been a drifter or dealer, or a protégé. He has been a projector, and a promoter, and may have been a grubby proprietor of an alley shop. He is accustomed to living precariously day-to-day in a hand-to-mouth existence.

He may by now be something of an old dog, but he is going to have to learn new tricks. He is going to have to learn to think in terms of diversifying lines, of departmentalizing operations, of regularizing financing, of expanding capitalization, of integrating forward to control outlets, of integrating backward to control supplies, and of making mergers and combinations to keep surplus cash working. He must learn a new way of acting if he is to survive in his new environment.

Unless he can do so, quickly and well, he and his enterprise are in mortal danger. He may be forced out in a fight for control of the organization; or the firm may top out on a plateau of small operation, with little profits, and these profits being eaten up by freeloaders and intruders. The firm, lacking long-range design and firm commitment to its own future, may become confused, founder, and fail.

The problems he now faces can be discussed at the level of formal organization, and as technical problems in business administration; but at the level where the entrepreneur must live they are interpersonal problems. We see the entrepreneur behaving according to the model used in courses in institutional economics, management, and decision theory. At the cognitive level, he is reshaping his strategy to meet the contingencies of a new phase in an always emerging process. There is no question but that his behavior is patterned on that of the rational man in a free enterprise system.

Holding, here, strictly to technical aspects at the organizational level, we can generalize that three tasks must be successfully handled. There is, of course, in reality, all manner of blends of the "mix" of these tasks. Here we are simply separating them for analytical purposes.

The first task (depending on the situation of the individual firm), is regaining control of the firm and driving intruding elements out of it. Almost from the moment of projection, the entrepreneur has had to make compromises. In originally setting up the firm, he may have been in control. While going through the knothole he has traded on his mastery of the situation to keep his undertaking afloat. He may have traded away major ownership in order to get working capital. Debtors may have been using threats of bankruptcy or foreclosure to dictate to the entrepreneur. A customer may have—because he is the only sales outlet—muscled his way into the firm to inspect equipment, examine finances, and to "advise" the entrepreneur. In all these instances, the entrepreneur may have lost virtual control of the enterprise. Now he must move back, asserting authority. He must, by one means or another, force these intruders out.

A second task arises from the structure that the entrepreneur gave his enterprise when he first set it up. This structure was established, by and large, as the most expedient device for getting the enterprise through the knothole. In some instances, this structure may have been evolved carefully and thoroughly, but more often it may have been thrown together simply to get things moving. The basic imperative was to bring together resources for the initial push. Having passed the critical phase, the entrepreneur now finds this jerrybuilt organization inadequate and stifling. He must alter or eliminate it either by dismantling it, or—as is sometimes necessary—placing a demolition charge under it.

A third task is what we can call "rationalizing the system." Here the entrepreneur has to learn to play the role of administrator and manager. This may be difficult. In going through the knothole, he has a highly personal and immediate relationship with the firm. Every event is dealt with personally. Nothing is too small for his attention. He makes all the decisions. He feels anything which happens to the firm happens to him personally, as though the firm were his biological child. His knowledge of and concern for the firm is immediate. He is concerned with what is happening now, and with what will happen in the next few hours or days. Both he and the firm operate on a highly pragmatic, emotional, and hand-to-mouth basis.

Now, with the knothole behind him, the entrepreneur must begin to disengage himself from minute problems, sever his bonds of close emotional involvement with the present, and devote increasing amounts of his time and energy to the overall reorganization of the firm and to structuring it to deal with futures of the intermediate and longer range.

At the cognitive level of administrative action, these are the tasks that (for reasons of analysis and description), can be isolated. For most entrepreneurs there is a golden moment when these problems can be acted on. Action cannot be premature. The entrepreneur, for example, who moves to expel intruders before he has laid the groundwork, may find that instead of regaining control of the firm he has lost out entirely. On the other hand, the entrepreneur who waits too long may find that he has lost—sometimes psychologically, at other times, situationally—the capacity to move. He may also find that the firm has settled into the mold of a small alley shop creeping along on marginal orders which larger establishments do not want. The entrepreneur must have developed, through his long period of training and experience, the ability to identify the moment and to move decisively.

These problems exist in reality at several different levels. We have discussed them as problems in rational and technical administrative action. They exist at this level for the entrepreneur, and if he does not have the sensitivity and intelligence to cope with them as technical problems, his own career and the growth of his firm become atrophied.

Being able to identify these problems and pose solutions to them at the intellectual level, however, is not enough. Professors of business, trained engineers, and accountants can perhaps see these problems in a much more rational and objective way than can many entrepreneurs. For this reason, entrepreneurs may hire or consult with such specialists to help them.

The entrepreneur must be able to perceive and to act upon these problems at a second level—the "interpersonal level." It is here that both the character structure and the early training of the entrepreneur become really essential. We have seen that the entrepreneur comes from a childhood situation where he has learned to be distrustful of powerful figures, and fearful of peers who may assume positions superordinate to him. We have seen that, as a child and as a young adult, the entrepreneur has learned to keep relationships with such figures on a temporary basis, developing techniques either for escaping from or driving these figures away. During the phase we call "basic dealing," he has learned the positive mode of this technique, grasping the transactional model of interpersonal relationship as one in which he can continue relationships—so long as they are of value—and sever them when they lose their value or become threatening.

GETTING RID OF PARTNERS

It is precisely this mode of operating that the entrepreneur, in moving beyond the initial phase, must bring into play again. He must get rid of those people who have, during this transitional phase, used his temporary weakness to intrude upon him. He must get rid of these figures for two reasons. At the organizational level, he must get rid of them because they block further development of the firm. At the level of internal and interpersonal dynamics, he must get rid of them because they inhibit him, because they restrict the autonomy for which he constantly searches, and because they recall to him those obscene, undependable, and frightening images, flight from which has been so instrumental in shaping his odyssey.

We can more fully understand the dangers by looking at one man who failed and at one man who did not. Mr. Chalmers, primarily a promoter, had during his career set up several firms and nursed them through the knothole. Each time he had lost out. Perhaps we can understand why he failed if we contrast him with Mr. Littler, his arch rival at the time of the field work.

These two men were fighting for control of a firm, with a Mr. Whiffle (Chalmers' original partner) holding the balance of power. Littler handled the technical side. He was interviewed in his office, and his interview was mostly about the firm and its operations. Jack Chalmers handled customer and vendor relationships and he might be described as the "outside" man. He talked about college:

> Then, after I was with this ice box company just for a short period of time, I started college. The way I got interested, well, I went to a J-hop at the college with a friend of mine. Hell, I had a ball. I thought that was the thing for me. I should go to college. My hero at that time was the treasurer of the company. He sort of took me under his wing. He infused the idea into me. "Take finance," he said. "That's the important thing. Get as much finance as you can." So I did. I took more damn finance than you can shake your fist at—every course they had there. As a matter of fact, I got to know this one economics professor. This professor was a man of seventy years old, and he used to come over to my fraternity house in the morning and wake me because I couldn't wake up. Then I'd help him out: he would come in there with his fly undone and I'd have to tell him about it. But this professor I got to know very well. As a matter of fact, one time on the train I played bridge with him. I played bridge with him for a grade, whether I got an A or a B. I lost, and got the B. But, hell, I really hadn't even earned a C in that course. Also, while I was in college, I used to buy alcohol from a medical student. Then I'd sell it to the students, and make a few bucks this way.

Mr. Chalmers was interviewed in a bar, which seemed to be his natural habitat. Chalmers had carried over his attitude toward college, into his business life. He saw his work as taking place primarily in informal, social settings.

In contrast to Chalmers, Littler was interviewed in his office. There, amid the paraphernalia of his profession, he described his own education:

> In high school, I was the manager of six other high school students who had a business of renting a hall and putting on basketball games with a dance following it. I played basketball and musical instruments—the piano, the clarinet, and one other instrument. I believe it was the drums. In this way, I was able to finance my way through school. I took the examinations to enter West Point. My three choices were, in order, to go to West Point to be an artillery officer, to be a doctor, and to be a chemical engineer, with some thoughts of becoming a corporate patent lawyer.
>
> I passed all of my tests to go to West Point, and even obtained congressional permission to go up there for their summer prep series. They put me on the firing range, at which time I found that I could not fire a gun correctly because I could not read the signals. I was color blind. This also ruled out for me any hopes of studying to be a doctor. Therefore, I decided to go to college and take Chemical Engineering. I took the five-year professional course, graduating with a Chemical Engineering degree. During my college days, of course, I was very busy supporting myself, particularly by playing in an orchestra three and four nights per week. However, one night getting on the subway, I stumbled and spat blood. At the age of twenty-two, I had a perforated stomach ulcer which has plagued me from that time and will plague me for the rest of my life.
>
> Following graduation, I meandered from job to job and found nothing of particular interest to me. Then I went in the evening to law school at the university, where I completed three out of the four years necessary for the law degree. But, due to the pressures of my jobs, studying at night, and the incessant problem of the ulcer, I was forced to drop out.

The contrast between the two men is evident. Chalmers plays at life. He played at it in college, and he plays at it in his career. For Littler, on the other hand, education was the grim forerunner of a grim career. Thoughout, he has had cold determination and a capacity for hard work.

During a long and damp afternoon in the bar, Chalmers used the interviewer as a sounding board, going back in his recollection to when Littler first came on the scene:

> Well, do you know how we first got him out here? Well, I don't know the first thing about (name withheld). I can move the stuff. I can sell it; but I don't know a damn thing about how to make it. So this customer told me, "Get Littler—he's a bastard—but he knows what he's doing." So Littler came out, and he was going to help us out so we could have decent material. So, I was taking him through the plant and he said, "My God." He got half way through the plant and he said, "God, this is awful. I couldn't help you guys. This is lousy. It's the poorest stuff I've ever seen." So I got him to come out here, and he was coming out bit-by-bit consulting with us and I finally got him to move out here.

Littler's price was a third of the business and an understanding that he would commute to New Hampshire on weekends, with the firm paying the tab. The Littlers were playing for keeps:

> You know the reason he wouldn't come out? It was his wife. They thought anything out of New England—she thought we were savages out here—there is nothing out here but Indians—the people out here are nothing. Well, now we are good friends. My wife and her are very good friends. Well, not very good friends. They're friends, but they're not real close friends. Well, for example, the other night we were going to the theater but at the last minute they called and said she wasn't feeling up to it.

> But, actually, when she came here, the first weekend here, I took her up north, her and a group of us—a party to go fishing for the weekend. Hell, I thought everybody liked fishing. We got up there, and the first morning we go out in the boat. She goes out in the boat, she gets seasick—just like that. My God, we were going to stay for the whole weekend, but we have to drive thirty miles and put her on the train and send her back.

At this point in Chalmers' monologue, the third partner, Whiffle (the man Chalmers had brought in at the beginning), came into the bar. Chalmers shouted to him, "Hey, Nick, come over here. Here's somebody I want you to meet." Whiffle, either not hearing Chalmers or choosing to ignore him, sat down at the end of the bar. Chalmers remarked, "Well, I wanted you to meet him, but I guess we'd better not. Nick's been pretty sick lately."

The interviewer remarked that Littler—with whom he had spent the morning—had taken the interviewer into a restricted area where a new and highly original process was being perfected. Chalmers seized upon this:

> Littler took you down there? My God, I've only been down there once. My God, that's the first time anyone has ever been down there. I had to sneak down there myself.

That Chalmers was not allowed to examine development of a process vital to the firm was a piteous admission that things were not going well for him. Perhaps for this reason he laid out his plans to the interviewer:

> Whiffle and I are going to throw that bastard out on his ear. We're going to pull a surprise meeting on him and vote him out of the vice-presidency. We'll be doing this real soon now, and I'll make the plant off limits to *him*.

A few weeks after this interview, Littler and Whiffle voted that Chalmers resign as president. We learned about six months later that Chalmers was lining up capital with which to begin a new venture. His is the case of the perpetual promoter.

In Chalmers we have a portrait of a failing man. If we ask ourselves why, we see that no one pat answer is good enough. He failed because he lost control of the technical side of the operation. He also failed because, somewhere along the line, he lost Whiffle's loyalty. This is explaining the failure only in a superficial way. More basically, he failed because he recognized that the Littlers were exacting too high a price, but could not act decisively on this understanding. Perhaps, after the fishing trip, he should have bought both the Littlers one-way tickets back to their beloved New Hampshire. Chalmers could not break off the relationship at the right moment because he lacked the character necessary to making a firm decision and sticking to it.

The following incident, told us by a Mr. Fielding, underscores both the need for seeing the moment and the use of the transactional model in severing the relationship:

> I'd been nursing this thing along. For two years, I'd been nursing it along, filling an order whenever I could get it. You see, it

wasn't a paying proposition. It was top quality in every way—the best that could possibly be made. It got on Ed's [his equal partner] nerves, and we fought about it continuously. I couldn't give it up because everything else we were doing—I couldn't be proud of it—Everything else was just junk.

Fielding tells us that the business was then doing well, in a small way, but that both he and his partner had come to realize they would never really grow in a highly competitive market. Then, one day, "I guess I was lucky because Ed was away when this letter came in from this mail-order house. They'd had some testing done, and had come up with the decision that they wanted to list our product as their top quality line."

Special knowledge being an important advantage, Fielding did not mention the letter to his partner. Instead, he did what he thought was the fair thing. He opened negotiations with his partner by offering to sell his half of the business. When Ed did not take this offer:

Then I made an offer to him. You see, I'd offered to get out with only a small profit. This gave him a chance if he wanted it. He turned it down, so then it was my turn. His original investment was ten thousand, and after three years it had probably doubled in value. It was probably worth twenty to twenty-five. I offered him thirty to get out. He said, "thirty-five," and I said "sold." That was in the bar of the Adams Hotel.

Had Fielding really done the "fair thing?" Perhaps in the years since this little drama he has sometimes wondered. Looking back, however, he thinks that he was justified.

We finally split up because I got disgusted with this guy. He was a guy. He was a drunk, a gambler, and a woman chaser. He got thirty-five thousand out of it. He really made it tough for me. It was just a nasty situation. You see, he always wanted to take the profits out, but we couldn't do this because then we wouldn't have any working capital. We had all sorts of arguments here. For example, he didn't want to allow any depreciation on equipment. Hell, you have to depreciate equipment.

The ruthless behavior which these men believe necessary at this crucial stage is further illustrated by Mr. Litchfield. Fred Litchfield had brought his firm through the knothole and now faced the problem and opportunity of expansion. He needed money fast, but before he could bring in new money, he had to clear away old debris. His problem, which dated from the firm's origin, was that he had an equal partner who would not sell and who would not allow Litchfield to buy:

> I located this guy who was interested in buying me out, and I took him around to the office. I told him [the partner] I was selling out to this guy. After he [the potential buyer] left, I had it out with Joe [the partner]. He tried to tell me I couldn't sell to an outsider unless he approved the sale. It was in our agreement. I said, "To hell with that, I'll sell and we'll put it in the courts." I pointed out he might win the case but it would ruin both of us. Finally, he agreed to sell. That's what I wanted. I wanted to get rid of Joe. He was like a bloodsucker about this—he didn't want to let go.

Most entrepreneurs, talking about manipulating partners out, take care to explain why these actions were justified. These justifications fall into a pattern. First, there is talk about the partner and why his weaknesses made necessary his going. The entrepreneur also makes it clear that he really had no choice, since dumping the partner was a necessary step in saving and further developing the firm.

THROWING OUT INTRUDERS

In the last section we looked at some straightforward power struggles in which the entrepreneur either gained or lost control. If the firm is a partnership, or incorporates with only two or three shareholders, the fight for control may be bitter but relatively uncomplicated.

Mr. Austin, expanding prematurely, sold stock to a number of investors. He believed that the stock was sufficiently spread so that, owning thirty percent of it, he was safe. There was, however, a revolt:

> They then called this meeting, at the behest of the majority, and they didn't even tell me about it. Well, they elected a new president replacing me. Then they called another meeting and they set up this committee—an executive committee; and they were closing me out so they said this committee was for control of the plant and could make any decisions without referring it to the Board of Direc-

tors. They came around and asked me to be vice-president for operations; and what could I do? If I'd refused, they'd have frozen me out entirely.

Probably this bloc, having control of the company, should have completely gotten rid of Austin. Austin bided his time while going about running the business. He was not dismissed, he says, "for I was the only one of them that knew the business. If I went, the business would fold. They were absolutely dependent upon me in this way." Austin then got an unexpected break, and he tells us about it with relish:

This banker friend called me up, and said this guy had borrowed $90,000 from the bank and put up his stock as collateral. The banker said this guy was going into a deal and had taken this money, but hadn't met his commitments. He said, did I want the stock, and that if I did I could have it for $45,000. I said, "Well, that's a little tough, isn't it?" and he said, "Well, business is business. I want to get rid of it to close this loan out. It's in default."

Austin purchased the stock by paying off the loan and making a settlement with the stockholder. In the course of this transaction, Austin learned that another piece of stock could be pried loose:

Then I had a meeting of my own, right here in the office. Jim sat here, and the rest of them, the attorney and the accountant, and all of them. I started by saying to Jim, "This is it. I'll buy you out for fifteen dollars a share." and he said, "Okay, it's a sale." I was a little hasty on this because it cost me a hundred thousand, and I found out afterwards that he was pressed for funds and I could have bought at a better price.

The price may have been high, but the day of reckoning had definitely arrived:

"Okay," I said to Jim. "You're through here. Get out and don't come back." And then [here Austin points from chair to chair around the circle as he talks], and then the attorney, "You're through," and then the other owners [who had elected themselves officers], "You're through." And then the accountant, "You can make out their resignation slips, and while you're at it you may as well make out your own." This accountant said, "Well, won't you need some accounting help? Maybe I should stay on as an advisory." I said, "That's the trouble. I've had your help for twelve years and that's what I want to get rid of."

Austin was on a thorough housecleaning spree. He tells us that he went "through the plant and fired anybody who had ever been friendly with that crowd in any way, shape, or form." Although he has since sold much of the stock he accumulated to regain control, he has "seen to it that it is widely distributed. My wife has the biggest block next to me, and my nephew has some. The rest I keep a careful eye on. I know pretty well where it is all the time."

Intruders are not the only people who muscle in as investors. Customers may also get unduly interested in the operations of a firm. One purchasing director for a large corporation said:

> When I myself or one of our analysts go into a plant we look first of all for neatness. If I see some dies stashed over in a corner and the owner is asked about it and says he will get around to it someday, this creates a very bad impression on me. This is in contrast to the man who has tool cribs, and in the work area has shelves erected and well built and has his tools and parts on these shelves and all neatly positioned and clearly labeled. This gives a totally different impression of the man and the way he runs his business.

We happened to talk with an entrepreneur who had had a run-in with one of these self-appointed inspectors:

> We had that big machine over there down—the one with the four heads. We had a little slack, and I told the boys to tear her down and check her out completely. They were doing this, and they had parts all down the aisle. Well, this guy from Gigantic came in here. We were running an order for them, and they came in like they owned the place. Well, he came in here and he sees all this stuff on the floor, and he says right to my face, "You'll have to clean this up. We don't approve of our vendors when they do business like this." Words to that effect. I told him to clear out, and then I called his boss and told him what I thought about their whole outfit. Actually, I've never bid in with them since.

The entrepreneur who is dependent upon one source of supply may find himself in an equally irritating situation:

They have these sales engineers which they call management consultants. They are supposed to tour the country, and when you ask for it they come in and help you with your management problems. This, of course, is supposed to be voluntary on your part. You're supposed to ask for help and they give it because you're an outlet for them; but actually you're saddled with these guys. They know your whole business exists because you can get supplies from them, so they wind up telling you how to operate. They let you know unless you agree you won't stack up very well as a customer if supplies get short. They let you know they won't ship to you.

This man had gone into business to utilize the output of a large chemical corporation. At the time of the interview, he was seeking diversification which would make possible breaking this natal bond.

Another man hit back at the excessive paper work demanded by one kind of customer:

This had been getting worse through the years. They ask for these elaborate bids. It will sometimes take two or three weeks to prepare one. They want to know all about you. Hell, they don't need to know all that. All they need to know is your price. It's also fair to say they need to know whether you can deliver, but if you've delivered before, that ought to be enough.

What's worse, this is all hocus-pocus. We submitted a bid to Mastodon, and it took three men a week to prepare. I knew it was absolutely rock bottom. Well, we didn't get it so I called up and asked, "How come?" This guy laughs and says, "You know how to get business out of us." Hell, I'm not going to do business by bribing anybody.

REVAMPING THE SYSTEM

Getting rid of partners and throwing out intruders is seldom conceived by these men as an end in itself. Usually, they make these moves as part of an emerging line of action. They are clearing away the debris of history to make room for the future. The organizational devices needed to get the firm on its feet are both inadequate and stifling:

I had for a long time been turning this over in my mind, but I was aware that it was premature. We were undercapitalized and

I could see this was going to keep us small. We needed more money in the business. The initial investment we had put in wasn't nearly adequate and none of us [the three partners] could add to it. All three of us were taking our expenses out, and there was nothing to leave in. On that basis, we were never going to grow. We needed new money, especially the kind of money we could use to expand.

This man had organized a tight partnership and had begun operations on a shoestring. During the first two or three years his firm had edged along, slowly improving its relations with a few customers and developing its production operations. During the latter period, it had been borrowing working capital on ninety-day loans. By repaying these loans on time, it had improved its credit situation. All this time the real entrepreneur among the three partners had been nursing the situation along. He was not going to be premature in his action, but he foresaw the next move:

> Although things were getting better, they were also getting worse. We were coming up against a stone wall. Ed and Bill [his two partners] were getting increasingly restless. They had sunk their savings in this thing, and they were getting less out of it than if they were on wages somewhere else.

Another man put the problem more succinctly: "We needed to get into our own building, and we needed tooling. In other words, we needed to get new money in by reorganizing." And still another man said: "Grow or die. If you stand still, you're dead."

All of these men were contemplating, now that their firms had negotiated the first hurdles and were more attractive financially, taking in new money. Taking in new money may at this stage be attractive in itself, but it may also be a means to an end:

> These little costs: we were being dimed to death—a nickel here and a nickel there. And depreciation—I wasn't allowing a nickel for depreciation. Of course, you might say there wasn't any depreciation on that stuff we picked up when we opened for business, but we still had to figure on replacing it. Those [machines] were a millstone around our necks.

This kind of statement is often followed by a little introspection by the entrepreneur. Joe Stoodley, who at the time of the field work retired as president of the company he had founded to become board chairman at a large salary, is one such example:

> I've never had any money sense. Money as such has never in-terested me. Why, in those days before I got Tom [who seems to be a personal secretary], I would have several thousand in my personal account at the bank, and I would be getting duns from collection agencies. I'd get bills and I'd stuff them in a pocket and forget about them. I'd tell myself, "I'll have a little time tomorrow. I'll write some checks then."

Such increasing awareness of a need to put things on a more systematic basis may lead to a "grand strategy" type of reorganization in which the firm is recapitalized and at the same time a new and more formal organization structure is introduced. Finance experts and teachers of business administration like to see it done this way.

Entrepreneurs, however, seem to move into systematizing the or-ganizations they have made in a much less rational way. One problem or another comes up, this causes reevaluation, and only gradually does the idea of complete revamping emerge. Take, for example, Elmer Kleit. Mr. Kleit tells us that when he first created his firm, he had employed a certified public accountant to handle his bookwork:

> I took my checkbook over there, and we had an agreement; neither O'Neil or I [O'Neil was the partner at this stage], were going to write any more checks. Checks or bills came in, and I'd put them into an envelope and send them over to him [the CPA]. He'd come in once a month and go over what had happened—how much had come in and how much had gone out—then he'd have O'Neil and me sign the forms he'd made up. We wouldn't even read them, we'd sign. He came over one day and he said, "How about you and O'Neil taking a salary cut? How about each of you taking five thousand less for about a year. Your business could use the saving." I looked at O'Neil and I said, "Okay, you're the boss."

Kleit offered to sell a fourth of the business, which by now had excellent prospects, to the CPA for $25,000. The CPA turned this offer down, but he said that if the partnership was dissolved and shares issued, he would come in for a fourth. This proposal led to an even more elaborate plan for reorganization.

Kleit needed additional capital, but he also needed a man who understood financial problems. It is typical of the entrepreneurial mode that Kleit did not go out and hire a financial expert. He sought, rather, to get the man of his choice involved in the firm. He wanted the man deeply motivated to make the financial side successful.

Another entrepreneur had a similar need at this stage, although his problem was engineering rather than finance. Mr. Graham says:

> I'm nothing but a working man and I can make anything as long as I can work with my hands. Give me any problem, and give me the tools and I can figure it out. After Jim [a partner with whom he had been having difficulties] pulled out, I needed to get somebody else. I'd been figuring out the machining problems, but I was seeing with this I could only get so far. Now I needed a really trained engineer. I picked up Frank, and at this time he was only five years out of [a prestigious technical school], and I brought him in at a handsome salary—really high. He had no cash, so I said, "Save some out each month and buy a piece of the company." We set a price on what the firm was worth then and that's what he pays. No matter how much the value goes up, he can still buy in at the original figure. That way he's protected. We signed an agreement to this effect.

To facilitate this arrangement, Graham decided to incorporate. A lawyer "friend" pointed out that if this step was to be taken, Graham could capitalize at much more than he had dreamed by selling stock to outsiders. Thus gradually Graham learned about finance.

EXPANDING THROUGH FINANCE

The temptation is great to go on playing the strictly entrepreneurial game at this stage. The entrepreneur, instead of building his organization, may exploit it as a tool for acquiring personal holdings. Such men may enhance their own wealth by buying and selling businesses; but this may inhibit the growth of the firm they created.

Mr. Peck started the Peck Company, but wound up with several firms all taking something out of his original company. After having gotten his original company through the knothole, Mr. Peck saw an opportunity:

> This outfit was on the ropes and I heard about it. I went down to Akron and looked it over, and from the outset I told them they

had nothing to sell. I said I would take an option and gave them a check for this. This guy, he'd inherited the business and didn't know what he was doing. That check looked big because they were strapped at the time. I said I'd send my auditors in to look it over and set a price, and that I'd give them an answer in five days. Actually, I stalled this along for about three months, and all the time things were getting worse for them. I had only to wait. Finally, I offered $45,000. They didn't like it but they took it.

Peck then tells us how he decided against having Peck Company make the purchase:

It could be turned into a good property, and I decided the profitable thing to do was buy it for myself. Actually, my wife and I set up a corporation for this purpose. By buying ourselves, we could keep the anticipated gains.

Mr. Peck did, however, send his management "team" in to straighten things out:

Several things—the inventory was much too high and this had to be liquidated, and there was a lot of deadwood that had grown on while the father had the business. These people we let go, and then I started with the union members. This was tougher, but I made it stick. I went to see the local president—right to his office—and I laid it out: "I'm the new owner and I have a choice here. I can either close the place down and sell off the real estate and building; or we can cut out this featherbedding and try to make a go of it. Give me a year and I'll be hiring more people by double out of your local than I am now."

This little property, renovated by the Peck Company's team, might have been a fine subsidiary for the Peck Company. Mr. Peck, however, did not see it this way. For him it was only the first of several holdings which he was to keep separate. The Peck Company will never grow into a large enterprise simply because Peck himself does not see this as a desirable objective. Contrast Mr. Peck with Mr. Martin:

I had sole ownership up until that time. I borrowed heavily, but had always fought shy of selling stock. Then I was approached by John Gifford. You've heard of John Gifford? He was almost seventy at the time and wanted to retire but could not because he had no one he could trust to take over. At first he offered me a salary and offered to buy me out; and when I turned this down, he said, "Well, then let's set it up so you buy me out." This staggered me, because, of course, you know how big he was. He showed me how we could do it. This took some doing, because he was maybe twenty times bigger than I was. But I kept faith with him, and even in retirement he made one hell of a bundle.

As a result of this deal, Martin Enterprises became, overnight, a quite respectable industrial empire. Through the years, Martin has added to it. His logic has always been one of diversifying and integrating with other ventures, and Martin Enterprises controls a group of subsidiaries.

With Martin we come close to the perspective these men must achieve if they are to go beyond being owners of small manufacturing businesses. Perhaps six or eight men out of over a hundred in our sample have fully achieved this perspective, although others approach it in varying degrees. Only when a man comes to see the organization as an instrument outside has he achieved that detachment essential to the manager. Once they achieve this perspective they are transformed into a kind of organization maker which lies outside the scope of our interest here.

At the point where we leave him, the entrepreneur is the dominant and controlling force in his own firm. The chain of events released by his projection of the firm have reached culmination. Now he is a full-fledged businessman with his own enterprise firmly under his control. The entrepreneur and his firm have "arrived." Or have they? The interview material shows that this is simply another way station—that this is not the end but only the beginning. At this point the entrepreneur, in a genuine sense, starts over. He starts this time, however, from a new plateau.

The entrepreneur is engaged in expanding, integrating, and structuring the instrument he has brought under control. In a real sense the existence of the instrument makes him feel more secure and protected than he has ever been in his entire life. In an equally real sense, however, nothing has changed. The very fact of having in his possession as valuable and desirable a thing as his own business increases his vulnerability. The old powerful and all-pervading figures are still there, and they at once threaten him with taking his possession away and indicate that they will at any moment withdraw the nurture and support that he and the firm need. The faces of these figures are changed. They now wear the masks of purchasing agents, of officers of finance houses, of government officials, of larger competitors poised to gobble him up.

As he has always done, the entrepreneur moves to ward off the threatening blows of these figures, or to drive them away. As long as he has his business, he cannot use his old escape through flight. Protection of the enterprise holds him. He is like the bishop in chess, "pinned" against the queen whom he must at all costs protect. The entrepreneur can no longer cut and run.

If he has created imaginatively, organized wisely, and made a sustained effort in the years following his act of entrepreneurship, the firm he has made will take its place within the network of business enterprise. It may steadily expand its operation, diversifying its lines and accumulating subsidiaries. One out of perhaps a hundred thousand new enterprises will continue its growth until it has become a great corporate power with far-flung markets and vast holdings.

By the very process of growth through time, the nature of the firm will change, and as change takes place the "founder" will cease to be the driving force. A new generation of men will emerge and take over the reins. These men will have their own competences and their own way, but the competence and the way of the entrepreneur will no longer be either sufficient or necessary.

The new phase of the firm will have set up new role demands, and these the independent entrepreneur as leader may find increasing difficulty in playing. Either gladly or reluctantly he will pass on the power to the younger generation, a generation of administrative entrepreneurs who create by extension.

The original entrepreneurial figure will be woven into the mythology of the firm. Relegated into retirement or into the role of elder statesman and chairman of the board, the creator is no longer the central figure. Standing at the window of the chairman's office, he may look out and down upon the yards, buildings, and equipment he has brought together into a great enterprise. And as he looks he may ask himself, "Why did I do it? What did I get out of it?"

When the interviewer from the university comes to call, he will be eager to answer these questions because they are questions of great interest to him as a person, but if the independent entrepreneur has really sought insight, he may come to believe that there are no simple and direct answers.

PART FOUR

INDEPENDENT AND ADMINISTRATIVE ENTREPRENEURS: A COMPARISON

Business Hierarchs:
Men Who Rise in Established Businesses

How do independent entrepreneurs differ from business hierarchs—that is, administrative entrepreneurs in established businesses? To answer this question we must first examine the business hierarchs, analyze the organizational and entrepreneurial environment in which they operate, set forth some of the research findings regarding successful performance of the executive role in established businesses, and finally assess the implications.

MANAGING A BUSINESS

The entrepreneurial environment of any business—large or small, well-established or newly-established—is in broad structure the same. Certain kinds of problems and challenges must be met regardless of the size or age of the enterprise. Entrepreneurial tasks typically involve building or generating new exchange relationships where none existed before, and maintaining or consolidating existing relationships. The entrepreneurs in our sample have undertaken and completed one act of building. The same round of activity characterizes executive behavior in large-scale, established companies. Their efforts to develop new products, conceive of new market structures, finance expanded activities, and develop organizations of people, tools, and machines in the pursuit of new entrepreneurial objectives are all part of the same picture. Big businesses act the same way as little businesses. In order to survive, they must be equally entrepreneurial, perhaps even more so because of the immense resources that must constantly be revitalized by organization extensions.

There are, however, certain obvious differences between the executives of large-scale, established companies and the entrepreneurs in our sample—especially in the circumstances in which entrepreneurial tasks are performed. The established organizations have the resources of an existing and viable business on which to build. They have capital and credit upon which to draw, and, even more important, they have high-talent manpower organized around the key entrepreneurial activities. They have research and development laboratories, marketing organizations for launching new products, ₅and existing production facilities that considerably reduce the expense of developing new product lines. Moreover, they have well-trained management personnel who can move in and take over new developments.

INFLUENCE OF THE ORGANIZATION STRUCTURE

Establishd companies by definition are characterized by organization involving a complex division of labor and a hierarchy of authority and control. This structure represents not only a functional division of labor but is also a social structure. The various functional and hierarchical positions in the organization take on social significance and meaning to the participants. Employees and executives alike become identified with the various functional interests and frequently internalize the values of their occupations. In addition, the hierarchy of control in the established business is viewed as a status ranking involving power, prestige, and expectations of deference. Finally, there are strong tendencies to view the entire organization as a self-contained entity in which the individual plays a greater or lesser part.

While the key entrepreneurial activities of the established company must still be successfully performed, these become an organizational undertaking that is not necessarily clearly perceived by the individual participant—in some cases even at the executive level. Rather, we find a focus on specialized job activities and career interests—a narrowing of interests that sometimes obscures the ultimate entrepreneurial goals of the business. In other words, the entrepreneurial activities are built into the organization and the actual interests of employees are primarily those of successful job performance within the structure.

The significance of this transmutation of entrepreneurial interests to organizational and job interests can be observed by examining the career line of the typical big-business executive. When he first enters a company, he is not concerned with running a business as much as he is with holding a job. His interest lies in finding a niche where there is a potential for advancement. To him, ultimate success is the top of a ladder which is to be climbed rung by rung. Each step up the ladder represents not only effort on his part but the willingness of those higher on the ladder to allow him, and even help him, to move up. He quickly becomes aware that he is operating within a system where job performance pays off but also where acceptance by those above him is of crucial importance. More than this, he learns that the climb is not just a matter of acquiring new job skills but also of developing social skills associated with higher status and organization power.

During most of the typical executive's career, the climb is confined to one occupational area. He moves up as a manufacturing executive, or sales executive, or personnel officer. Within this activity he typically becomes an expert.

There is in established companies a continuous trend toward increasing complexity in the various functional areas. What could be done a generation ago by high school graduates now requires college trained personnel or even graduate training beyond the college level. This grading up of educational and personal requirements is, in part, a reflection of the real and growing complexities of modern business; but it also results from job competition, trends toward the professionalization of key occupations, and the outright status exclusion that frequently develops within hierarchical structures.

CHARACTERISTICS OF ESTABLISHED ORGANIZATIONS

Prior Existence. An obvious fact about established organizations is that they existed prior to the individual executive. Sears, Roebuck and Co., for example, is currently being managed by its fourth generation of executives. Richard W. Sears and Julius Rosenwald are by this time historic figures of the dim past—known directly by few, if any, of the current crop of top executives. Coming into a business after its establishment gives one the feeling that the organization has an existence of its own. Executives come and go, but the organization goes on forever. In this connection, the demise of a well-known, established business is—for those who know it—very much akin to the death of a great and noble figure.

The fact of prior establishment and historic continuity gives the individual executive a "generational" view of managerial succession. He develops a sense of son succeeding father. The world of work and of personal success to him is one of occupying a position in an established structure with the hope of rising in an existing hierarchy.

Hierarchical Organization and Division of the Entrepreneurial Function. A second characteristic of established businesses—which we have already pointed out or alluded to in several places—is that they are hierarchically organized. In addition, the overall entrepreneurial function is divided into several major functional areas and into a great variety of subordinate tasks. The hierarchical structure and functional division result in a complex of occupational circles within circles of ever-widening scope. At each higher level of the administrative hierarchy, the circle expands to include a broader segment of the business.

The young junior executive usually begins his career within a narrowly circumscribed functional activity. He sees himself as holding a job, occupying a niche, rather than running a business. Until he reaches the very top of most organizations, his success depends on his occupational and professional competence. As a consequence, the demands in most established organizations for occupational or functional competence are very high indeed. A man simply cannot achieve success in large-scale, established organizations without extensive formal education and long years of experience in a particular field. Yet with all his experience and education he can often climb to the upper echelon of management knowing less about running a total business than many pushcart merchants.

The hierarchical structure of power and control in the established business automatically makes climbing the hierarchical ladder the main avenue to success. There are, of course, blind alleys which may represent positions of moderate success. A man can become, for example, a great scientist or technologist in his organization and may even enjoy considerable respect and recognition for his sense of duty and his persistent pursuit of occupational competence. These are always respected virtues in our occupationally oriented society. But the main line is straight up in the administrative hierarchy. Vertical mobility, accordingly, means climbing a ladder of positions of increasing administrative power over larger and larger segments of the functional activities of the business.

It is only when a man has risen through many levels that he may find himself engaged in weighing project proposals, and in bringing together men to launch a program which requires creating either a new "internal" unit or a "spin-off" external organization. Such an executive's major attempt at organization making may occur as the capstone to his career. It is this which accounts for the "project president"—the official who is elevated to the presidency with only four or five remaining career years with the understanding that he will devote those years to the creation of a new product or international division, or that he will relate his organization with other firms by helping create an "interstitial" structure.

Social Organization. To understand fully the significance of vertical mobility in a hierarchical structure, we must call the reader's attention to yet a third characteristic of established businesses. We are referring to the social organization that typically develops whenever there are continuous relations among people over long periods of time. Under these conditions, the administrative hierarchy becomes a structure of status levels. Expectations develop both from topside and from below regarding the behavior and demeanor of persons occupying the various levels. These expectations not only include notions regarding a man's occupational competence but also encompass various beliefs about his appearance, use of language, expressive skills, mode of dress, life style outside the organization, and so on. In other words, he must "make sense" socially as well as occupationally. Indeed, the social expectations become so intricately intertwined with the occupational and functional demands that it is virtually impossible to separate them. It is very possible that the demands, especially in big business, for more and more education among those in the top ranks arise out of social considerations as much as from the increasing complexity of the executive role. Or perhaps a more accurate way of viewing it is that the increasing need for education and the growing complexity of the executive social role in big business go hand in hand, one giving rise to the other.

The social organization developing in the established business has other important implications. It gives rise to a sense of unity and overall purpose not only at the executive level but down the line among employees, supervisors, and middle-management. Thus, management and employees alike develop the feeling that they are part of a unified structure of action, working together to achieve broad goals and purposes. This impression is enhanced by the cooperative work systems developing around the productive efforts of the organization, for technological activities are goal-directed and purposeful with individual efforts organized around a common objective.

The sense of unity and purpose arising within established businesses transforms the executive function from the strictly entrepreneurial one of developing exchange-relationships and negotiating differences in interests and values, to a leadership function. This alteration cannot be too strongly stressed since it is a key factor in shaping the role of the modern business executive. A leader interprets the unfolding reality against the needs of his group. His interpretations and the decisions he reaches must be effective if the group's needs are to be successfully met. In established organizations, the leadership function follows such a pattern.

The needs of the group, however, are viewed in terms of the occupational specialty. The executive within each functional specialty attempts to develop action programs that will enhance the relative position of the larger organization. Typically, these programs are aimed at making the entire organization more effective and successful. Thus, what begins as an expression of narrow functional interests is broadened to include the common interests of the entire organization.

The leadership concept places great demands on the executive in the established organization to develop an action program, posture, or stance that serves as the basis of his decisions and actions in the organization. He is expected to have a sense of direction—to know what it is all about and to be on top of the situation. His decision function is accordingly conceived as one of developing and launching programs which will excite the interest of those whom he leads and which can, at the same time, be "sold" to higher levels of management. Success can often be measured by the ability of the executive to gain an allocation of resources favorable to the interests of his department or division. Not only does he as an individual gain power, status, and prestige by securing such resources, but the morale of the entire group is typically enhanced by the heightened sense of status and recognition.

The demands on the executive in the established organization for leadership and direction place a premium on personal courage, conviction, and ego-strength. No matter what a business looks like as a result of the social organization that develops and the sense of unity and purpose that accompanies its development, it is still a system of exchange and transaction—a complex structure of interaction in a continuously changing, and often conflicting, world. Its unity and purposefulness are illusory and its directions circular and self-fulfilling. The sense of direction developing among executives accordingly is largely a subjective phenomenon; it is, to put it another way, a projection of the individual's own sense of purpose and his own interests. Ego-strength, therefore, becomes a very important consideration in the choice of executives for established organizations.

Management by an Executive Team. Another characteristic of established, large-scale organizations—which has been suggested in the foregoing comments but needs greater emphasis—is the pattern of team management. The executive team is essentially a competitive but interdependent structure of relationships. Each executive competes with the others for a greater allocation of resources; but, at the same time, each recognizes that he controls and directs only one segment of the total business. Successful performance of one function accordingly requires the support of other key executives. This leads to a variety of activities in mahogany row which may, at first glance, seem like unnecessary political shenanigans, but which are really very much a part of getting a job done in a large-scale business. Executives in some instances attempt to form coalitions in order to dominate the management organization. There is often a good deal of mutual good fellowship to avoid making enemies who can sabotage programs at crucial points. In some cases, there is an almost conscious trading of favors. Some of the emphasis on good human relations at the executive level is little more than sophisticated bargaining. We have known executives who kept lists of the mistakes of others in the organization ready for use if they themselves were accused of errors and inadequacies.

Rather typically, there are various bids for leadership in the executive team. Some executives strive to give the impression that they have topside support from high-level executive officers or even from the board of directors. Sometimes they truly have this support. Others strive for leadership on the basis of the strength of their programs. Still others strive on the basis of their personal qualities of leadership.

In the struggle for domination of the executive team, executives typically assume the various strategic roles possible for them. Thus, we will almost always find at least one executive who places heavy emphasis on "tight" administration—the "t-crosser," the "i-dotter" par excellence. Another will stake his claim to leadership on innovation and new ideas. Another will emphasize expansion and increased sales, while yet another will talk consolidation and increased profits. As in any political arena, the potential roles are limited; but also, as in politics, each possible role is occupied by an ardent proponent of the strategic position it represents. If the role is emptied by death, retirement, or other turnover, someone typically moves in to pick it up.

Part of the creativity of executive behavior is conceiving and promoting new strategic positions in the organization. Interestingly enough, the proliferation of new executive positions at the top of established businesses represents the successful efforts of men to conceive and develop new executive roles. The way this is done is a story in itself, involving the whole process through which a particular occupational specialty is validated. We do not have the space here, however, to develop this theme.

The competition within the executive ranks considerably narrows the innovative possibilities. Ideas are supposed to be practical and plausible, which often means simply conventional and safe. Too much of a deviation from the perceived reality is likely to be criticized. Any idea that threatens to restructure the executive organization and the existing pattern of occupational and strategic positions will be openly fought, for the success of such an idea will diminish and even eliminate current centers of power. Yet, great new advances are made precisely in this manner.

PSYCHODYNAMICS OF THE EXECUTIVE ROLE

With this somewhat sketchy outline of the characteristics of large-scale, established businesses and their demands on the executive role, we can turn now to a consideration of the psychodynamics of the executive role. What is the personality configuration of those who are successful? We shall refer first to research by Professor William E. Henry of the University of Chicago.[1] Professor Henry studied a group of more than one hundred business executives using the Thematic Apperception Test (TAT). The interpretations of the TAT data were done "blind"—that is, without any prior knowledge of the individuals who were being assessed. Surveys of past job performance, summaries of current job behavior provided by others, and certain existing test information were used to distinguish a group of "successful" versus "unsuccessful" executives. Successful executives typically had a history of continuous promotion, were still regarded as promotable, and at the time of the study held major administrative posts.

Professor Henry identified a personality pattern that seemed almost specific for those individuals who achieve success in the executive role in established businesses. This unique configuration, he says, is not found among "men in lower-level supervisory positions, men who are considered 'failures' in executive positions and men in clerical and laboring jobs." He states:

> From the research it became clear that the "successful" business executives studied had many personality characteristics in common. (It was equally clear that an absence of these characteristics was coincident with "failure" within the organization.) This personality constellation might be thought of as the minimal requirement for "success" within our present business system and as the psychodynamic motivation of persons in this occupation. Individual uniqueness in personality was clearly present; but, despite these unique aspects, all executives had in common this personality pattern.

What are some of the characteristics of successful hierarchs Professor Henry identified? We shall discuss them in relation to our previous discussion of the demands made on the executive role in established bureaucracies.

Mobility Drive. We have already described the hierarchical struc-

---

[1] William E. Henry, "The Business Executive: Psychodynamics of a Social Role," *The American Journal of Sociology*, LIV (January, 1949), pp. 286–91. All quotations of Henry are from this article.

ture of the established business organization. Success in a hierarch means climbing a status ladder. A man isn't likely to climb unless he has the desire—not just the inclination, but real desire. It is, therefore, not surprising that Professor Henry found that his successful executives were all mobile, feeling "the necessity to move continually upward and to accumulate the rewards of increased accomplishment." By mobile, we interpret Professor Henry to mean "desirous of getting ahead in the organizational hierarchy." The term *mobility* usually refers to social class mobility—that is, movement from one class level to another. A number of these executives are no doubt also socially mobile in this sense, but certainly not all of them.

Mobility in the hierarchy can take two forms. First, there are those who desire mobility as evidence of increasing competence on the job. Second, there are those who are motivated by a desire for increased power and prestige. Whatever the source, the motivation is strong. No one gets up there who isn't willing to make a strong effort.

Positive Attitude Toward the Boss. The climb up depends on acceptance by those at higher levels in the organization. Without a nod from the boss, a man doesn't move. More than this, movement upward ultimately means taking the place of those in higher authority. Both of these considerations indicate the advantage of liking the boss and the boss's style. Professor Henry says that the successful executive "looks to his superiors as persons of more advanced training and experience whom he can consult in special problems and who issue to him certain guiding directives. He does not see the authority figures in his environment as destructive or prohibiting forces."

Obviously, such men are going to have real advantages in building effective relations with superiors, particularly over those associates who believe that their superiors are "jerks" and who view authority as essentially prohibiting and destructive. The latter are apt to have very inadequate relations with their superiors—they won't like the boss, and, what is more important, the boss won't like them.

Work and Activity. Hard work never hurt anyone's chances. The man who can channel his energies effectively, and can turn out more than the next man is likely to be spotted by his superiors. The successful executive is an eager beaver who really likes to work and keep moving. In other words, it isn't just show for the boss. According to Professor Henry, these are men "who must accomplish in order to be happy." They gain their satisfaction from the actual doing of the work rather than "merely from contemplating the completed product."

The advantage of being able to work on a piece of a total task and gain satisfaction just from the doing goes without saying. The young junior executive starts his career on a small segment of the total job of the organization. If he can find motivation in these limited tasks, he is more likely to do a good job and gain the support of higher authority. If he can go on to other tasks with equal drive and energy, he is more likely to gain new, and he hopes, broader assignments.

Professor Henry finds that the successful hierarch is basically an aggressive individual who channels his energies "into work or struggles for status and prestige." In other words, his motor is always running—it is only a question of gearing it into the work or other activities at hand. He doesn't have the problem of motivating himself and striving continuously to find work inspiration and new sources of energy.

Decision-making Ability. Previously we discussed the heavy demands placed on the executive role for direction and action programs. The executive is supposed to know what it's all about, and is supposed to be a stalwart source of stability and structure in what could be a chaotic, ill-defined situation. The successful executive has the ability to "organize unstructured situations and to see the implications of their organizations." Professor Henry says, "They have the ability to take several seemingly isolated events or facts and to see the relationships that exist between them." More than this, they are future-oriented, and are "concerned with predicting the outcome of their decisions and actions."

Some executives structure events in very conventional, mundane, and uneventful ways. Others are capable of integrating many considerations into plausible pictures of reality. Some force familiar patterns on new and unfamiliar events. If they don't quite fit, they "bang" the facts around until they do. Others are more flexible and capable of altering existing structures in order to adapt to change. But however they do it, the successful executives at least think that they know what's going on and are never at a total loss for an answer—even though it may take the more deliberate ones some time before they find one.

Closely related to the ability to structure events and come up with a picture of what is going on and what is likely to occur is the ability to make decisions. Decision involves choice among alternatives. There are inevitably more ways than one of structuring a situation and certainly more ways than one of acting on it. The choice is seldom between good and bad, since the various alternatives typically will have both good and bad consequences. It is here that courage and conviction are clearly required. Professor Henry indicates that the successful executive has the ability to act effectively in decision situations. He is quite capable of pushing through to conclusions even in very trying circumstances. If he loses the sense of certainty and decisiveness and becomes confused and distraught, others lose confidence in him.

Deeper Psychological Considerations. The foregoing constellation of factors in the personality of the successful executive are fairly obvious and directly related to the requirements of the executive role. Professor Henry, however, based his observations on a deeper, clinical analysis of the personality of the respondent. Rather typically, the psychologist analyzes current behavior in terms of the subject's earlier adjustment to childhood experiences. The established organization is a hierarchical, social system not unlike the family structure—at least in general form—in that there are authority figures (parents), colleagues and associates (siblings), and subordinates (the children in relation to the parents). Almost always, higher levels of authority are identified with masculine figures. The organization is sometimes viewed as essentially feminine. The relationship with authority—the direct authority of higher levels of management and the idealized authority of the organization—is determined by prior patterns of adjustment with one's parents.

Professor Henry describes the successful executive as "a man who has left home." He has broken his emotional feelings of dependency on his parents. Most important, he has severed these ties without any strong feelings of resentment. To put it another way, the successful executive is independent and capable of handling his relationships with authority figures and with the organization without emotional involvement, without feelings of hostility or antagonism, or without overriding feelings of dependency.

Narrowing his analysis down, Professor Henry points out that the tie is most clearly cut with reference to the mother. These are not men who are tied to their mother's apron strings. There is a residual tie to the father, but this remains positive. The successful executive is positively oriented toward an admired and more successful male figure.

Pursuing this consideration further, Professor Henry suggests that the successful executive is not totally independent of the father. Indeed, "there must remain feelings of dependency upon the father image and a need to operate within an established framework." Thus we gain a picture of a man who, in fact, does not set his own ultimate goals but who prefers to work within an already established framework where overall goals at least are provided. Professor Henry points out that those executives who were truly independent and more narcissistic in their views would probably feel loyalty only to themselves and find themselves "unable to work within a framework established by somebody else." This observation obviously has some bearing on our analysis of independent entrepreneurs.

Middle-class Beliefs and Values. The deeper psychological influences on the personalities of successful executives must also be related to cultural beliefs and values. As we saw in Table 2-2, a large percentage of successful executives come from the middle class. In this segment of our society, child rearing and early family relationships are such that a larger percentage of personalities of the successful type may be produced. If nothing else, the father of the upper-middle-class family is likely himself to be successful and therefore a powerful source of inspiration and emulation. But, in addition, certain values inculcated in the children become a major part of the system of beliefs characterizing the executive. Professor Henry says:

> The successful executive represents a crystallization of many of the attitudes and values generally accepted by middle-class American society. The value of accumulation and achievement, of self-directedness and independent thought and their rewards in prestige and status and property are found in this group. But they also pay the price of holding these values and of profiting from them. Uncertainty, constant activity, the continual fear of losing ground, the inability to be introspectively leisurely, the ever present fear of failure, and the artificial limitations put upon their emotionalized interpersonal relations—these are some of the costs of this role.

CHAPTER FOURTEEN

Two Pathways

At some time in their careers, administrative and independent entrepreneurs both become organization makers. If they do not, of course, they are not entrepreneurs as we have defined them in this book. In thinking the matter through, we have arrived at a conception of two kinds of entrepreneurship occurring at quite different "places" in the organizational network. We have come to conceive of the administrative entrepreneur making his projections and creating within the structural imperatives of existing social and economic relationships. We have come to think of the independent entrepreneur as making his projection, having broken away from such relationships and finding himself "outside" the existing structures.

Once organization making is conceived of as taking place in two quite different contexts, there is a strong temptation to think in terms of two diverging pathways—one leading to administrative entrepreneurship and the other being the way of the independent entrepreneur. Such a "map" is, indeed, helpful as a model for examining the routes to one or the other destination.

The danger exists, however, that having arrived at such a mental map we may come to think of the two pathways as diverging at some specific point, and to think of men as electing at one specific point in time to follow one rather than the other. Although it may be fruitful to think of the pathways as distinct from each other, to think of men following exclusively one rather than the other is a distortion of reality.

There is, rather, a steady flow of traffic back and forth between the two pathways. There is no single point at which all men leave one pathway for the other. There are, rather, many points at which

215

men switch back and forth. Independent entrepreneurship does require, however, a leaving of the well-blazed paths through the bureaucratic structures. The imperative here is quite simple. Unless a man does at one or another point break away, he will never make an independent organization.

In modern society the way to high executive position and to administrative organization making is highly "structured." The administrative entrepreneur arrives at his position because he is "mobile" in several senses of the word. As a person—to take one meaning of the word—he is ambitious to "succeed" and has strong drives to achieve. He is also mobile in the sense that he is quite willing to move around geographically—to go where the job takes him. Still again, he is mobile in that he sees each job as preparation for the next one higher in the structure (and he is willing to accept the challenge). He constantly prepares himself for movement up the scalar order of a hierarchy.

His orientation is, however, to what sociologists call "vertical mobility." He comes to believe that "success" is best achieved by staying within established structures and by working out his own destinies within those structures. His is a "staying pattern." In the face of crisis, his first impulse and continuing pattern are to seek a solution within the structured order. This does not mean that he is a passive recipient of demands imposed upon him by the structure. As Eugene Jennings has shown, a man with such passive characteristics cannot rise far in such structures. In fact, as such a man achieves power to do so, he must learn to change the structure, extending it by creating new instruments to carry forth his emerging programs and purposes.[1]

Independent entrepreneurs are also forceful and ambitious men. As a group, however, they are peculiarly confused by problems of mobility through existing scalar structures. As the TAT analyst says in Chapter 4, "What is lacking here among these entrepreneurs seems to be the value of 'getting ahead,' rising in a social hierarchy, and achieving positions of authority and rewards. . . . Moreover, the instances of mobility aspirations that do occur tend to be negative rather than positive—i.e., the hero is mobile because he is attracted to some richer and more satisfying way of life." Such men, in their internal orientation not ambitious to climb vertical ladders, are prone to make

[1] Eugene Emerson Jennings, *The Mobile Manager* (Ann Arbor: Bureau of Industrial Relations, The University of Michigan, 1967).

two kinds of mistakes in attempting to work out solutions within bureaucracies.

First, they do not fit their own desires and ambitions into a time schedule for movement up the ladder. We saw in Chapter 6 that these men had many temporary successes in their ventures into bureaucratic life, often—through a sponsor—arriving at high levels very early in their careers. They could not, however, accept the demand placed upon them that their further progress be more orderly. As Mr. Schull, who was passed over for a major promotion because he was still in his early twenties, said, "Why wait? Wait for what? . . . It was true that I was very young, that I was ahead, and that therefore I could gamble." Schull here does not see a career as a series of orderly steps up a ladder. He is not unambitious, but he does not understand the mobility game as it is played in large organizations.

Furthermore, these men cannot see large and formal structures—and their superiors in them—as basically nurturing and protective. To the contrary, in moments of crisis they are likely to see the structure and the people in it as basically stifling, threatening, and untrustworthy. If the administrative entrepreneur learns to trust the structure and to stay within it in times of danger, the independent entrepreneur distrusts the structure and seeks to avoid danger by escaping from it. The administrative entrepreneur has a staying pattern, but the independent entrepreneur has a "leaving pattern." As we saw in Chapter 8, although this leaving pattern creates many immediate difficulties for the independent entrepreneur, it is a functional necessity. Unless he breaks away from the pathway leading to administrative entrepreneurship, he can never make an organization of his own.

Where is it that men first begin to learn these two patterns—that of staying and that of leaving? All our evidence is that the patterns are not learned at one time, once and for all. They are, rather, learned through a slow process in which there is accretion in the man's perspective of the desirability of one as contrasted with the other pathway. We have to return to early childhood to look at the point at which men first start along one rather than the other route.

DIVERGENCE IN CHILDHOOD

A first major divergence occurs in the kind of families into which these men are born. We recall that independent entrepreneurs are not recruited either from minor or major occupations in the established bureaucracies. They come from the ranks of the urban and rural blue-collar workers and poor families. Unlike administrative entrepreneurs, then, independent entrepreneurs are not born into families where at an early age they can observe and learn to value the bureaucratic way of life. Since they do not internalize these values, the world of large-scale structures has to be learned as something "outside" the early experience—as a land into which the man may sojourn but in which he does not really belong.

If we consider farmers and most professional men to be owners of small enterprises, fully fifty-five percent of our independent entrepreneurs come from entrepreneurial families. Twenty-five percent of independent entrepreneurs were the owners of small businesses—a hard core of the entrepreneur tradition. This suggests that for many independent entrepreneurs patterns were set at an early age.

If we assess the economic level of the families of origin from the interviews, we find that almost two-thirds of them described their early family life as poor or even underprivileged. Twenty-nine percent recalled being "well-off," and six percent said they were "affluent." Most independent entrepreneurs have moved a long way from impoverished backgrounds.

For many men, therefore, the pathways diverged at an early age. Proportionally many more independent than administrative entrepreneurs were born into families where bureaucratic traditions and middle-class values were not "taught." It is not the figures on occupational origins, however, which are of central significance. It is, rather, the manner in which these occupational origins nudged men in the direction of learning staying or leaving patterns.

It is within such families that independent entrepreneurs learn to distrust authority figures—the parents who went away through death, withdrawal, or betrayal. It is also within such families that independent entrepreneurs learn not to put their faith in established order—in the family and in the larger world of community, education, and work bureaucracies. The reader has in this book met many men whose movement into the pathway of independent organization making really began with this negative perspective.

Other men in their early childhood learned a more positive lesson. They learned the transactional model of interpersonal relations. The independent entrepreneur builds his own structure. More than this, the structure he builds—at least as he perceives it—is not hierarchical and bureaucratic, but is rather a system of exchange and transaction— one that he put together by making deals. He does not perceive his role as one of leadership so much as being the key figure in an exchange system.

For both negative and positive reasons, many independent entrepreneurs have already at an early age learned to survive in the open. These men have learned to use their wits and have acquired the ability to make deals. From the materials presented in this book, however, it is evident that not all independent entrepreneurs find the pathway to independent organization making at this early age.

DIVERGENCE IN FORMAL EDUCATION

For most men, leaving formal education at the grade or high school level is to leave the pathway leading to executive status. To say, however, simply that these men without college were "barred" from the executive route is to ignore the dynamics of the process. Why do so many independent entrepreneurs leave education so early?

Stories told by entrepreneurs suggest that brute poverty may sometimes be involved. Men born into families which cannot provide them with adequate food or adequate clothing have little chance of staying long on the education escalator.

The stories, however, also suggest that poverty in some instances may have been more of an after-the-fact rationalization than a true determiner, and that many independent entrepreneurs "failed" in formal education because they had already rejected formal structures and adult authority figures. Unlike their administrative counterparts, they were not at home in the bureaucracy of formal education. Many men who climb the executive ladder preface this climb by performing well on the education ladder. They enjoy schoolwork for its own sake because it earns them rewards from admired teachers and parents, and because they have the time perspective to move through the grades step-by-step. Many entrepreneurs "fail" for all three reasons.

Furthermore, we have seen that one group of independent entrepreneurs were precocious in their understanding of the world of occupations. Such men are neither pushed off nor fail on the education escalator. They leave quite voluntarily because the world of work seems to offer more immediate challenges and greater rewards. Here men who are to become administrative entrepreneurs may have greater internal restraints. They may dream about career "success," but they have sufficient self-discipline to work through formal education before beginning their careers.

Sometimes independent entrepreneurs who did achieve higher education recall that they did so because no occupational opportunity intervened. Several such men went to college—and one even through college—while they were waiting around for something to break in the world of work. Such men, more or less educated by accident, do not share with their administrative counterparts a map of higher education as one stage along the road to career achievement.

In formal education, as in early childhood, the pathways diverge for some men but not for others. In recounting their experiences, many men who were to create their own organizations recalled that during formal education they were still on the main road to success in one or another bureaucratic structure. It was only later that they took the diverging pathway.

DIVERGENCE IN EARLY CAREER EXPERIENCES

Most men who are to become business executives have, at the time when they take their first jobs, already learned to identify themselves with "standard" role definitions. They have with varying success played the role of son, grade and high school student, and professional student such as in engineering or law. In taking their first jobs they usually continue this process of strong self-identification as junior engineers, as employees of law firms, or as one or another kind of management trainee. Few of these men, according to Warner and Abegglen, ever hold blue-collar jobs.

Such men learn early in life—and have this lesson reinforced many times—to think of themselves as having a place in a large design—to regard themselves as job-holders contributing a speciality within a larger structure. They have learned the arts of maintaining sustained relations with peers, of playing both the role of protégé and sponsor, and of seeing the organization as a hierarchy through which they can move, with each job a preparation for the next step.

The majority of independent entrepreneurs have never learned to identify themselves so firmly in terms of "standard" roles. For many, this incapacity begins in early childhood when they do not learn to be "sons" to fathers, either because the father is not there or because of mutual rejection. This incapacity is again for some, but by no means all, reinforced by the failure to play the role of student well.

At that moment when they begin their careers, independent entrepreneurs redisplay their inability to play "standard" roles. We have shown them during the period of drifting as they wander from firm to firm, never satisfied. We have shown how they become protégés to sponsors but fail because they are too fervent, because they try to hang on too long, or because they try to undermine and supplant the sponsor. We have shown how they make their first exploratory business attempts, winding up in bankruptcy courts. And we have shown how they find initial success in hierarchies, but lose out because they cannot accept the patterned system of step-by-step advancement.

Here again the pathways diverge, but not for all men. A few of the independent entrepreneurs—after getting through college and even graduate school—went on for a few years into the professions or into the executive ranks. A few people came to independent organization making as quite rational extensions of careers begun in the bureaucracies. Most independent entrepreneurs, however, have by this point crossed over to the independent way.

DIVERGENCE BY ROLE DETERIORATION

It seems axiomatic that any man who creates an independent organization must be free at some point in his life of bureaucratic restraints and controls. From this point of view, the moment of role deterioration may be the most crucial point tactically at which the two pathways diverge. It presents the man with an opportunity to act on his own. Stories told by these men suggest that the period of role deterioration is significant as a precipitating factor.

No matter which pathway men follow, they come to those points where their security is threatened, where their forward movement is blocked, and where events seem to be in the hands of inimical figures. At such crisis points men may elect to stay on the pathway and try to overcome the obstacles, or they may strike out on their own. Which pathway a man may choose at this point to follow most certainly depends in part on the objective reality of the immediate situation. We have reported on men who, because of sustained periods of role deterioration, seem to have had no viable alternative to the entrepreneurial way. We have also reported on men who, suddenly thrust into a moment of crisis, came to choose independent organization making only after careful—although often emotional—evaluation of possibilities. The way a man will elect in such moments depends on what he has learned long before the crisis confronts him.

Men who are to become administrative entrepreneurs have learned to cope with such crises within the established order. They marshall their forces, plot their powerplays, and execute their designs with an eye to the imperative of continuing climb through the existing structure. It is in this crucible that their leadership qualities are forged, and it is out of it that they emerge as leaders who can extend their organizations into new dimensions of activity.

Men who are to become independent entrepreneurs have learned to break away. They have learned to cope with danger and frustration by leaving the threatening situation, and they have learned to find their way through even greater insecurity by operating on their own until they can come home to their own peculiar havens.

The pathways to administrative and to independent organization making diverge at many different points. Men elect one or the other because of a complex of personal characteristics and situational imperatives. The election is, however, at no single point completely irrevocable. Men may rise high in the bureaucratic structures, and may then become independent entrepreneurs as a further extension of their administrative careers. Men may start their careers early as independent entrepreneurs, and, through success in creating their own firms, they may, during the final stages, become administrative entrepreneurs.

CHAPTER FIFTEEN

The Independent Entrepreneur
and the Large Corporation

Our interest in the entrepreneur as an organization maker is related to broader conceptions of the free enterprise system. Free enterprise, like all ideological notions, means many things. Certainly one image of free enterprise is a picture of resolute, intrepid men going into business for themselves. This is by no means an inaccurate portrayal, for it is true that each year in alley shops, in basements, and in abandoned lofts and warehouses, Americans follow the prototypic pattern and seek their fortunes in their own businesses. A vast number of these new activities are doomed to death almost before they begin. Some, however, survive the first hectic months and years during which they must secure financial support, find productive and efficient modes of organization, relate themselves effectively to the larger market economy, and enter a period of growth and development. An exceptionally small number of these new enterprises, having weathered the storm of the earlier years, go on to become industrial and commercial giants. One in thousands becomes a power to be reckoned with on the national scene. For the vast majority of new enterprises, a point is early reached from which further development is extremely difficult. Such firms find an equilibrium and level off with a local and small clientele and with little prospect for further growth.

We see in the notion of the free enterprise economy a continuous entry of new enterprises—a picture of venturesome men, often without resources, launching small and leaky craft on the entrepreneurial stream. At the same time, there is the little-understood attrition of the large corporations. These giants viewed from the knife-edge present seem to be rolling on forever. They have built huge and specializd bureaucracies, accumulated vast resources, and extended their activities into international markets. Yet some get pushed up on the sand bars of the entrepreneurial stream and lie abandoned like rotten hulks for all to see. Some, it is true, were simply gobbled up through purchase and merger by the bigger fish in the pool. Others, however, having lost touch with the production and distribution reality of their times, failed to maintain their competitive position, and went under.

On the other hand, great industries and businesses of America, for the most part, were initially projected and created in humble circumstances. Sears, Roebuck and Company started in a railroad station in a small Minnesota town. Ford Motor Company was literally created in the proverbial back alley shop. United Air Lines was formed from a clutter of airmail pioneers scattered in tin-shack hangars on bumpy dirt runways throughout the country. It is difficult to imagine now that these large corporations had small beginnings.

Indeed, there are those who feel that free enterprise as a competitive process in this country is dead. There are no longer—so the argument goes—opportunities for men to strike out on their own. Who, for example, could organize resources, build an organization and capture even a small share of the market now carved up by the big three in automobiles?

This pessimistic view finds support in several trends which in combination appear to lead toward the disappearance of the independent entrepreneurial process. The increasing role of government—especially the federal government—in regulating and controlling activities of private business is often cited. An increasing concentration of power in the hands of a few large corporations is believed to indicate that vast domains of activity have already been staked out. The newcomer, the argument runs, must content himself with crumbs and leavings. Big government, big business, and big labor are pictured as having so preempted the areas of production and distribution that there is little left for a person operating on his own. High rates of taxation, it is firmly believed, limit entrepreneurial activity because men cannot accumulate savings and venture capital.

The picture thus painted is a sobering one. It is made more so by citing statistics on the high rate of mortality of new businesses. Students have long been concerned with these statistics, and have conducted many investigations into the financial, production, and personal factors leading to this failure of so many businesses. One implication of their findings has been that this high failure rate means the end of the small and independent entrepreneur. Attention has accordingly shifted to the corporation's role in research and development, innovation, and venture capital. If there is little or no opportunity for the individual, then bureaucratic, corporate enterprising must take over. Much is made recently of the role of giant private bureaucracies in technological and marketing change. Here again there is supporting evidence. Business and industry have in the past twenty years enormously increased expenditures for scientific and technological research. Efforts are made by large corporations to gain better understanding of the market through research in consumer behavior. It would appear that the little guy has no chance in a world so dominated by giant corporations.]

In the face of such arguments, however, great and successful businesses have been built in the past thirty years and great businesses have gone under. We may be witnessing here a process of monumental design which has considerably greater vitality than seems evident at any other time. Over the long haul, a few little back alley shops do grow to bigness and power—and giants do shudder, falter, and collapse. The capacity for adjustment is not infinite, even for the largest and most powerful of corporate giants.

These a priori arguments that opportunities for the creation of new businesses are disappearing are contravened by statistical evidence.[1] In 1946, immediately after the war when many men in our sample were creating their businesses, there were 3,487,200 business firms operating in the United States. By 1957, this figure had been increased by almost 1,000,000 new firms. The increases shown were largely in retail trade, contract construction, and service industries, but all lines of endeavor showed some increase. The number of corporations, as indicated by Bureau of Internal Revenue statistics, increased by approximately 400,000 between 1946 and 1956. In 1962, the year closest to the time of our fieldwork, there were approximately

[1] Data in this and the following paragraph have been drawn from *Historical Statistics of the United States, Colonial Times to 1957: A Statistical Abstract Supplement* (U.S. Department of Commerce, Bureau of the Census, 1960).

4,752,000 business firms in operation.[2] Most of these new firms are small.

New firms established each year averaged close to 400,000 between 1946 and 1957, the decade in which most of our entrepreneurs were getting started. In 1957, there were 405,100 new businesses started and 341,500 businesses discontinued. Yet, there was a gain of approximately 90,000 new businesses a year between 1946 and 1957. These new businesses were quite small—employing on the average fewer than seven employees—but in the eleven years could have accounted for well over ten percent of the paid employment among operating firms in the United States in 1957.

A few hours spent examining the manufacturing records of giant corporations in aerospace, automobiles, or in almost any other field dramatically reveals the role of the small firm in the emergent economy. Such records list both sources of components and customers for finished products.

The giants—and this trend seems to be accelerating—draw on the smaller firms as sources of components and depend upon them as outlets for their products. Any design engineer in a large corporation has at his finger tips dozens of manuals listing thousands of makers of the components he may need in his design. It is true that many of these components will be supplied by other large corporations, but a large proportion must be produced by those small firms which specialize in the engineering and the production of small orders. Consequently, "vendor relations" are today often handled in large corporations by departments set up to develop and maintain close bonds with specialized suppliers. Such departments are often staffed with men claiming special experience in dealing with the small entrepreneur.

The same process takes place in the search by corporations for customers. A chemical corporation, to take one example, is dependent upon thousands of small firms who fabricate and use its synthetic materials. Such a corporation may have a department charged with recruiting and training representatives to such consumers of plastic materials. One such corporation runs regular seminars for its people on the problems of small business firms.

Large corporations swim in a sea of small business, with increasing technological complexity. The dependence of the giants on the

[2] *Survey of Current Business* (U.S. Department of Commerce, Office of Business Economics, June 1962), p. 24.

small firms seems to be increasing. For example, thirty years ago the policy in the airplane industry was "integration backwards" with the objective of making "in shop" every part of the airplane. Today, the policy is reversed. Planners seek to purchase "outside" as many components as possible, reserving for their own "make shops" the production of experimental parts on which "lead time" must be cut to a minimum, and the making of production parts when a vendor of them cannot be found or fails to make delivery.

The corporate giants in the more highly developed technological fields are moving toward the specialized functions of design, coordination and planning, and responsibility to the customer for the finished product. This is the essential meaning of the term "prime contractor." The prime contractor in the more advanced fields tends to become the control center of a network of productive activities carried on by hundreds or even thousands of firms. Even the responsibility for final assembly may—in such fields as aerospace—be contracted out to an organization created to specialize in such work.

Today, small enterprise is created to do those myriad tasks which are either too small, too specialized, or too complex to be undertaken by the corporate big fish in the sea. Such small firms do not always stay small—a few of them get big.

By the same token, the more successful of these small firms do not long remain dependent upon one giant as a source of supply or as a customer for products. In Chapter 13 of this book, we found that one task of the independent entrepreneur is to sever such initial ties by seeking alternative sources of supply, by diversifying his activities, and by attracting a range of customers.

In a real sense, therefore, the two ways of organization making in our society are increasingly complementary one to the other. As our technology becomes more complex, opportunities for filling a specialized niche are increasingly abundant. We can expect to see more and more men leaving the protective cup of bureaucracy and striking out to make an organization of their own.

This continuing opportunity for independent entrepreneurship has profound implications for the future shape of our society. A society having no room for the independent organization maker must be one having values fundamentally different from those existing today in America.

THE INDEPENDENT ENTREPRENEUR AND
THE AMERICAN DREAM

⌈ The term *entrepreneur* evokes many different images. In the popular conception and to some extent in the historical literature of America, the independent entrepreneur is a risk-taker—a man who braves uncertainty, who strikes out on his own, and who—through native wit, devotion to duty, and singleness of purpose—somehow creates business and industrial activity where none existed before. In some respects, he is the heroic figure in American folklore akin, perhaps, to Daniel Boone and to other truly indigenous epic types—stalwart independents who hewed forests, who climbed over the tops of mountains, who built new communities, who rose from nothing to something, and who did all the things American heroes had to do to build a great nation. ⌉

At the same time, the term *entrepreneur* engenders certain negative overtones. There is a connotation of manipulation, greed, avarice, and grasping acquisitiveness. While it is true that the entrepreneurial hero built railroads, canals, communities, industries, and great systems of trade, there is also the implication that in the process he befouled nature, sullied valleys, denuded forests, muddied and contaminated the rivers and streams, scarred mother earth, and generally ravished the natural order of things. Nature and God's creatures—including ordinary folk—all suffered at the hands of those who sought to impose their will on the natural order.

The symbolism expressed in the American image of the independent entrepreneur is a profound reflection of our national history and character. We are a people who for nearly twelve generations went through the recurrent process of imposing man's will on a wilderness of primeval forests, rugged mountains, mighty rivers, unending plains, and waterless deserts. Although this resurgent effort at the moving edge of the frontier has long since ended, the spirit and the imagery live on. Professor W. Lloyd Warner in analyzing the symbolic life of Americans has the following to say about our views of nature[3]:

---

[3] W. Lloyd Warner, *The Living and the Dead: A Study of the Symbolic Life of Americans* (New Haven: Yale University Press, 1959), p. 157.

. . . the forest primeval was a symbol of quiet, tranquility, eternal timelessness, when nothing happened and all was still. Femininity, inactivity, virginity, and timelessness are clusters of meaning expressed by the "Spirit of the River and the Wilderness," while after "her" contact with the dominant male civilization of the West, she becomes the "mother" out of whom a great nation sprang.

Thus, in American symbolic life, the natural order—the wilderness—is essentially feminine. It is the "mother" out of which man has built and created things—the natural resource from which man shaped his civilization. At the same time, there is the implication of ravishment and rape. Thus, the entrepreneur as the heroic representation of the positive American theme of building and constructive effort inevitably evokes the negative image of destroying nature. Even the historians cannot make up their minds—sometimes viewing the entrepreneur affirmatively and other times seeing him as a robber and pirate.

However we may personally feel about the entrepreneur, he emerges as essentially more masculine than feminine, more heroic than cowardly, and in the long run more constructive than destructive. Like him or not, he is still fascinating to Americans. The reasons are not hard to find. For one thing, all fortunes in America were created by independent advances into administrative entrepreneurial activity. America's social structure is a product of the milling efforts of thousands who came to these shores seeking their fortunes and hoping that Lady Luck would beam upon them. Those upon whom she smiled became great figures of power and, in many cases, established family dynasties persisting through many generations. The way up in America was largely through business and industry. Accordingly, the fascination with both kinds of entrepreneurs is—in part, at least—a fascination with men of power and prestige, and with the history of our first families.

But there is considerably more than this behind the allure of the independent entrepreneur. His values and activities have become part of the character of America and intimately related to our ideas of personal freedom, success, and—above all—individualism. He represents the rags to riches theme in its purest sense, for he rises on his own by building a solid structure beneath him, not by social climbing. He gets there by what he knows, not by whom he knows. His resources are all inside, not outside. The story—or, if you wish, the myth of the independent entrepreneur—is a drama in which the protagonist challenges the established order and forges ahead toward the glowing light called "success" using only native wit, ability, and hard work—with perhaps a bit of luck and Calvinistic fate thrown in for good measure. He is successful because he sticks to the simple and obvious American virtues. He builds a better mousetrap or provides a better service, and he does these things in the best way he knows. He is resolute, disciplined, and utterly devoted to the narrow goals he has set for himself. He is literally a limited-purpose man striving to build a limited-purpose organization. He is a combination of ambition and simplicity. Writing in the 1830's, Alexis de Tocqueville noted both the ambition and the uncomplicated aims of Americans:[4]

> The first thing which strikes a traveler in the United States is the innumerable multitude of those who seek to throw off their original conditions; and the second is the rarity of lofty ambition to be observed in the midst of the universally ambitious stir of society. No Americans are devoid of a yearning desire to rise; but hardly any appear to entertain hopes of great magnitude, or to drive at very lofty aims. All are constantly seeking to acquire property, power, and reputation—few contemplate these things upon a great scale; and this is the more surprising, as nothing is to be discerned in the manner or laws of America to limit desire, or to prevent it from spreading its impulses in every direction.

Thus, the independent entrepreneur in the American pantheon of heroic types is truly the successful common man. As such, each independent entrepreneurial performance recapitulates, at the level of the individual, the revolt of the common man against the established order. Each performance is a renewal of the democratic notion that all men are born equal and that the value of the individual to society does not depend upon family or social class position. It is not by chance that independent entrepreneurial activity remains the haven for the common man. It offers an escape, on the one hand, from an established and overly complicated social order; and an opportunity, on the other, to build a place within our society. Nor is it by chance that the American worker today—trapped in a dead-end production

---

[4] Alexis de Tocqueville, *Democracy in America,* Galaxy Edition (New York and London: Oxford University Press, 1947), p. 245.

job—dreams about getting out of the shop and into his own business. Ely Chinoy, in a study of automobile workers, found the following: "Most of the talk of leaving dealt with the traditional avenue of success, some kind of small business venture. Of the forty-eight who had thought of quitting, thirty-one suggested a 'business of my own' as their goal; six wished to become independent farmers."[5] Such dreams are for most, as Chinoy found, simply rationalizations.[6]

Of particular importance from our point of view is the fact that talk of leaving the factory—especially when focused upon traditionally sanctioned goals—serves to reinforce the worker's identification with the dominant success values of American culture. Even if he recognizes—in those occasional moments when he looks at things clearly—the emptiness of his talk of buying tourist property or a turkey farm, the risks of failure in business, the likelihood of low income in an automobile repair shop or a small grocery store, this worker has not surrendered to the difficulties of his position. In his own mind he may appear to be persevering and hopeful, ambitious and hard working, just as he is encouraged to be. He, too, wants to get ahead as others have done before him—and, perhaps, as his children will do after him. By seeking to convince others of the reality and strength of his aspirations, he fosters his belief in his own ambition and perseverance—and he continues to believe in the reality of opportunity.

Rationalization or not, the dream sometimes becomes a reality. Professor Chinoy studied only the workers who stayed and dreamed on; but in this book we have looked at men who followed through on their ambitions and who achieved a degree of success and independence.

The ambition to get into one's own business—whether dream or reality—serves as an effective safety valve in our society. It is in a sense a kind of "permanent revolution," which does not involve direct attack on the established citadels of power. It represents for the ambitious man an acceptable route for advancement and one that places upon him and his own efforts the responsibility for his success or failure. Instead of having to move up in a hierarchy—or, failing that, to revolt against the established order—he can leave the established struc-

[5] Ely Chinoy, *Automobile Workers and the American Dream* (Garden City, N.J.: Doubleday, 1955), p. 157.
[6] *Ibid.*, p. 95.

ture and go out on his own. The deeper traditions of our society, its history, myths, and many of its heroic figures all point in this direction. The stability of America with all its dynamics and chaotic change is bound up with these traditions and beliefs.

Bibliography

Carroll, John J., S.J., *The Filipino Manufacturing Entrepreneur: Agent and Product of Change* (Ithaca, New York: Cornell University Press, 1965).

Chinoy, Ely, *Automobile Workers and the American Dream* (Garden City, New York: Doubleday & Company, Inc., 1955).

Cochran, Thomas C. and William Miller, *The Age of Enterprise* (New York: Harper & Brothers, Harper Torchbooks, The Academy Library, 1961).

Cole. Arthur H., *Business Enterprise in Its Social Setting* (Cambridge, Massachusetts: Harvard University Press, 1959).

Ginzberg, Eli, ed., *What Makes an Executive?* (New York: Columbia University Press, 1955).

Harbison, Frederick and Charles A. Myers, *Management in the Industrial World* (New York: McGraw-Hill Book Company, Inc., 1959).

Henry, William E., "The Business Executive: Psychodynamics of a Social Role," *American Journal of Sociology,* LIV (January 1949), 286-91.

Mayer, Kurt B. and Sidney Goldstein, *The First Two Years: Problems of Small Firm Growth and Survival* (Washington, D.C.: Small Business Administration, 1961).

Newcomer, Mabel, "The Little Businessman: A Study of Business Proprietors in Poughkeepsie, New York," *Business History Review,* Vol. 35, No. 4 (Winter 1961), pp. 477-531.

O'Donovan, Thomas R., "Contrasting Orientations and Career Patterns of Executives and Lower Managers" (Unpublished Ph.D. dissertation, Michigan State University, 1961).

Riesman, David, *The Lonely Crowd* (New Haven: Yale University Press, 1950).

Smith, Norman Raymond, "The Entrepreneur and His Firm: An Exploratory Study to Examine the Relationship Between Entrepreneurial Types and the Initiation, Maintenance and Aggrandizement of Their Companies" (Unpublished Ph.D. dissertation, Michigan State University, 1965).

Tocqueville, Alexis de, *Democracy in America,* Galaxy Edition (New York & London: Oxford University Press, 1947).

Warner, W. Lloyd, *The Corporation in the Emergent American Society* (New York: Harper & Brothers, 1962).

Warner, W. Lloyd, *The Living and the Dead: A Study of the Symbolic Life of Americans* (New Haven: Yale University Press, 1959).

Warner, W. Lloyd and James C. Abegglen, *Big Business Leaders in America* (New York: Harper & Brothers, 1955).

Warner, W. Lloyd and James C. Abegglen, *Occupational Mobility in American Business and Industry* (Minneapolis: University of Minnesota Press, 1955).

Warner, W. Lloyd and Norman H. Martin, *Industrial Man* (New York: Harper & Brothers, 1959).

Warner, W. Lloyd, Paul P. Van Riper, Norman H. Martin, and Orvis F. Collins, *The American Federal Executive* (New Haven: Yale University Press, 1963).

Whyte, William H., Jr., *The Organization Man* (New York: Simon and Schuster, Inc., 1956).

Index

Abegglen, James C., 18, 50
age of independent entrepreneurs at
    time of study, 17
Age of Enterprise, The (Cochran
    and Miller), 8
AID, 2
assets, securing physical, 147-149
authority, attitudes toward
    administrative entrepreneurs, 210
    independent entrepreneurs, 44-46
*Automobile Workers and the Amer-
    ican Dream* (Chinoy), 231

*Business Enterprise in its Social
    Setting* (Cole), 8, 9
"Business Executive, The: Psycho-
    dynamics of a Social Role"
    (Henry), 209

Chinoy, Ely, 231
Cochran, Thomas C., 8
Cole, Arthur H., 8, 9-10
Collins, June, x
cost barrier, breaking the, 168-169
Coup, Roger, x, 39
creation phase, 5-6, 138-139
    and projection phase, 137-138
customers
    building up, 170-172
    lining up initial, 152-153

dealing, as education for independ-
    ent entrepreneurs, 79-84
death, as a theme in independent

entrepreneurs' childhoods, 24
decision-making ability
    administrative entrepreneurs, 211
    independent entrepreneurs, 42-43
Defoe, Daniel, 95
Democracy in America (Tocque-
    ville), 230
Department of Commerce, U.S.
    Bureau of the Census, 50, 225
    Office of Business Economics,
        226
drifting, as education for independ-
    ent entrepreneurs, 64-66

educational levels of administrative
    and independent entrepre-
    neurs, 50
entrepreneur
    administrative and independent
        compared, 3, 6-9, 201-202
    as organization builder, 10
    as organization maker, 2
entrepreneurs, administrative
    occupational origins, 18
    education, 50
    psychodynamics of, 208-213
    mobility drive, 209-210
    positive attitude toward the boss,
        210
    work and activity, 210-211
    decision-making ability, 211-212
    middle class beliefs and values,
        213

entrepreneurs, independent
  defined, 85
  age at time of study, 17
  occupational origins, 18
  psychological profile
    value system, 40-41
    lack of social mobility drives,
      41
    chronic fatigue, 42
    lack of problem resolution, 42
    relations with subordinates, 43
    relations with partners, 43-44
    relations to authority, 44
    remoteness of male authority
      figures, 45-46
    views of females, 46
entrepreneurial function and hierarchical organization, 203-205
entrepreneurship, basic dilemma of,
  91-92
executive team and administrative
  entrepreneurs, 207-208
expanding, through finance, 194-
  196

Ford Motor Company, 1, 224

government intervention, 169-170

Harbison, Frederick, 7-10
Henry, William E., 209-213
Historical Statistics of the United
  States, Colonial Times to
  1957: A Statistical Abstract
  Supplement (Bureau of the
  Census), 225
hot lines, riding, 175-178

ideas and projections, 115
initial acts, discussed, 141-142
intervention, government, 169-170
intruders, throwing out, 188-190

invention, idea of and projection,
  117-120

Jennings, Eugene, 216

knot hole, through the, discussed,
  159-160

Living and the Dead, The: A Study
  of the Symbolic Life of Americans (Warner), 228
loans, meeting short term, 160-162

Management in the Industrial
  World (Harbison and Myers),
  7, 8, 9, 10
Manhattan Project, 1
March, James C., 8
market, idea of and projection, 129
Marshal, Alfred, 8-9
Miller, William, 8
Mobile Manager, The (Jennings),
  216
mobility, blocked, 50-51, 96-98
mobility, social
  administrative entrepreneurs and
    vertical mobility drive, 205,
    209-210, 216
  independent entrepreneurs and
    lack of mobility drive, 41
money, getting as initial act in creation, 142-147
  holding old, 165-168
  making, idea of and projection,
    130-133
Myers, Charles A., 7-10

NASA, 1, 15
new blood, taking in, 162-165

Occupational Mobility in American
  Business and Industry (Warner and Abegglen), 18, 50

occupational origins of administrative and independent entrepreneurs, 18
opportunities, intervening, and education of independent entrepreneurs, 51
organization, limited purpose, 1-2
Organizations (March and Simon), 8
organization making,
  by extension, 3
  independent, 3
  main phases, 4-6
orphaned and alone, as a theme in independent entrepreneurs' childhoods, 20

partners, getting rid of, 182-188
Peace Corps, 15
People of Plenty (Potter), 7
Potter, David M., 6-7
poverty, escape from as a theme in independent entrepreneurs' childhoods, 23
product, idea of and projection, 120-123
projection phase, 4-5, 115-117
  and creation phase, 137-138
projectors, 95
psychodynamics
  of administrative entrepreneurs, 208-213
  of independent entrepreneurs, 40-46
protégéship, as education for independent entrepreneurs, 66-79

resources, 123-129
revamping the system, 191-194
role deterioration, 96, 111-113
Rosenwald, Julius, 203

Schumpeter, Joseph A., 10
Sears, Richard W., 203
Sears, Roebuck and Company, 203, 224
Simon, Herbert A., 8
Small Business Administration, ix
Social Research, Inc., x, 39
strategic action, 153-157
supply, assuring sources of, 172-175
Survey of Current Business (Office of Business Economics), 226

talent, enlisting special, 149-152
Thematic Apperception Test, 39, 209
Tocqueville, Alexis de, 230
transactional mode of interpersonal relations, 88-92
TVA, 15

values, 40-41, 213

United Airlines, 224
Unwalla, Darab B., ix-x

Warner, W. Lloyd, 18, 50, 228
Work attitudes toward
  administrative entrepreneurs, 210-212
  independent entrepreneurs, 42